Mourning Freud

PSYCHOANALYTIC HORIZONS

Psychoanalysis is unique in being at once a theory and a therapy, a method of critical thinking and a form of clinical practice. Now in its second century, this fusion of science and humanism derived from Freud has outlived all predictions of its demise. **Psychoanalytic Horizons** evokes the idea of a convergence between realms as well as the outer limits of a vision. Books in the series test disciplinary boundaries and will appeal to readers who are passionate not only about the theory of literature, culture, media, and philosophy but also, above all, about the real life of ideas in the world.

Series Editors:
Esther Rashkin, Mari Ruti, and Peter L. Rudnytsky

Advisory Board:
Salman Akhtar, Doris Brothers, Aleksandar Dimitrijevic, Lewis Kirshner, Humphrey Morris, Hilary Neroni, Dany Nobus, Lois Oppenheim, Donna Orange, Peter Redman, Laura Salisbury, Alenka Zupančič.

Volumes in the Series:

Mourning Freud
Madelon Sprengnether

Does the Internet Have an Unconscious?: Slavoj Žižek and Digital Culture
(forthcoming)
Clint Burnham

On Dangerous Ground: Freud's Visual Cultures of the Unconscious (forthcoming)
Diane O'Donoghue

Born After: Reckoning with the Nazi Past (forthcoming)
Angelika Bammer

The Analyst's Desire: Ethics in Theory and Clinical Practice (forthcoming)
Mitchell Wilson

At the Risk of Thinking: An Intellectual Biography of Julia Kristeva (forthcoming)
Alice Jardine

Mourning Freud

Madelon Sprengnether

Bloomsbury Academic
An imprint of Bloomsbury Publishing Inc

B L O O M S B U R Y
NEW YORK • LONDON • OXFORD • NEW DELHI • SYDNEY

Bloomsbury Academic
An imprint of Bloomsbury Publishing Inc

1385 Broadway	50 Bedford Square
New York	London
NY 10018	WC1B 3DP
USA	UK

www.bloomsbury.com

BLOOMSBURY and the Diana logo are trademarks of Bloomsbury Publishing Plc

First published 2018

© Madelon Sprengnether, 2018

All rights reserved. No part of this publication may be reproduced or transmitted in any form or by any means, electronic or mechanical, including photocopying, recording, or any information storage or retrieval system, without prior permission in writing from the publishers.

No responsibility for loss caused to any individual or organization acting on or refraining from action as a result of the material in this publication can be accepted by Bloomsbury or the author.

Library of Congress Cataloging-in-Publication Data
A catalog record for this book is available from the Library of Congress.

ISBN: HB: 978-1-5013-2800-8
PB: 978-1-5013-2799-5
ePub: 978-1-5013-2801-5
ePDF: 978-1-5013-2802-2

Series: Psychoanalytic Horizons

Cover design: Daniel Benneworth-Gray
Cover image © Kunstmuseum, Basel, Switzerland/Peter Willi/Bridgeman Images

Typeset by Integra Software Services Pvt. Ltd.

To find out more about our authors and books visit www.bloomsbury.com. Here you will find extracts, author interviews, details of forthcoming events, and the option to sign up for our newsletters.

*For Jessica Lee Gohlke,
James William Anstey,
Beatrice Nellie May Anstey, and
Arthur John Anstey*

CONTENTS

Preface viii
Acknowledgments xi

Introduction: Insight and Blindness 1

PART ONE Biography and Theory 19

1 Reading Freud's Life 21
2 Mourning Freud 65
3 Freud, Irma, and the Dream of Psychoanalysis 93

PART TWO Transitions 117

4 Undoing Incest 119
5 Freud as Memoirist 139
6 Literature and Psychoanalysis 163

PART THREE Ghosts and Ancestors 187

7 Reflections on Melancholia and Mourning 189

Conclusion 241

Works Cited 246
Index 260

PREFACE

This book originated in 1990 with the publication of *The Spectral Mother: Freud, Feminism, and Psychoanalysis*, when I thought I had more to say than I could fit into that argument.

In particular, my reading of the standard biographies of Freud (Ernest Jones and Peter Gay), along with many biographies of his followers, e.g. Anna Freud, Melanie Klein, and the first English translations of his letters (to Martha Bernays, to Wilhlem Fliess, and to Eduard Silberstein), initiated a new line of thinking. I was struck then by how Freud's construction of the Oedipus complex (seemingly derived from his personal experience) was belied by the conditions of his early life. Pursuing this train of thought, I composed "Reading Freud's Life." Little did I know how abiding my interest in this subject would become, nor how many essays I would write to address what I saw then as a divergence between Freud's theory and his life.

The three essays that I subsequently published ("Mourning Freud," "Undoing Incest," and "Freud, Irma, and the Dream of Psychoanalysis") helped me to develop my train of thought on how Freud both addressed and avoided some of his more pressing personal concerns, as evidenced in the details of his biography, his writings, and his correspondence. At that time, I seriously considered writing another book on Freud. I even had a title for it: "Reading Freud's Life: Revisionary Biography and Psychoanalytic Theory." I didn't, mainly because I was unsure of the conclusion I wanted to draw: yes, Freud failed to theorize the preoedipal period, but why does this matter?

At the same time, I was very engaged by the rapid transformations occurring in the field of psychoanalytic theory, e.g. intersubjective and countertransference theory, Lacanian psychoanalysis, French feminism, the work of Jacques Derrida, the emergence of attachment theory, the rising prominence of trauma theory and its relation to

Holocaust studies, not to mention the contributions of cognitive neuroscience, the newcomer on the scene.

All of these developments, as I perceived them, pointed to a profound paradigm shift, not only in the development of psychoanalysis (a field with multiple converging and conflicting strands) but also in the world of literary studies. I attempted to tease out some of these strands and how they mutually interact in the following publications: "Freud as Memoirist: A Reading of 'Screen Memories,'" and "Literature and Psychoanalysis." Each of them helped me to push my thinking further—in the direction of literary critical theory but also toward a new awareness of how psychoanalysis intersects with cultural studies.

These essays, in turn, led me to another series of revelations, ones I could not have articulated when I was immersed in the question of how Freud's theory diverged from his life experience. Rather, I began to think about how psychoanalysis as a discipline has evolved (and dramatically altered) in the wake of Freud's magisterial presence and influence.

I did not come to such an awareness quickly or easily, as there are many interrelated factors involved: Freud's biography (which is only now becoming more evident through recent biographical studies and the editions of his correspondence stemming from the Freud Archives); the major shift in theory from oedipal to preoedipal concerns; a corresponding emphasis on the earliest stages of life—per Lacan, French feminism, poststructuralism, and current emphases on unrepresented and unrepresentable experience; coupled, at last, with the insights of contemporary neuroscience. Gradually, I began to see how these seemingly divergent trends intersect and interact.

The investigation of the preoedipal period post-Freud is profoundly inter-involved with other sociocultural concerns that have emerged in the twentieth century, continuing into the twenty-first: the evidence of historical trauma and increasing focus on violent political movements and their complex origins—matters that Freud might have referred to as the "death instinct." But naming is not the same as explaining. Attributing the history of violence in the twentieth century and beyond to an unfathomable "death instinct" is like saying that people cause destruction because they are destructive.

I prefer to pursue a submerged line of Freud's thought pertaining to his speculations about the work of mourning that characterizes the earliest stages of development, a line of thought developed by his followers Karl Abraham and Melanie Klein and further explored in the theories of Jacques Lacan, Jacques Derrida, their adherents and others. I see this movement, moreover, as critical to the development of trauma theory, which addresses the realm of unrepresented experience in many of the same terms as do theorists of early childhood development.

We come into the world lacking language and the kinds of boundaries that language imposes between self and other. While this manner of thinking does not "explain" the kinds of devastation that human beings inflict on one another, it does attempt to address this issue as a problem. In this sense, I see Freud's inability fully to explore the preoedipal period as having enabled the efforts of his followers, who extended his fragmentary thoughts on mourning into their own investigations regarding the earliest stages of ego development, the evolution of language and representation, and the effects of trauma on nations and societies as well as individuals.

Ironically, Freud's failure to mourn his own childhood losses stimulated the creativity of his followers, leading to new ways of understanding mourning as crucial to the development of individual subjectivity, in addition to being a lifelong process. "Reflections on Melancholia and Mourning," the final chapter in this book weaves all of these strands of thought into a cultural, historical, and psychoanalytic narrative, which involves mourning as a body of theory that pays tribute to Freud's power and influence, while acknowledging his blind spots and vulnerabilities.

My intention throughout this book, and as expressed in its title, is not simply to examine Freud's personal occasions and evasions of mourning but also to consider how we might respectfully and creatively mourn Freud.

ACKNOWLEDGMENTS

As with any project of long gestation, I have innumerable people to thank for their support. Each chapter of this book was read in earlier versions by many friends, writers, and editors, all of whom offered critical commentary along with their encouragement. I will recall them, as I reconstruct the circumstances of my writing.

I composed "Reading Freud's Life," while living in Oakland, California in the early 1990s, where I had the good fortune to join the newly formed Psychobiography Group, founded by Peter Ostwald, Diane Middlebrook, and Stephen Walrod. This group, which met for several years in San Francisco, has since moved to the East Bay and continues to this day. In addition to its founders, its early members included (to the best of my recollection): Daniel Benveniste, Jim Breslin, Liz Cara, Alan Elms, Marilyn Fabe, Bruce Heller, John MacGregor, William Runyan, and David Sundelson. Some members moved away, new members joined, and some have passed away since the group's founding. Although I no longer live in California, I remain in touch with many of its original and subsequent members. Later, when I submitted this paper to *American Imago*, I benefited from the keen editorial eye of Martin Gliserman, who agreed to publish it despite its length. This essay later drew the attention of Anthony Elliott, who included it in his volume titled *Freud 2000* (1998).

I wrote "Mourning Freud" at the request of Peter Rudnytsky for a conference titled "Psychoanalyses/Feminisms," which he organized at the University of Florida Gainesville in 1994. Peter's interest in my work, then and now, has served as a constant stimulus for me to develop my thinking about Freudian and post-Freudian psychoanalytic theory. I was very pleased that he included "Mourning Freud," a pivotal essay in the development of this book, in *Psychoanalyses/Feminisms* (1998). In a shorter form, "Mourning Freud" was also published in the volume edited by Anthony Elliott and Stephen Frosh titled *Psychoanalysis in Contexts* (1994).

"Freud, Irma, and the Dream of Psychoanalysis" came about as a result of an invitation to present a paper at a conference titled "The Dream of Interpretation: Dreams of Interpretation" (2000), in honor of the four-hundredth anniversary of the publication of Freud's *The Interpretation of Dreams*, organized by Rey Chow and Thomas Pepper, both members of the Department of Cultural Studies and Comparative Literature at the University of Minnesota at that time. To this conference, I owe my attempt to organize my thoughts about Freud's areas of blind-sight in regard to the possible meanings of his own dreams. I am grateful (once again) to Peter Rudnytsky, who had succeeded Martin Gliserman as editor of *American Imago*, for perceiving the merit of this essay and fostering its publication under the title "Mouth to Mouth: Freud, Irma and the Dream of Psychoanalysis."

I wrote "Undoing Incest" at the request of the editors of *Modern Philology* to review the collection of essays edited by Lynda Boose and Betty S. Flowers titled *Daughters and Fathers* (1989). I "mistook" their invitation to write a review essay rather than a simple review. The editors were kind enough to overlook my error and publish "Undoing Incest" in its entirety.

I am happy to be able to include it here, as it extends my thinking about the "traffic in women" into my speculations about Freud's involvement in triangular relationships throughout his life. This essay also allowed me to pay tribute to the work of numerous feminist scholars of Shakespeare, whose groundbreaking analyses provided me with my first understanding of how women (and other) scholars may support one another in intellectual ways. I spent my formative years as a literary/social critic in their good company and owe them all for the vibrant community of discussion and debate they introduced me to. I have sustained lifelong friendships with many of them: especially Shirley Garner, Gayle Greene, Coppélia Kahn, Carol Thomas Neely, and Murray Schwartz. Although I have not published on Shakespeare for many years, I think about his work nearly every day and feel grateful for my friends' companionship and support.

The gestation of "Freud as Memoirist" is complex and spans many years. In 1998, I enrolled in a program titled New Directions in Psychoanalytic Thinking, founded by Sharon Alperovitz MSW and Robert Winer MD, which had formed under the aegis of the Washington Center for Psychoanalysis. I had been seeking a way to supplement my work in academia, which focuses primarily on theory, with an understanding of how clinicians make use of these theories in their consulting rooms. I participated in this three-year program, graduated from it and continued to attend, first as a group discussion leader, then as the organizer of one of its weekend conferences. Throughout, I had anticipated writing a "capstone" essay on the case history as a variant of fiction writing. But I delayed.

In 2006, I was invited to join a Freud Discussion Group, the brainchild of Anton Kris and Elisabeth Young-Bruehl, which met for several years in New York City for the purpose of discussing and theorizing "The Historiography of Psychoanalysis." I participated in this lively discussion for many years, until Elisabeth moved to Canada, where she died suddenly (of a pulmonary embolism) in 2011. The members of this group included (in addition to Elisabeth and Tony) the following distinguished company: Samuel Abrams, Harold Blum, Marcia Cavel, Peter Neubauer, Murray Schwartz, and Eli Zaretsky. I was lucky to be a part of their high-powered conversation. We had all promised to compose an essay on the topic of our discussion, but Elisabeth, Murray, and Eli were the ones who came through first on this promise. The rest of us went our own ways. I did, however, submit about five pages of a prospective essay derived from my original idea about the rhetorical form of the psychoanalytic case history, but did not complete it then. I remember vividly, however, the comments of Tony Kris. Years later, when I took up this topic again, I refined my preliminary train of thought (in relation to what I was then learning about the neuroscience of memory and my teaching of memoir writing) into a broader essay on Freud's understanding of how memory alters over time and in relation to one's personal wishes and needs.

I presented this essay, at the invitation of Peter Rudnytsky, Chair of the APsaA History of Psychoanalysis Discussion Group, at its annual meeting in 2012, where I benefited from the group's questions and comments. Lou Rose, the incoming editor of *American Imago* (and current Executive Director of the Sigmund Freud Archives), offered publication, which I gratefully accepted.

I composed "Literature and Psychoanalysis" at the request of Anthony Elliott and Jeffrey Prager for their jointly edited volume *Routledge Handbook for Psychoanalysis in the Humanities and the Social Sciences* (2016). I knew them both by this point in time, deeply respected their work and was delighted to be asked to contribute to this distinguished collection of essays. It has always been a pleasure for me to work with Anthony and Jeffrey.

The final chapter in this volume came about as a result of Anthony Elliot's invitation to participate in a conference he organized at the University of Flinders, Adelaide, Australia, titled "The Paradox of Melancholia: Paralysis and Agency" (2012). Although I'd worked with Anthony and the other keynote speaker Jeffrey Prager long-distance, I'd never met them in person. This was a very memorable occasion for me. Not only did it lead to my expanding my ideas about Freud's theories of mourning and melancholia but also to a wider range of thought about how psychoanalytic theory, post-Freud, has shifted focus from oedipal drive theory to the realm of preoedipal theory and to the related fields of attachment and trauma theory.

As I write this, I realize two things: how important it has been to me over the course of my career to participate in three very different, yet equally vital, intellectual communities, each of which has fostered my deepest personal and professional commitments: to literature, to feminism, and to psychoanalysis. I want to express my gratitude, once again, to the following: the Psychobiography Group in the Bay Area, the New Directions Program in Washington DC, and the Freud Discussion Group in New York. To this list, I want to add two more: the Program for the Psychological Study of the Arts, founded by Norman Holland at SUNY Buffalo in the 1970s, and the Minnesota Psychoanalytic Society and Institute, of which I have been a member since the mid-1990s.

Norman's program at SUNY Buffalo held an annual conference for many years, which served to foster my interest and education in the changing field of psychoanalytic theory while also offering me a congenial environment for trying out my own ideas. In more recent years, my participation in the Minnesota Psychoanalytic Society and Institute has broadened my relationships with theorists and clinicians in my home environment. I am thankful in particular to Hal Steiger MD for hosting the ongoing discussion group on "Interdisciplinary Studies in Psychoanalysis," which seeks to bridge the worlds of psychoanalysis and the academy.

Nearly last but not least, I am deeply grateful to the Department of English and the University of Minnesota for assisting my research and writing through numerous grants and funded leaves

ACKNOWLEDGMENTS

over time. In particular, my being named Regents Professor in 2008 (through its generous research budget) has supported the preparation of this book.

I have more debts than I can possibly name. In closing, however, I want to single out some especially important people who have not only fostered my intellectual life but also become lifelong friends. Among and in addition to the ones I've already named, I wish to pay special tribute to the following: Janet Adelman, Ramsay Breslin, Nancy Chodorow, Marilyn Fabe, Shirley Garner, Gayle Greene, Claire Kahane, Anton Kris, Carol Thomas Neely, Peter Rudnytsky, Murray Schwartz, Stephen Walrod, and Brenda Webster. Others who know how much they have contributed to my personal development and well-being include: Jessica Gohlke, Sybil Houlding, Alice Jones, Toni McNaron, Robert Littlejohn, Mardi Louisell, Wendy Martin, Leslie Morris, Mariann Regan, Steven Snyder, and Michael Young.

Every one of you has played a significant part in contributing to the person I am today and the one I have yet to become. None of you is responsible for any errors of fact, judgment, or infelicities of expression that remain in this book.

Introduction:
Insight and Blindness

> *All literary works contain one or more ... sub-texts, and there is a sense in which they may be spoken of as the "unconscious" of the work itself. The work's insights, as with all writing, are deeply related to its blindnesses: what it does not say, and how it does not say it, may be as important as what it articulates.*
>
> TERRY EAGLETON, *LITERARY THEORY: AN INTRODUCTION*

After Freud, no author may be understood to be the master of his or her texts or meanings. The readings that I offer in this book address the blind spots in Freud's own thinking as a means of exploring the trajectory of psychoanalysis over the course of the twentieth century and beyond. In its broadest terms, I see this movement as a shift from oedipal to preoedipal concerns, with corresponding emphases on the mother–infant relationship, the drama of separation and individuation, preverbal/unrepresented states of being, and related theories of trauma and mourning.

The subject that Freud most clearly failed to confront in his life and his work, I maintain, is mourning. To his credit and to our lasting benefit, he attempted a theory of ego development grounded in the infant's struggle to cope with the frustrations and disappointments of separation from its mother, but did not delve deeply into these issues as he considered them too shadowy and elusive to pursue. The first four chapters in this collection explore Freud's reluctance to investigate the dynamics of the preoedipal period as one of the possible results of his own childhood history of traumatic loss.[1] The Oedipus complex, I maintain, was a more cheerful, optimistic, and ego-syntonic construct for him to theorize than that of mourning.

Post-Freudian developments in psychoanalytic theory focus precisely on the areas that Freud neglected. Taking cues from his work, they also probe the blind spots in his thinking to develop new concepts of human development—ones that respond in a mobile way to the social, cultural, and historical dilemmas of our time. Theories of trauma and mourning, I maintain, have emerged as especially powerful tools in conceptualizing some of the problems we face today as a global society. The process of culturally mourning Freud—separating from his magisterial image, ideation, and influence, while also respecting the uniqueness of his achievement—offers a means of utilizing psychoanalysis in an evolutionary way to address questions of individual and collective subjectivity, otherness, mass violence, and human suffering.

Terry Eagleton (1983) writes about the unconscious of a text in much the same way that Freud wrote about dreams, works of art, slips of the tongue, and the free flow of his patients' associations. None is transparent; all are subject to interpretation. Eagleton's debt to Freud is obvious. What is less evident is the challenge implicit in his insistence that all texts (including Freud's own) may be examined for their symptoms of ambivalence, blindness, or omission. While Freud's investigation of the dynamics of the unconscious provides the framework for Eagleton's statement about interpretation, Eagleton turns the tables on him by directing our attention to the unconscious dimensions of Freud's own writings. Authorized by Freud, Eagleton's hermeneutic stance serves at the same time to question his authority.

Jacques Derrida (1975, 1976, 1978), the primary theorist of deconstruction (the interpretive mode advocated by Eagleton), was an assiduous reader of Freud, finding in his texts the same dynamics that he discovered in other great writer/philosophers from Aristotle to Nietzsche. To this extent, he read Freud (and others) against the grain, pointing to the moments of hesitation, avoidance, or silence in their texts that demonstrate their internal disharmony and instability. Freud, a master decoder of his patients' dreams, symptoms, and personal narratives, would have resisted attempts on the part of others to decode his own. He alone, he believed, held the key to the meanings of his unconscious. Freud's position as the founder of a new discipline coupled with his personal authority discouraged his followers not only from deviating from his views but also from reading his texts for evidence of their blindnesses as well as their insights. Yet *The Interpretation of Dreams* (1900) opened a Pandora's box for future readers and interpreters.

That Freud wrote like a writer, that is to say, in oblique, metaphoric, nonlinear fashion, making rich use of the power of myth, hypothesis, allusion, and analogy, not only assures his place in modern literature but also opens his texts to endless interpretation. Analysis, as Freud himself admitted, is never fully terminable. We read Freud not simply for his ideas but for the intricacy and artfulness of his prose. Few today, for instance, would accept his fantastical constructions of history, biography, and anthropology as represented in his portrayal of Moses as a non-Jew (*Moses and Monotheism* 1939), his depiction of Leonardo da Vinci's early life (*Leonardo da Vinci and a Memory of His Childhood* 1910b), or his concept of the patricidal primal horde (*Totem and Taboo* 1913b). Yet Freud's texts continue to attract readers as those of many of his adherents do not.

Freud's analysis of his patient Dora, considered a seminal text because of his discovery and articulation of the concept of transference, is a case in point. A key text in the development of psychoanalytic practice, "Fragment of an Analysis of a Case of Hysteria" (1905), unfolds less like a scientific treatise than a short story. The narrative, even for Freud, is exceptionally convoluted, involving a family constellation that places Dora as a teenager in the position of being propositioned by the husband (Herr K) of her father's lover (Frau K).

What seems glaringly obvious to a contemporary reader is the inappropriateness of Herr K's advances to Dora, which border on child molestation. Guided by his incipient oedipal theory, which assumes that children normally experience sexual desire for one or the other of their parents, Freud bypasses the issue of Dora's helplessness and vulnerability to insist on her repressed wish to have sex not only with Herr K but also with her ailing and impotent father. Freud's argument proceeds through *a priori* assumption (oedipal desire), displacement (Dora's fingering of her reticule represents masturbation), hypothesis (Herr K is impotent, hence enjoys fellatio with Frau K), and dubious analogy (Dora's desire, like that of Frau K, centers on fellatio). There is no question that Freud's portrayal of this intricate domestic drama, involving adultery, sexual predation, and (fantasied) incest, makes for a good story. But does it ring true? In particular, does it sustain Freud's conclusion that Dora suffered from repressed desire for him as well as the other men in her life and fled treatment out of anger, frustration, and revenge? If not, what happens to the concept of transference?

Alternatively, is it possible to affirm the validity of the idea of transference, while seriously questioning Freud's interpretation of Dora? I am inclined to argue this case, as transference (and its corollary countertransference) makes sense in its own terms, quite apart from Dora's sad story. While the particular circumstances of Dora's history could not and cannot be replicated with another analyst in order to demonstrate the validity of Freud's hypotheses, the condition of a patient expressing feelings toward his or her analyst that derive from other sources *can* be duplicated. Even ordinary people in the course of daily life can observe the phenomenon of "transferring" an emotional response from one person to another, just as they can observe the dynamics of repetition compulsion (behavior that does not vary regardless of the situation) in everyday encounters.

Despite the questionable nature of many of Freud's interpretations of Dora's wishes, fantasies, and desires, he arrived at a very valuable perception, whose use value does not depend on the specifics of his case presentation. In this sense, "Fragment of an Analysis of a Case of Hysteria" offers an instance of insight in the midst of blindness.

In *The Spectral Mother: Freud, Feminism, and Psychoanalysis* (1990), I investigated the near-absence of the figure of the mother in Freud's writing as an implicit blind spot in his thinking. It is not that he could not imagine the existence of a period preceding the oedipal but rather that he could not theorize it. As a result, the figure of the mother is spectral: obscure, shadowy, haunting, and somewhat threatening. As a consequence, Freud cannot adequately address the issue of female sexuality and does not even begin to investigate the question of maternal subjectivity or desire.

What seems absent, marginal, or ambivalent in Freud's texts provided fertile ground for subsequent psychoanalytic theorists to speculate about the figure of the mother and the drama of early childhood development, in essence, all things preoedipal. Because Freud hinted at but did not pursue these matters at length or in depth, he left an open field for his successors. Many schools of thought have emerged to occupy this field: Kleinian, Lacanian, object relations, self-psychology, and attachment theories among the most prominent. These schools, despite their differences from one another, do not seek to displace Freud's concept of the Oedipus complex but rather to supplement it. Over time, however, the Oedipus complex (along with the drive theory that informs it) has waned in significance as issues pertaining to the earliest phase of life, including loss, trauma, and mourning, have moved center stage. Viewed from this standpoint, contemporary psychoanalysis has "flipped" Freud, exploring the shadow side of his work as opposed to its explicit structures of meaning.

In *The Spectral Mother*, I argued that Freud's inability to focus on the figure of the mother and, by extension, to theorize the preoedipal period stemmed from his association of women and femininity with castration. The oedipal construct, in contrast, offered a model of phallic masculinity that he could more easily conceptualize and embrace. The first four chapters in this book take this argument further. In them, I maintain that Freud's biography does not support his self-analysis as represented by its outcome: the Oedipus complex. Instead, it reveals an early history of traumatic loss that Freud alludes to without exploring. His inability to recognize and mourn these losses, I maintain, resulted in his failure to theorize their origin in the preoedipal period.

"Reading Freud's Life" examines the standard biography of Freud as articulated by Ernest Jones (1953–57) and Peter Gay (1988). Both take Freud's self-analysis at face value and use it to structure and interpret his life. Freud's biography, they maintain, demonstrates the dynamics of the Oedipus complex, hence affirming the validity of Freud's insight. Such a line of reasoning is not only circular but it also ignores Freud's investment in his self-image as the lonely and beleaguered founder of psychoanalysis, whose heroic endeavors in the face of opposition resembled those of a military commander or "conquistador." Freud sought to fashion his legacy in part through this self-portrayal but also through his resistance to formal biography, to the point of purging his files of personal papers on at least three occasions.

Evidence of Freud's daily life (apart from his writings) does exist, however, in the form of correspondence preserved not by the sender but by the receiver. I examine his correspondence with his adolescent friend Eduard Silberstein (Boehlich ed. 1990) and a selection of his letters to his fiancée Martha Bernays (E. Freud ed. 1975) to explore the dynamics of two intimate relationships at significant moments in his early adult life. What these letters reveal, I maintain, is a young man exquisitely attuned to expressions of sympathy or rejection who longs for a confidant, if not an actual soul mate. His friendship with Silberstein founders when Silberstein falls in love with a woman Freud considers his inferior. His rocky courtship of Martha goes through cycles of anger and reconciliation, suggestive of a need on Freud's part to push Martha away in order to pull her back again. Later in life, in *Beyond the Pleasure Principle* (1920), Freud described this kind of behavior as repetition compulsion, without however relating it to his own circumstances. In the push/pull game with a spool played by his grandson Ernst, Freud perceived a child's attempt to master (through repetition) the trauma of his mother's departure. What he was unable to recognize was the extent to which Ernst's dilemma mirrored his own history of early loss.

Whereas the official biography of Freud focuses on the oedipal drama of his life, I redirect the reader's gaze to its preoedipal dynamics, taking clues from what we know about his mother's character and the multiple disruptions of his early life. This record reveals a series of painful ruptures and upheavals that Freud could not acknowledge, and hence failed to mourn.

In "Mourning Freud," I examine Freud's response to his father's death in the light of his development of the Oedipus complex, which served to obscure a tangled set of emotional responses centered on the feeling of being painfully "uprooted." Jacob Freud died in 1896, in the midst of Freud's most profound period of inner turmoil and self-questioning. Not only was Freud suffering from a host of neurotic symptoms but he was also struggling with the idea of the seduction theory, which attributed his own and his patients' hysteria to childhood sexual abuse. If the seduction theory is true, Freud reluctantly concluded, fathers are to blame.

Finding this hypothesis difficult to credit, Freud opted (theoretically) for a reversal of the trajectory of desire. Parents do not want to have sex with their children; rather children harbor erotic feelings toward their parents. This shift of focus, which entailed a transposition of his patients' stories of sexual abuse from the realm of actuality to that of fantasy, not only set the course of Freud's future theorizing but also exonerated his father from the charge of having molested his children—a relief to Freud in the midst of his grief.

At the same time, Freud appeared to have slighted his father's memory in choosing a simple funeral ceremony (over the objections of his family) and in arriving late for the ceremony itself. Freud analyzes at length a dream that contains the phrase "You are requested to close the eyes" in the light of his behavior but does not connect this injunction to his seeming indifference to the gravity of the occasion. Later, he misquotes Hamlet "to be cheerful is everything" to his friend Wilhelm Fliess, as he writes to inform him that he has renounced his seduction theory (Masson ed. 1985, 265). Further distorting the plotline of Shakespeare's play, Freud interprets Hamlet's delay in killing Claudius as evidence of his murderous wishes toward his (deceased) father. Freud, in effect, bypasses the subject of mourning (Hamlet's and his own) in the face of his father's death—to focus on filial lust and aggression.

Freud's articulation of the Oedipus complex, consisting of erotic wishes directed toward the mother and hostility toward the father, acts as a screen or defense against a more problematic set of concerns, as represented by the condition of mourning, which Freud associated with helplessness and vulnerability. When Freud addressed the subject of melancholia in 1895, a year prior to his father's death, he described it as a "wound" or "hole" in the psychic sphere (Masson ed. 1985, 103–104). Later, in "Mourning and Melancholia," he repeated this metaphor, comparing the dynamics of melancholia to that of "a painful wound which calls for an extraordinarily high anti-cathexis" (1917, 258). It is clear that Freud's response to his father's death stimulated his thinking in creative ways. Yet psychoanalysis as a discipline rests not on the feeling of being "uprooted," much less on the metaphor of the wound, but on the Oedipus complex. How might it have developed differently had Freud probed more deeply into his grieving process?

"Freud, Irma, and the Dream of Psychoanalysis" examines Freud's "specimen" dream in *The Interpretation of Dreams* (1900) as an instance of phallic interpretation imposed on oral material.

Freud's self-analysis, here as in other respects, focuses on oedipal themes while ignoring preoedipal avenues of interpretation.

Irma, the subject of Freud's dream, complains of pains in her throat, stomach, and abdomen. Reluctantly, she opens her mouth for examination, where Freud observes whitish patches and scabs covering structures that resemble the turbinal bones of the nose. He understands these signs of infection as due to a contaminated injection of trymethylamin administered by a friend.

Irma calls up many associations: to Freud's wife Martha; his daughter Mathilde; women patients in general; and Emma Eckstein in particular, who suffered from nasal hemorrhages due to a bungled operation performed by Freud's friend Wilhelm Fliess. The association with Emma Eckstein is particularly relevant, I maintain, due to Freud's own subjection to nasal surgery at the hands of Fliess. Rather than pursue his implicit "feminine" identification with Irma/Emma, however, Freud emphasizes the "masculine" meanings of the dream. His summary interpretation focuses on his wish to disclaim responsibility for Irma's distress, attributing it instead to the unclean injection.

Freud's interpretation emphasizes his role as Irma's physician and his anxiety about his failure to relieve her of her afflictions. While his interpretation makes sense in terms of his recommending surgery to Emma and his feeling of responsibility for its outcome, it obscures the degree to which Freud may have feared for his own safety at the hands of Fliess. Had he pursued this line of association, he would have placed himself in the position of a suffering, orally/nasally violated woman.

Ironically, Freud suffered later in life from cancer of the mouth and jaw, an actual (and finally fatal) form of oral violation. There is no question, moreover, that his cancer was fostered, if not induced, by his addiction to smoking, specifically to cigars. The painful operations necessitated by Freud's condition also caused him to hemorrhage (not unlike Emma Eckstein) on more than one occasion. In this sense, Freud's Irma dream seems eerily premonitory.

I suggest that Freud's addiction to cigars (which persisted despite his cancer diagnosis) represented an unsatisfied oral craving, not unlike the one he attributes to Leonardo da Vinci in his fantasy recreation of Leonardo's infancy. The bastard Leonardo, he posits, was once aggressively kissed and fondled by his mother, then abruptly abandoned when she relinquished him to the care of his well-born father. Deprived of his mother's nipple, Leonardo developed in its place a fondness for sucking at the male organ, which contributed to his adult homosexual disposition. Freud, who imagined a vivid and complex scenario of Leonardo's relationship with his mother, radically simplified the narrative of his own. His mother Amalia rarely appears in his writing, except in idealized form, as the beautiful young mother who believed in the destiny of her "goldener Sigi," her beloved first-born son.

The reality of Freud's early life did not conform to this ideal. Rather, his position at the center of his mother's attention was soon disrupted by the birth of his brother Julius, followed by Julius's death and (presumably) Amalia's mourning. Six other siblings were born in rapid succession, each calling for maternal care. While Freud's first nanny may have provided a substitute for his mother's love, she too proved unreliable. Caught stealing from her young charge, she was abruptly dismissed. Nor did Freud's father offer a bulwark of protection against these childhood misfortunes. Business problems forced Jacob to relocate his family twice within a period of two years, first to Leipzig and then to Vienna. Freud's early life was filled with loss.

If Freud *did* not theorize the preoedipal period (as I have argued in *The Spectral Mother*), it was because he *could* not (as I argue here), due to his inability to acknowledge the painful feelings evoked in him by the disruptions of his childhood, coupled with his understanding of melancholia (unresolved mourning) as an open wound. His emphasis on the Oedipus complex screened this awareness from his self-scrutiny, which acted instead to confirm the identity he strove to construct, inhabit, and bequeath to posterity. Ernest Jones's and Peter Gay's oedipal readings of Freud's biography reaffirm Freud's own carefully articulated self-image. A preoedipal interpretation of his life, such as the one I present in the first four chapters in this collection, offers a different picture. Reading on the margins of the official biography and in the interstices of Freud's own writings, one can discern the figure of a man who struggled with and against mourning, in theory as in life.

The next three chapters locate psychoanalysis in contexts (social, cultural, and literary) that broaden the discussion of Freud's work to demonstrate its continuing relevance to contemporary theory and practice. Here, I explore trends in psychoanalytic, sociocultural, and literary theory that intersect with, challenge, and extend Freud's thinking into areas he either failed to imagine or chose not to pursue. My assumption is that psychoanalysis, as a product of human invention, is historically contingent, hence subject to alterations in culture and society. Together these chapters demonstrate how psychoanalysis has evolved in response to significant social developments as manifest in second-wave feminism, critical theory, and postmodernism.

"Daughters and Fathers" (1989), a review of an anthology of essays by the same title, examines the Oedipus complex in relation to its corollary the exchange of women, viewed by Lévi-Strauss as fundamental to the structure of human society. As Lynda Boose, one of the editors of this collection, points out, Freud's assumption that the father prohibits incest between mother and son in the patriarchal family offers no particular protection to the daughter. Rather, the father's authority over his daughter's choice of a mate not only assures her subordination to him but also facilitates his use of her as a sexual object. While Freud presumed that daughters desired their fathers, as sons wished to possess their mothers, he did not perceive the mother as a blocking figure, that is to say, one who could prevent father–daughter incest.

According to Freud, the father's threat of castration is sufficient to deter the son from acting on his desire for his mother. Daughters, in contrast, are not subject to such a threat, as Freud considered them already castrated by virtue of being female. Nor did Freud imagine the mother as a figure of power in her own right. Although the incidence of mother–son incest is relatively low in Western culture, father–daughter incest (a subject that Freud abandoned along with his seduction theory) is not uncommon. The Oedipus complex, with its emphasis on the son's desire for his mother curbed by the father's threat of castration, provides no barrier, in theory at least, to father–daughter incest. Unlike the mother–son relationship, the father–daughter bond, as Boose argues, "has no effective internal mechanisms for negotiating its dissolution" (1989, 46).

Many of the contributors to *Daughters and Fathers* view the patriarchal family as one that not only subjects women to paternal control but also makes them vulnerable to paternal lust. The exchange of women, designed to prohibit intratribal or intrafamilial marriage, does not, as they observe, obviate incest. Freud's attention, I maintain, to the drama of male sexual development obscured his understanding of girls and women, including their status within the patriarchal family. It also prevented him from exploring with any degree of subtlety his relationship with his mother and the early stages of his own life. Freud's unmourned losses from this period of time contributed to the structure of his relationships with women in his adult life.

As in Lévi-Strauss's understanding of the exchange of women necessitated by the incest taboo, women in Freud's life often served as mediators of male bonds. This structure may be observed in the Dora case history, where Dora is the object of exchange between her father, Herr K, and Freud; in Freud's relationship with Emma Eckstein, whose near-fatal nose operation at the hands of Wilhelm Fliess inspired Freud's theory of hysterical longing; and in the roles of Sabina Spielrein, Loe Kann, and Helene Deutsch in Freud's rivalries with Carl Jung (Sabina's mentor and paramour), Ernest Jones (Loe Kann's lover), and Victor Tausk (Helene Deutsch's analysand).

In these instances, Freud either colluded with significant men over the fate of suffering women or contended with them for sole possession of their loyalty. His relationship with his daughter Anna displays these tendencies in their most explicit and disturbing form. There is no question that Freud's analysis of Anna bound her to him in intimate and powerful ways. Although she formed a close adult attachment to Dorothy Burlingham, Freud also analyzed Dorothy, hence enjoying the role of a privileged "third" in their relationship. In later life, he depended entirely on Anna for the daily nursing care he required due to his multiple surgeries for oral cancer. Freud's emphasis on the Oedipus complex as the foundation of the patriarchal family obscured his awareness of the degree to which he participated in the exchange of women that subjects them to paternal authority and (quasi-incestuous) control.

In "Freud as Memoirist: A Reading of 'Screen Memories,'" I examine Freud's concept of "screen memories" in relation to the contemporary neuroscience of memory, current controversies about the use of fiction in the memoir genre, and Freud's own autobiographical writing practices. Freud, who pioneered the genre of the case history (a synopsis of a patient's symptoms and treatment) as a new form of nonfiction writing, sometimes made use of his own experience in lieu of a patient's history in order to make a theoretical point. While candid in some instances about the degree of self-analysis involved in his speculations, at other times he chose to disguise the autobiographical basis of his thought. His essay on screen memories (1899), which represents memory itself as a complex form of disguise, falls into this category.

In it, Freud presents a dialogue between himself and a psychologically inclined young man about a memory from the young man's childhood. Together they arrive at the conclusion that the memory in question is not a faithful representation of an actual sequence of events but rather an elaborate reconstruction based on adult fantasies, wishes, and desires. Freud extends this insight to include all childhood memories. Indeed, he maintains, it may be questioned "whether we have any memories at all *from* our childhood: memories *relating* to our childhood may be all that we possess" (1899, 322).

The young man's ready assent to this proposition should come as no surprise, as he is none other than Freud himself. Here Freud engages in an unusual form of fictionalized memoir in the guise of nonfiction. As in *The Interpretation of Dreams*, Freud derives theory from self-analysis, writing a new form of autobiography. Since his subject is memory, he creates a conundrum: if memory is as fallible and untrustworthy as Freud maintains, how are we to view his generalization about screen memories, given that it is based on a childhood memory of his own? The appeal of Freud's concept, I suggest, is more literary than scientific, although that does not serve to discredit it. On the contrary, Freud's understanding of memory as a reformulation of the past in the light of present experience has proved prescient. It resonates, in particular, with the understanding of memoir as a specialized form of fiction and with developments in the neuroscience of memory.

The memoir genre, currently enjoying immense popularity with the reading public, has drawn criticism in recent years for instances of an author's conscious alteration of the facts of his or her life to create a more appealing story line. Some readers have protested the blurring of fiction and nonfiction in these kinds of memoir practices. At the same time, most readers understand that memoir writers make use of many of the fiction writer's techniques, such as the invention of dialogue, creation of composite characters, and compression of events, for the purpose of dramatic effect. Where does memoir stop and fiction begin? Individual authors draw this line in different ways for themselves, some with greater latitude than others. Yet none would maintain that memoir offers a simple transcription of the past, rather than an imaginative reconstruction.

Contemporary studies in the neuroscience of memory confirm Freud's understanding of memory as an unstable product of an individual's current experience, while extending it in more radical ways. According to the neural network theory of personal memory, there is no such thing as an uncontaminated memory that can be retrieved intact. Rather, memories are encoded in neural network connections, which when activated make new neural connections, thus altering the previous memory formation through the very process of retrieval. The neuroscience account of personal memory attributes the fluidity and flexibility of memory to neural network activity rather than to the work of the unconscious, yet it affirms Freud's insight that we have no pure memories from our childhood, only ones that we reconstruct in relation to the present moment.

"Literature and Psychoanalysis" explores areas of convergence and divergence between two very powerful modes of interpretation: psychoanalytic theory and literary criticism—as they have evolved more or less in tandem over the course of the twentieth century. Early adherents of Freud in the field of literary criticism (like the first generation of psychoanalysts in the United States) made use of his oedipal theory to elucidate the meanings of classic literary texts. Such habits of reading neatly conformed to the social reality of postwar 1950s America, where men and women were expected to play clearly defined gender roles in society. Social changes accompanied changes in psychoanalytic theory, leading to the rise of women writers and a focus on women as mothers and daughters in literary investigation. Post-Freudian concepts invaded not only the realm of literary criticism but also that of literary production. Women writers (modern and premodern) began to enter the mainstream of public awareness and to command critical attention, in the form of book reviews as well as high school, college, and university course syllabi.

The development of object relations theory, Lacanian theory, and intersubjective theory, in parallel with the evolution of deconstructive literary criticism, led, in turn, to more flexible means of interpreting women's experience of themselves as women and their social realities. Certain avant-garde forms of writing were redefined as examples of "l'écriture féminine," a form of writing that resonates with the preverbal, prelinguistic phase of the Imaginary as conceived by Jacques Lacan. In these instances, as in others, it is clear that psychoanalytic terms and theoretical constructs have entered the mainstream world of literary writing and criticism.

No one, in effect, in today's interconnected cyber-culture is "innocent" of psychoanalysis or of Freud. Writers (like Nabokov) may fight or (like Philip Roth) appropriate him, but there is no question that Freud has profoundly influenced and altered the way that individuals in Western culture think about themselves as psychological, social, and historical beings.

Deconstructive theory coupled with developments in trauma theory have led, in addition, to an emphasis on preverbal or unrepresented aspects of human experience that challenge traditional categories and methods of interpretation. Whereas Freud sought to replace unconscious wishes, urges, and compulsions with conscious awareness and control, contemporary theorists stress the difficulty in providing narrative shape or form to experiences that bypass or elude representation.

For practitioners of deconstruction, texts inevitably undermine themselves due to the dynamics of representation, which suppresses one set of meanings in order to highlight another. Deconstructive interpretation seeks to subvert or undo the hierarchy of meaning in classic texts in order to demonstrate the instability of the meaning-making process itself. Trauma theory rests on the assumption that certain kinds of extreme experience fail to achieve narrative representation in terms of ordinary memory formation. Without adequate symbolization, these experiences find expression in flashbacks, nightmares, and other forms of intrusive anxiety states. Trauma theory rests in part on psychoanalytic observation and in part on neuroscientific investigation, both of which posit a failure of narrative memory function.

Questions of narrative organization and representation have emerged as major issues for our time, given the traumatic history of the twentieth century as a result of two world wars, intractable ethnic conflicts, global human rights violations, and multiple instances of genocide, most notably the Holocaust. How, we want to know, can victims of individual or collective trauma "integrate" their experiences into the ongoing narrative of their lives? How also can an adequate account be rendered of acts of mass cruelty enacted by human beings toward members of their own species? Such questions challenge not only the forms and techniques of personal narrative (such as the psychoanalytic case history, memoir, and autobiography) but also the larger structures of fiction writing and history.

Freud's concept of the "death instinct" did not resolve these issues, although it did attempt to designate the magnitude of the questions they raise. Post-Freudian developments in psychoanalytic theory have not only "flipped" his oedipal construct in favor of the preoedipal period but they have also dissolved Freud's assumptions about mastery, analytic, and otherwise. To this extent psychoanalytic theory, like that of literary theory and practice, has embraced the perspective of postmodernism, which unhinges our expectations about reason, order, narrative coherence, and integrity of meaning not only in our individual lives but also in the realms of social culture, politics, and history.

The last chapter in this volume traces the concept of mourning from Freud's "Mourning and Melancholia" (1917) through a sequence of transformations wrought by subsequent theorists, who focus on the dynamics of the preoedipal period.

Karl Abraham (1927) and Melanie Klein (1935 [1940]) regard melancholia and mourning as aspects of one another and relate both to the earliest phases of life and the struggles they entail. Jacques Lacan (1977a) makes a sharp distinction between the preverbal state of the Imaginary (associated with the mother) and the Symbolic (related to the father). For Lacan, language and culture are necessarily oedipal and patriarchal, although the Imaginary exerts a seductive (and disruptive) influence. Following Lacan, Julia Kristeva (1989) regards melancholia as the residue of the subject's failure to negotiate the transition from the Imaginary to the Symbolic. Mourning, in contrast, signals the achievement of "negation," a turning away from the languageless state of fusion with the mother toward the father's world of symbolic representation. Melancholia, in this view, constitutes a failure of mourning, resulting from the inability to acknowledge loss, which originates in the infant's primary loss of its mother.

Nicolas Abraham and Maria Torok (1994) introduce the terms "incorporation" and "introjection" as a further means of distinguishing between the stasis of melancholia and the evolutionary process of mourning. Whereas incorporation attempts to negate the reality of loss by swallowing the object whole, introjection absorbs it gradually into the mourner's subjectivity. Like Kristeva, Abraham, and Torok regard incorporation as a strategy for denying loss, hence a form of melancholia, whereas introjection instigates the process of grieving.

Trauma theory, initiated by Freud in *Beyond the Pleasure Principle* (1920), has become increasingly prominent, due in part to studies of stricken war veterans and survivors of genocide. This body of thought distinguishes between states of representation and nonrepresentation, as trauma is understood to bypass the subject's capacity for narrative integration. Much like melancholia, trauma resists language and change. Instead, it resides in the subject in an encrypted state, impervious to the process of symbolic representation, like a ghost, haunting from within. I draw on Hans Loewald's (1960) distinction between ghosts and ancestors to describe how trauma, like melancholia, resembles the condition of haunting.

The contemporary focus on trauma in psychoanalysis, literature, sociology, history, and neuroscience indicates its importance for our time. I explore Freud's contribution, as well as its limitations, to this important field of study. What Freud could only glimpse or focus on in a fleeting way has become the subject of sustained attention today. Freud's failures of mourning in his early life inhibited him from developing fully articulated theories of mourning and trauma in his adult life. They also prevented him from investigating the preoedipal period, which includes our first experiences of separation and loss, which lead, in turn, to a subjective sense of individual selfhood.

Understanding the ways that Freud approached and avoided the subject of mourning helps us properly to mourn him. Regarding Freud's legacy in this way in no sense diminishes his achievement. Rather, it releases us, as his heirs, into the stream of our own lives, times, and individual histories.

Note

1 Louis Breger regards Freud's childhood as traumatic, as do I (*Freud: Darkness in the Midst of Vision*, 2000). He includes my essay "Reading Freud's Life" (1995a), where I first articulated this idea, among his references, stating that he encountered it, along with my book *The Spectral Mother* (1990) and my subsequent essay "Mourning Freud" (1995b), when his own book was nearly

concluded. I am sorry that he does not recall our meeting in California as he was in the midst of writing his book, when I shared with him the text of "Reading Freud's Life." Needless to say, our interpretations of Freud's early life, despite their resonances, diverge in the uses that we make of them.

My views are more in tune with those of Joel Whitebook, whose recently published biography of Freud, titled *Freud: An Intellectual Biography* (2017), traces the impact on Freud's thinking of his inability to incorporate feelings of helplessness and vulnerability (stemming from his early childhood losses) into his theoretical activity.

PART ONE

Biography and Theory

1

Reading Freud's Life

Naturally the writer's life will be seen as irrelevant to his works if you reduce biography to the level of gossip. But if you respect the biographer's art, a better alternative presents itself. Rather than maintain that a philosopher's moral character has no bearing on his thinking, wouldn't it make more sense to suppose that the life and thought of a philosopher, a writer, or a literary theorist must interact in numerous complex and significant ways?

DAVID LEHMAN, *SIGNS OF THE TIMES*

In a series of essays on the life and death of Sylvia Plath, Janet Malcolm draws the following distinction between fiction and nonfiction. "The facts of imaginative literature," she writes, "are as hard as the stone that Dr. Johnson kicked. We must always take the novelist's and the playwright's and the poet's word, just as we are almost always free to doubt the biographer's or the historian's or the journalist's" (1993, 138). The shock value of this statement derives from its reversal of the usual alignment of poetry, drama, and fiction with the realm of illusion, non-fiction with fact. "In imaginative literature," she continues, "we are constrained from considering alternative scenarios—there are none. This is the way it is. Only in nonfiction does the question of what happened and how people thought and felt remain open" (138). The point she is making is that biography is a matter of interpretation, a particular construction of the available evidence, from a special angle of vision. This should not be news to a contemporary practitioner, yet the striking thing to me about the standard biographies of Freud (Ernest Jones 1953–57 and Peter Gay 1988) is precisely their consistency, their failure to present competing perspectives on the same (and gradually expanding) body of materials.[1]

Freud himself, I believe, is largely responsible for this phenomenon, having first created, then promulgated a construction of his life that continues to circulate in the work of his major biographers. The effect of such unanimity not only sustains Freud's own self-image but also implies a homologous relationship between his theory, insofar as it derives from his labor of self-analysis, and his life. Should Freud prove to be a fallible narrator/interpreter of his own life, certain aspects of his theory might also come into question.

In my own practice of reading Freud's life, I wish to disrupt the canonical version of his biography by demonstrating the way it derives from and legitimizes Freud's own heavily invested self-construction, and then to offer an alternative and competing version of two episodes of Freud's life based on existing evidence. I hope to make clear how much is at stake not only in the interpretation of Freud's life but also in the construction of biography generally.

Freud's self-fashioning

Writing to his fiancée, Martha Bernays, in the spring of 1885, Freud declares that he has nearly completed a purge of his personal papers, having destroyed "all my notes of the past fourteen years, as well as letters, scientific excerpts, and the manuscripts of my papers," an action "which a number of as yet unborn and unfortunate people will one day resent" (E. Freud 1975, 140). That Freud had in mind his future biographers becomes evident in the following comment:

> I couldn't have matured or died without worrying about who would get hold of those old papers. Everything, moreover, that lies beyond the great turning point in my life, beyond our love and my choice of a profession, died long ago and must not be deprived of a worthy funeral. As for the biographers, let them worry, we have no desire to make it too easy for them. Each

of them will be right in his opinion of "The Development of the Hero," and I am already looking forward to seeing them go astray. (141)

According to Ernest Jones (1953, xii), Freud conducted a similar purge in 1907 on the occasion of his making some changes in his living arrangements, while his departure from Vienna offered Anna Freud and Marie Bonaparte the opportunity (presumably at his direction) to sift through his papers and correspondence, "burning masses of what they considered not worth taking to London" (Vol. 3: 223).

Freud was consistent in his hostility toward the notion of being discovered or anatomized by his biographers. When Bonaparte approached him in 1936 with the idea of purchasing his letters to Wilhelm Fliess from a Berlin bookseller, Freud countered with a proposal to obtain them himself, with the clear intention of destroying them. "I want none of them to come to the notice of so-called posterity," he told her, warning her further that "with the very intimate nature of our relationship, these letters naturally dilate on just anything" (Gay 1988, 614). Bonaparte (with her eye on history in this instance) resisted Freud's urgent pleadings to allow him to dispose of the letters, depositing them instead in the Rothschild Bank in Vienna, where they remained until after the Anschluss.

When Arnold Zweig suggested, on the basis of his close acquaintance with Freud and reverence for his work, that he write his friend's biography, Freud acted quickly to squelch the idea. "No, I am far too fond of you to permit such a thing," Freud responded with genial finality, adding somewhat testily that "anyone who writes a biography is committed to lies, concealments, hypocrisy, flattery and even to hiding his own lack of understanding, for biographical truth does not exist, and if it did we could not use it" (E. Freud 1970, 127).

The exuberance of Freud's comment to Martha concerning the obstacles he has set in the path of his future biographers, whose task it will be to construct a narrative of heroic development, contrasts sharply with his admonition to Zweig, which concludes with the sardonic observation: "Truth is unobtainable, mankind does not deserve it, and in any case is not our Prince Hamlet right when he asks who could escape whipping were he used after his desert?" (127). Whereas early in his life Freud imagined his biography in somewhat mythic terms as "The Development of the Hero," later he seems to have feared not only the depredations of false flattery and outright misrepresentations of fact but also the kind of critical judgment that the disclosure of his intimate life circumstances might bring. While Freud is undoubtedly right to emphasize the "impossibility" of biography, its pursuit of an unobtainable truth, his own efforts to lead his biographers astray, if not actually to prevent his life from being written, bears closer scrutiny.[2] Specifically, for someone whose major theoretical concepts derive from his labor of self-analysis and whose published writings repeatedly refer to aspects of his own experience, such resistance to the notion of his own biography virtually cries out for interpretation.[3]

When Freud, who never wrote a formal autobiography, finally did produce a work focused explicitly on himself (*An Autobiographical Study* 1925), it was almost exclusively an account of his professional life, devoted to a description of his medical career and the way in which he was led to the founding of psychoanalysis. Indeed, in his 1935 postscript to this essay, he avers that his life has no particular status of its own apart from the history of that movement. "Two themes," he writes, "run through these pages: the story of my life and the history of psycho-analysis. They are intimately interwoven." Further, "This *Autobiographical Study* shows how psycho-analysis came to be the whole content of my life and rightly assumes that no personal experiences of mine are of any interest in comparison to my relations with that science" (71). It seems that Freud wishes to subsume his life into his work and to be known henceforward only through this medium. Later, in the same postscript, he offers a rationale for this stance. "The public," he states categorically,

> has no claim to learn any more of my personal affairs—of my struggles, my disappointments, and my successes. I have in any case been more open and frank in some of my writings ... than people usually are who describe their lives for their contemporaries or for posterity. I have had small thanks for it, and from my experience I cannot recommend anyone to follow my example. (73)

Evidently wishing he had been more discreet, Freud now wants to spare himself further discomfort. By enfolding his life into the history of psychoanalysis, Freud not only protects his personal privacy but in the same stroke recreates himself as a cultural icon, no small accomplishment, given his designs on posterity.

Freud's self-portrayal in his *Autobiographical Study*, while strikingly unautobiographical in the commonly understood sense, does, however, convey significant information about how he wanted to be perceived by future generations. In this regard, his seeming detachment, and hence objectivity, betrays an undertone of urgent instruction. A cluster of statements dealing with issues of isolation, independence, and priority, for instance, attest to Freud's investment in his status as heroic founder or originator and hence his belief in his singular personal destiny.[4]

As a student at the university, Freud states that he stood apart from his contemporaries by virtue of his Jewishness, which conferred on him an alien identity. Refusing this characterization on the grounds that he has never felt any reason "to feel ashamed of [his] descent," Freud nevertheless admits that he suffered from a degree of social ostracism. "I put up, without much regret, with my non-acceptance into the community; for it seemed to me that in spite of this exclusion an active fellow-worker could not fail to find some nook or cranny in the framework of humanity" (9). Later, as if to congratulate himself for his ability to sustain himself in a hostile environment, Freud distinguishes between himself and his former friend and mentor Josef Breuer on the basis of the latter's thin-skinned response to criticism of their jointly published *Studies on Hysteria*. "I was able to laugh," Freud claims, "at the lack of comprehension which [Strumpell's] criticism showed, but Breuer felt hurt and grew discouraged" (23). When Freud finds Breuer, whose "self-confidence and powers of resistance were not developed so fully as the rest of his mental organization," unable to follow him in his research into the sexual origins of the neuroses, he clearly also implies that the older man falls short of his own standard of intellectual courage and stamina (23).

Freud returns to this theme in regard to the early reception of his psychoanalytic studies. "For more than ten years after my separation from Breuer," he states unequivocally, "I had no followers. I was completely isolated. In Vienna I was shunned; abroad no notice was taken of me" (48). Even after his work began to attract attention, Freud steadfastly maintains that its reception in Germany was "nowhere friendly or even benevolently non-committal" (49). "After the briefest acquaintance with psycho-analysis," he concludes rather bitterly, "German science was united in rejecting it" (49). Freud's description of his trip to the United States in 1909 contrasts with this portrait of nearly unrelieved isolation, yet it functions in part to draw out the full implications of his European disregard. "Whereas in Europe I felt as though I were despised," he tells us indignantly, "over there I found myself received by the foremost men as an equal" (52). Freud's summary of what he calls the "first phase" of psychoanalysis is considerably more blunt. "I stood alone, 'he states flatly,' and had to do all the work myself" (55).[5]

Freud's professions of his isolation, combined with his emphasis on himself as sole originator of psychoanalysis, constitute what I would call a profound labor of self-construction. In this otherwise modest summary of his life's work, Freud offers very clear instructions about how he wants to be viewed from the vantage point of history—as a quietly heroic figure who has virtually single-handedly brought about a revolution in consciousness. For the most part rhetorically successful, Freud's narrative efforts are punctuated, however, by two instances of conspicuous anxiety: the first when he all but blames his fiancée Martha for standing in the way of his achieving early fame for discovering the anesthetic properties of cocaine, and the second when he goes out of his way to dismiss the work of Pierre Janet as in any way anticipating his own.

In an otherwise smooth description of his early scientific activities, Freud makes a sudden detour to describe why he did not become famous for advocating the use of cocaine as an anesthetic in ophthalmic surgery. After introducing the subject of his marriage in 1886, he interrupts the flow of his narrative to dilate on the subject of this missed opportunity. "I may here go back a little," he begins, "and explain how it was the fault of my fiancée that I was not already famous at that youthful age" (14). His experiments with cocaine, he explains, were cut short by the prospect of a visit to his fiancée in Wandsbek from whom he had been separated for two years. In his absence, a colleague, Carl Koller, to whom he had spoken about his work, conducted the crucial experiments, which demonstrated the specific usefulness of the drug in anesthetizing the eye. Koller published a paper on the subject and thus earned credit for the discovery.

There is evidence that Freud did not immediately resent his failure to achieve this distinction, but rather that his annoyance at having been superseded by his friend developed over time, as he became aware of the full significance of the fact that the use of cocaine for a variety of medical problems had come into disrepute. Shortly after the publication of Koller's paper, for instance, Freud wrote to Martha that "a colleague has found a striking application for coca in ophthalmology and communicated it to the Heidelberg Congress, where it caused great excitement," concluding, evidently without rancor, that "it is to the credit of coca, and my work retains its reputation of having successfully recommended it to the Viennese" (Jones 1953, Vol. 1: 88). Three months later, his attitude toward Koller's celebrity seems unchanged. "On Sunday," he writes to Martha, "Koller was on duty at the *Journal*, the man who made cocaine so famous with whom I have recently become more intimate" (E. Freud 1975, 131). Most of what follows, as if to indicate Freud's lack of envy for his friend's success, is taken up not with cocaine but with Koller's response to a personal insult.

Freud's attitude toward the issue of priority seems to have undergone a gradual transformation, until he came to regard himself as the virtual author of Koller's discovery. In retelling this story many years later, Freud emphasized his own awareness of the anesthetic properties of cocaine, thus enhancing his role in the critical finding of its application to the eye, while downgrading that of Koller by laying stress on his rather narrow medical aims in conjunction with his obvious opportunism.

> One day I was standing in the courtyard with a group of colleagues of whom this man was one, when another interne passed us showing signs of intense pain. [Here Freud told what the localization of the pain was, but I have forgotten this detail.] I said to him: "I think I can help you," and we all went to my room, where I applied a few drops of medicine, which made the pain disappear instantly. I explained to my friends that this drug was the extract of a Southern American plant, the coca, which seemed to have powerful qualities of relieving pain and about which I was preparing a publication. The man with the permanent interest in the eye, whose name was Koller, did not say anything, but a few months later I learned that he had begun to revolutionize eye surgery by the use of cocaine, making operations easy which till then had been impossible. (Brackets in Jones 1953, Vol. 1: 86)

In 1924, when Freud composed his *Autobiographical Study*, he was perturbed enough by his failure to gain credit for the one property of cocaine that had proven of lasting medical use that he was willing to implicate his fiancée in his lapse. Calling it an "omission" ["mein damaliges Versäumnis"], however, he took the final blame on himself. By 1935, his judgment had once again changed. This time he concluded his discussion of this episode by saying that he "bore [his] fiancée no grudge for the *interruption*" ["die damalige Störung," emphasis mine], clearly implying that she alone was responsible for his not having pursued his research further (15, n. 2).

From this distance in time, Freud's need to assure his audience that only his love for his fiancée stood in the way of his having become famous at a relatively early age speaks more to his anxiety about his personal distinction as well as to his reputation for having indiscriminately endorsed cocaine than it does to the truth of his claim to have been the first to divine its specific anesthetic properties.[6]

Freud's tirade against Pierre Janet, in the midst of an otherwise dispassionate account of the early development of psychoanalysis, betrays similar self-promotional concerns. Here it is the vehemence of Freud's assertion that he owes nothing to the work of Janet, whose studies he and Breuer had once cited as bearing on their own, which suggests something more than an impersonal judgment.

After carefully distinguishing between his and Janet's understanding of the dynamics of hysteria, Freud claims, in something of a *non sequitur*, that "this distinction seems to me to be far-reaching enough to put an end to the glib repetition of the view that whatever is of value in psychoanalysis is merely borrowed from the ideas of Janet" (31). Once having embarked on this topic, moreover, he cannot let it go. "The reader will have learned from my account that historically psychoanalysis is completely independent of Janet's discoveries," Freud continues, "just as in its content it diverges from them and goes far beyond them" (31). Janet's works, next to his own, he states, are negligible and "would never have had the implications which have made psycho-analysis of such importance to the mental sciences and have made it attract such universal interest" (31). While Freud himself has treated Janet "with respect," moreover, Janet "behaved ill, showed ignorance of the facts and used ugly arguments," finally destroying the "value of his own work by declaring that when he had spoken of the 'unconscious' mental acts he had meant nothing by the phrase" (31).

Freud takes pains to deny Janet any claim to priority whether for the content of his ideas, his terminology, or the chronology of his publications—in spite of the fact that his and Breuer's *Studies on Hysteria* (1895), along with their *Preliminary Communication* (1893), postdated several of Janet's major case studies.[7] Breuer's discoveries, Freud unabashedly maintains, "had been made earlier but were published later than his" (31). While Freud seems to have no difficulty acknowledging Breuer's contribution to the development of psychoanalysis, he also makes clear the limited nature of his friend's participation, along with his difficulty in coming to grips with the sexual content of the neuroses and his consequent defection from the field. Whereas Breuer has long since vanished as a rival, Janet evidently continues to pose a threat.

Freud's self-characterizations in his *Autobiographical Study* benefit, no doubt, from hindsight. As early as 1914, however, he had established the main outlines of his later stance regarding himself as the prime originator of psychoanalysis and its beleaguered and solitary defender during its beginning stages. In his essay "On the History of the Psycho-Analytic Movement" (1914), Freud declares baldly that "psychoanalysis is my creation; for ten years I was the only person who concerned himself with it, and all the dissatisfaction which the new phenomenon aroused in my contemporaries has been poured out in the form of criticism on my head" (7). Much of what follows is taken up with Freud's response to the defections of his followers Adler and Jung. In anticipation of this discussion, where he does active battle with his former disciples, Freud established an image of himself as a man who is wholly devoted to the objective pursuit of science and completely imperturbable in the face of hostile criticism. "The void" that he claims formed itself around him due to the unpopularity of his position regarding the sexual etiology of the neuroses, for instance, only serves to confirm him in his sense of mission: "I made up my mind to believe that it had been my fortune to discover some particularly important facts and connections, and I was prepared to accept the fate that sometimes accompanies such discoveries" (22).

That Freud had an early and highly developed sense of personal destiny (he was born in a caul; he was his mother's favorite; predictions were made to his parents of his future greatness) has been commented on by many. What is less evident is the way in which Freud parlayed these family myths and expectations into a quasi-literary structure of self-portrayal, which not only served complex political aims in the development of the psychoanalytic movement but also substituted for the kind of deep self-analysis Freud claimed he had conducted on himself, yet refused (for the most part) to disclose.

Even Freud's name is a product of self-conscious manipulation. Like many adolescents, Freud experimented with his given name, alternating Sigismund (his birth name) with the shorter and more stylishly literary form Sigmund, until he finally settled on the latter.[8] As a child, moreover, he identified not with his father whose submission to a gesture of overt anti-Semitism permanently disappointed him, but with great military heroes of history: Alexander the Great, Hannibal, Cromwell, and Napoleon.[9] In later life, he was to form a passionate attachment to the figure of Moses, recreating him, however, according to a highly idiosyncratic fantasy of his non-Jewish identity (*Moses and Monotheism*, 1939). One might even argue that Freud's reconceptualization of the origins of religion, morality, and civilization itself in *Totem and Taboo* (1913) represents an attempt to recast his own history, from the beginning as it were. Not content with his specific family legacy—with its poverty, its ties to local Jewish culture, its lack of obvious distinction—Freud, first in fantasy and then in theory, refashioned it to suit himself.[10] It is in this context that his obsession with matters of priority and originality in his professional life reveals its urgency. Freud's whole theoretical endeavor was tied to his labor of self-creation.

Thus Freud himself set the parameters for the legend of the psychoanalytic movement and the cult of his personality that grew up around him. This was, I believe, a conscious (and partly retrospective) act to define his life which he offered to the world as autobiography, inviting his readers to identify him with his public existence, thereby effectively masking the private man, along with the details of his intimate personal life, while actively seeking to destroy the traces that might call his artfully constructed self-portrait into question.[11]

Self-analysis: Terminable or interminable?

In his essay "On the History of the Psycho-Analytic Movement" (1914), Freud credits his self-analysis with rescuing him from a period of uncertainty regarding the correctness of his technique and his belief in himself as a physician of the neuroses. "I often dreaded losing my bearings," he confides, "and also my confidence" (20). Pursuing his conviction regarding the interpretation of dreams as offering a point of stability in this unsettling state, he began to analyze his own, with markedly gratifying results. "I soon saw the necessity of carrying out a self-analysis, and this I did with the help of a series of my own dreams which led me back through all the events of my childhood," Freud explains, giving the impression that the process was not only complete but also relatively painless. So persuaded is he of the efficacy of this technique that he concludes by recommending it "for anyone who is a good dreamer and not too abnormal" (20).

Yet Freud was not always so sanguine. Bogged down in the midst of his self-analysis, he wrote in rather different terms to his friend Wilhelm Fliess. "My self-analysis is still interrupted," he complained, "and I have realized the reason. I can only analyse myself with the help of knowledge obtained objectively (like an outsider). Genuine self-analysis is impossible; otherwise there would be no [neurotic] illness" (Masson 1985, 281). Prior to composing "On the History of the Psycho-Analytic Movement" Freud had also cautioned about the usefulness of a self-analysis for analysts in training. In "Recommendations to Physicians Practicing Psycho-Analysis" (1912), he states: "this preparation is no doubt enough for many people but not for everyone who wishes to learn analysis." Not everyone, he warns, can "succeed in interpreting his own dreams without outside help" (116). As a result Freud recommends that anyone "who wishes to carry out analyses on other people shall first himself undergo an analysis by someone with expert knowledge" (116). Even so, such analysis "will, as may be imagined, remain incomplete," so that in continuing his self-examination on his own, the analyst will always be discovering "something new" (116).

Late in his life, Freud returned to these issues in an essay that vacillates as much as its title: "Analysis Terminable and

Interminable" (1937). Here both the efficacy of analysis and self-analysis come into question. On the one hand, Freud affirms that it is indeed possible to bring the analysis of a patient to a satisfactory conclusion. On the other hand, there are many obstacles that stand in the way of such a prospect, and in any case one can never predict what the future outcome of an apparently successful analysis will be. Carrying these concerns over into a discussion of the qualifications for *becoming* an analyst, Freud explicitly recommends a self-analysis conducted under the supervision of another. Yet "for practical reasons this analysis can only be short and incomplete" and "every analyst should periodically—at intervals of five years or so—subject himself to analysis once more," with the result that "not only the therapeutic analysis of patients but his own analysis would change from a terminable into interminable task" (248–49). As if to compound this series of difficulties, Freud concludes his essay with a reflection on a certain bedrock resistance regarding femininity in both male and female patients, which frustrates, when it does not altogether negate, the therapeutic process. Freud seems only half-facetious when he refers to psychoanalysis as one of those "'impossible' professions in which one can be sure beforehand of achieving unsatisfying results" (248).

In "Analysis Terminable and Interminable," Freud struggles to maintain the viability of analysis in the face of his own doubts about the possibility of self-knowledge, much less the feasibility of knowing the mind of another. He admits, for instance, that "the special conditions of analytic work do actually cause the analyst's defects to interfere with his making a correct assessment of the state of things in his patient," yet he has no other solution to offer than that the analyst display a "considerable degree of mental normality," a condition to be achieved through the medium of his own analysis (248). But the analytic situation is subject to infinite regress. If no analysis is properly speaking terminable, if both analyst and patient are immersed in a medium of unstable meanings, then what upholds the process of interpretation?[12] Furthermore, if the basic tenets of psychoanalytic theory derive from Freud's own, presumably incomplete, self-analysis, what guarantees their validity?

Freud addressed this set of problems in a marginal, but telling way, in a note dealing with one of his own slips of the pen. In "The Subtleties of a Faulty Action" (1935) Freud describes how he wrote the word "bis" in place of the preposition "für" in an inscription to a woman friend conveying the gift of a stone to be set in a ring. He analyzes this substitution on the basis of his not wanting to repeat the word "für" twice in rapid succession. "The chance identity in sound," he explains, "between the foreign word 'bis' which embodied the criticism of the original phraseology [because of its Latin meaning 'for a second time'] and the German preposition made it possible to insert 'bis' instead of 'für' as though by a slip of a pen" (233–34). Yet this clever linguistic interpretation does not suffice. "In self-analysis," Freud warns, "the danger of incompleteness is particularly great. One is too soon satisfied with a part explanation, behind which resistance may easily be keeping back something that is more important perhaps" (234).

Freud's daughter Anna offers another level of interpretation: he had given this friend a stone for a ring like that before and this was the repetition he wished to avoid. Seeing the aptness of Anna's comment, Freud incorporates it into his own analysis, pointing to the way in which his original interpretation with its emphasis on an esthetic difficulty served to mask an instinctual conflict. Taking things one stop further, he admits to an unwillingness to part with the stone at all and hence a deeper level of resistance to the idea of repetition. "I was looking for a motive for not making a present of the stone," Freud confesses, "I liked it very much myself" (234). Evidently content with having exhausted the meaning of this episode, Freud concludes with the observation that this seemingly minor slip "enables one to realize once more how complicated the most unobtrusive and apparently simplest mental process may be" (234).

Case apparently closed. Yet what about the "danger of incompleteness" to which Freud so problematically alludes? How can we know if he has overcome all resistances, that nothing more important has been held back? Perhaps the very ingenuousness of Freud's self-disclosure in his interpretation serves to disguise a more troubling and intractable motivation. How can we be assured that Freud is not deceiving us, that he is not deceiving himself?

I would like to suggest another reading of this incident as a means of demonstrating Freud's own insight into the interminability of analysis, self- or otherwise. A footnote to this essay in the *Standard Edition* identifies the woman friend in question as Anna Freud's close companion Dorothy Burlingham, who was by this time inextricably involved with the Freud household (233, n.1). Not only were two of her children in analysis with Anna Freud, with whom she had formed the most intimate ties of friendship, but she had further consolidated her fortunes with that of the Freud family by moving into the same apartment building and undergoing an analysis with Freud himself.[13] Hence there is reason to believe that the gift of a stone to be set in a ring may have been charged in this instance with special significance.

We know that Anna herself underwent an analysis with her father and that he relied on her in innumerable ways as a result of his suffering from cancer of the jaw. That Freud was not only dependent on his daughter in his old age but that he also had difficulty imagining her ever leaving him finds expression in his reference to her as his "Anna-Antigone," and his coded allusion to her in the "The Theme of the Three Caskets" (1913) as Cordelia.[14] There is every likelihood in this context that Freud perceived Dorothy Burlingham as a rival for his daughter's affections. For him to offer her the gift of a stone to which he himself felt attached could easily have invoked a symbolic level of response in which the precious object stood for something infinitely more dear.

Beyond this set of considerations, if we take into account the fact that the gift of a stone to be set in a ring was the means by which Freud accepted disciples into his inner circle, his gesture becomes even more richly overdetermined.[15] From this standpoint, one might argue that Freud was not only implicitly relinquishing to Dorothy some part of his claim to his daughter's love, but that he was simultaneously accepting the outsider into his family.[16]

Freud's analysis of his seemingly minor slip, taken one-step beyond his own, ironically validates his perception of the incompleteness of self-analysis. In this light, Freud's confidence in having explicated his parapraxis "without raising any great difficulties" seems a product of misrecognition. One cannot help feeling resistant to his desire to establish closure where the possibilities for further interpretation are so tantalizingly evident. Freud's own analysis invites further analyses, thus rendering the entire process effectively interminable.

Is self-analysis a theoretical impossibility, and if so, what does this say about the discoveries Freud made through this method? What happens to the validity of Freud's self-analysis, for instance, when interpreted through Jacques Lacan's concept of the mirror stage? According to Lacan (1949), the ego achieves a spurious integrity from the moment an infant first catches sight of itself in a mirror or (in D.W. Winnicott's view) perceives its image reflected whole in the gaze of a mirroring person, typically its mother. From this point forward, the child will conceptualize itself in terms of this imago, which will also remain forever alienated and unattainable, a product of false unity based on a fundamental misrecognition. Lacan's account of the mirror stage problematizes the formation of the ego to such an extent that self-knowledge is no longer meaningful as a realizable aim, but only as a trajectory of desire.

Nevertheless Freud's self-analysis has been taken as the ground of psychoanalysis, its point of unchallenged origin, the firm basis from which Freud elaborated his entire theoretical structure. As such, his self-analysis has performed an ontological function, enjoying the status of an unmoved mover in an otherwise mobile, evolutionary system, subject to more or less continuous readjustment and revision. If, however, we assume with Lacan that no one, including the exemplary Freud, can pretend to unmediated self-knowledge, then a host of habitual responses in regard to both theory and biography come into question.

Biographical phallacies

Ernest Jones (1953–57), in his monumental three-volume biography, established the myth of Freud's self-analysis as bold, unprecedented, and essentially unrepeatable. "In the summer of 1897," Jones solemnly announces, "Freud undertook his most heroic feat—a psychoanalysis of his own unconscious. It is hard for us nowadays," he adds, "to imagine how momentous this achievement was, that difficulty being the fate of most pioneering exploits. Yet the uniqueness of the feat remains. Once done it is done forever. For no one again can be the first to explore those depths" (Vol. 1: 319).

Others had tried, "from Solon to Montaigne, from Juvenal to Schopenhauer," only to succumb to inner resistances. Freud was alone, with "no one to assist the undertaking in the slightest degree." He risked the loss of his closest male friend. "What indomitable courage, both intellectual and moral, must have been needed!" But Freud was equal to the task. He was driven by "an overpowering need to come at the truth at all costs," and the rewards were ample. At the end of this soul-wrenching process "there emerged the serene and benign Freud," who worked in imperturbable composure, a man of "flawless integrity" (Vol. I: 319–20, 327).

The stages of this process are by now familiar. Jacob Freud died in October of 1896, precipitating a crisis in his son's mental life, which occupied him intensely for over a year and culminated in his formulation of what became known as the Oedipus complex. Along the way, Freud abandoned his earlier seduction theory of neurosis and gradually detached himself from his dependence on his friend Fliess. Jones's narration of this series of developments supplies the hidden links in Freud's own teleology, casting an aura of triumphant inevitability over the entire process. If the theoretical outcome of Freud's self-analysis is to be trusted, Jones implies, we must believe in its logical progression as well as its ultimate claim to psychological truth.

While Jones does acknowledge, in something of an afterthought, that few, if any, psychoanalyses are ever complete and that we cannot expect this of Freud's either, he does not challenge the central insights produced thereby. Thus, despite the admittedly fragmentary and oblique nature of its documentation, Freud's self-analysis is taken at face value, its theoretical conclusions accepted as dogma. Freud's life is not so much constructed or interpreted in this biographical labor as it is simply restated, albeit more smoothly and consistently, in Freud's own terms.

For all of its care to take account of recent scholarship and to include the most up-to-date documentary evidence, Peter Gay's (1988) biographical portrait of Freud is not much different from that of Jones. While Gay is more cautious than Jones in praising the solitary achievement of Freud's self-analysis, he does not seriously question its results. Gay wrestles, for instance, with the subjectivity of Freud's method only to reaffirm it on the grounds that Freud did not confine himself to his own experience but tested his observations against the reports of his patients. "What must matter to the student of psychoanalysis," he concludes, "is not whether Freud had (or imagined) an Oedipus complex, but whether his claim that it is the complex through which everyone must pass can be substantiated by independent observation or ingenious experiments" (90). Given the degree of Freud's investment in his own analysis, however, it is hard to imagine his actively seeking evidence of its disconfirmation, whereas to do so from within the psychoanalytic establishment would constitute a form of heresy. Nor is it obvious what sort of "ingenious experiment" might be devised to offer independent evaluation.

While conceding the problematic and self-contradictory nature of Freud's approach, Gay nevertheless manages to suggest its ultimate viability. "The private provenance of his convictions," Gay states, would not inhibit him "from developing a theory about mourning and, even more broadly, a theory about the ubiquitous family drama with its ever-varied yet largely predictable plot of wishes, gratifications, frustrations, and losses, many of them unconscious" (90). What Jones accomplishes through a rhetoric of hero-worship, Gay conveys through a tone of sophisticated rationality and urbanity.

Gay persuades, not so much by waiving objections to Freud's method, but rather by first admitting its inherent difficulty (if not the actual impossibility of such a task) and then (somewhat paradoxically) supporting its outcome. After acknowledging, for instance, that "self-analysis would seem to be a contradiction in terms" (96), he goes on to excuse Freud from this criticism on the grounds of the unprecedented nature of his undertaking. Freud had no precursors, he explains, "no teachers, but had to invent the rules for it as he went along" (98). Skillfully sidestepping the problem of the lack of a neutral observer (and hence the impossibility of transference) in Freud's self-analysis, Gay claims that Freud himself "did not consistently equate his self-scrutiny with a full analysis" (97).

Gay's adoption of the term "self-scrutiny," by lowering the stakes in regard to the question of subjectivity, also helps to deflect its negative charge. Yet for all his careful understatement, Gay praises Freud's achievement in much the same terms as Jones. "Compared to Freud," Gay asserts, "the most uninhibited autobiographers from Saint Augustine to Jean-Jacques Rousseau, however penetrating their insights and frank their revelations, had been somewhat reserved. Ernest Jones's 'hyperbole,' he freely admits, 'has much to commend it'" (98).

Next to the mythologizing labors of Jones, Gay's rhetorical strategies seem better suited to our skeptical times, yet the essential narrative remains the same: the work of mourning, abandonment of the seduction theory, discovery of the Oedipus complex, and break with Fliess all converge on the momentous and unique event of Freud's self-analysis. Basically unchallenged from within psychoanalysis, this narrative constitutes a myth of origins, which not only explains the birth of the psychoanalytic movement but also serves to elucidate further incidents in Freud's life. Jones, for instance, understands Freud's growing hostility toward Fliess as a displacement of his (as yet unrecognized) oedipal feelings toward his father (Vol. 1: 324), while Gay sees Freud reliving his oedipal conflicts in his writing of *The Interpretation of Dreams*: "he was defying his surrogate fathers—the teachers and colleagues who had fostered him but whom he was now leaving behind" (141). As if to validate itself, Freud's theory is used to construct his biography. The implicit circularity of this technique is troubling at best. Yet the alternative, for both Jones and Gay, appears to be unthinkable, as it would offer a challenge to Freud's self-analysis, the very foundation on which psychoanalysis rests.

Both Jones and Gay accept Freud's own characterizations of his mental activity during the period in which he undertook to analyze himself. Both, for instance, regard the death of Freud's father as the precipitating (and determining) event in the profound psychic labor that issued in the formulation of the Oedipus complex. While this explanation appears to be satisfying on an emotional level, it does not make sense at every step. It is not clear, for instance, why feelings of jealous rivalry and hostility should be the only ones to suggest themselves through the process of mourning, nor why their discovery should provide significant relief.

Gay sees Freud's mourning as not only "exceptional in intensity" but also exceptional "in the way he put it to scientific use ... gathering material for his theories" (88). He credits this process with Freud's understanding of survivor guilt, concluding that what he found through his self-analysis is that "it is as perilous to win one's oedipal battles as it is to lose them" (88–89). While this account confirms Freud's insight into his aggressive urges toward his father, it says nothing about his feelings of absence or loss, feelings that Freud himself articulated on more than one occasion. In a letter to Fliess, shortly after his father's death, for instance, he wrote:

> By one of the dark ways behind the official consciousness my father's death has affected me profoundly. I had treasured him highly and had understood him exactly. With his peculiar mixture of deep wisdom and fantastic lightness he had meant very much

in my life. He had passed his time when he died, but inside me the occasion of his death has reawakened all my early feelings. Now I feel quite uprooted. (Jones 1953: I, 324)[17]

Later in his preface to the second edition of *The Interpretation of Dreams*, Freud referred to his father's death as quite simply "the most poignant loss in a man's life" (xxvi).

As a product of mourning, the oedipal theory encodes Freud's discovery that he wanted his father to die, the usual assumption being that these feelings, repressed in childhood, reemerged under the pressure of his actual death. Yet Freud's statement to Fliess points in another direction, to his feeling uprooted, grieving, at a loss. What happened to this reaction? Is it possible that in stressing his incestuous desire for his mother and his murderous impulses toward his father Freud masked another level of response? Did he find aggression a more acceptable emotion than a feeling of helplessness or abandonment?[18]

The point here is not so much whether I am right in this interpretation as whether alternate constructions to Freud's own can be adduced from the same evidence.[19] Given the admittedly autobiographical nature of Freud's approach, his obvious attempts to fashion his public image, and the inherently problematic nature of self-analysis, it makes sense to scrutinize the process by which he arrived at some of his central insights. Yet Freud's most prominent biographers are willing to take him at his word. By exempting Freud from the psychoanalytic method of interpretation he advocated, Jones and Gay not only confer on him the mythological status he himself claimed, but they also (and perhaps more importantly) assume the inviolability of such a major hypothesis as the Oedipus complex.[20] In this way Freud himself becomes the guarantor of his theory, which thereby achieves transcendental signification.

Unauthorizing Freud

I want to try out a biographical approach that unauthorizes Freud, one, that is to say, which not only displaces Freud as the author of his own self-portrait but which also questions his theoretical mastery or authority. In order to do this, I will focus on relatively private (yet readily available) kinds of evidence, chiefly Freud's letters to his adolescent friend Eduard Silberstein (Boehlich 1990) and his letters to his fiancée Martha (E. Freud 1975) during the period of their engagement. I choose this material because it has not been discussed extensively and because it covers a period in Freud's life in which he had not yet arrived at the fixed image of himself he later took such pains to project.

Freud corresponded with Silberstein for a period of ten years, from the time he was 15 until he was 25. As adolescents they learned Spanish together, often writing to each other in this language, developed a coded means of address based on an episode in Cervantes's *Don Quixote*, and founded a secret society, which they termed the "Academia Castellana." Gradually their friendship waned, bringing the habit of regular correspondence to an end by the beginning of 1881. A year and some months later Freud met Martha Bernays, to whom he quickly became engaged. That Freud's involvement with Martha served in part to fill the gap left by Silberstein is evident from a letter to her in which he describes the course of this earlier attachment. Due to their temperamental differences, Freud explains, he and Silberstein drifted apart, "Then you appeared on the scene and everything that came with you: a new friend, new struggles, new aims" (97). In this light it makes sense to read the two sets of letters—to Silberstein and to Martha—in relation to each other.

Quite early in his correspondence with Silberstein, Freud expresses a desire for an almost encyclopedic exchange of information. Not content with the limitations of the letter format, he offers, on a trip to Freiberg, to keep a travel diary especially for his friend "in which all the outings I shall ever make will be crammed" (9). Even so, he feels impatient with the condition of separation, confessing that "our evening saunters and nocturnal visits have so accustomed me to communication that I find it hard to do without it now" (11). Often frustrated by the slowness of the mail or the tardiness of a reply, both of which contribute to the difficulty of sharing the fullness of his experience, Freud later reaffirms his desire to tell all, to know all, by proposing that both correspondents write once a week a letter "that is nothing short of an entire encyclopedia of the past week and that with total veracity reports all our doings, commissions and omissions, and those of all strangers we encounter, in addition to all outstanding thoughts and observations and at least an adumbration, as it were, of the unavoidable emotions" (57–58).

Normally somewhat shy in society, Freud opens his heart to Silberstein, taking care to warn him, however, "not to let these notes fall into anyone's hands" if he wishes to retain Freud's trust (12). Evidently anxious to protect his privacy yet eager to enjoy a freedom and totality of communication that he will later recommend to his analytic patients, Freud concludes another letter with the mild admonition: "I trust you do not show my letters to anyone ... because I want to be able to write with complete candor about whatever comes into my head" (24).

When Silberstein writes sparingly, Freud gently reprimands him. "But someone who is self-possessed and feels affection for his friends," he chides, "will always find something that engages his attention sufficiently to be considered worthy of taking up his friends' time," reminding him further that "selfless sympathy with everything that concerns or happens to the other is often the most valuable, indeed the sole, contribution of a friend" (62). Freud is correspondingly moved by "affectionate words," confessing that separation is sometimes useful because "writing makes it all easier," and "it does one good to read warm and friendly words addressed to oneself" (77). In an especially expansive mood, Freud himself attests to the intensity of the bond he feels with Silberstein. "I really believe that we shall never be rid of each other," he writes. "Though we became friends from free choice, we are as attached to one another as if nature had put [us] on this earth as blood relations; I believe we have come so far that the one loves the very person of the other and not, as before, merely his good qualities" (126).

What Freud strives for in his relationship with Silberstein is a condition of openness of communication in which he can feel intimately known or understood. His first experience of romantic love evokes a similar set of responses. Contrary to expectation, however, his interest migrates from its first object (a girl more or less his own age) to her mother. Writing to Silberstein from Freiberg on August 17, 1872, Freud confesses that he has "taken a fancy" to Gisela Fluss, the eldest daughter of his host family, although his reticence prevents him from speaking to her. Ignorant of his attraction, she departs on a trip. By September 4, Freud is moody due to her absence, but he has found a new focus for his admiration, the extraordinary Frau Fluss, whose charms surpass even those of her daughter. "It would seem that I have transferred my esteem for the mother to friendship for the daughter," Freud explains, "I am full of admiration for this woman whom none of her children can fully match" (17).

What follows is an encomium to Frau Fluss's virtues: her head for business, her culture, her easy management of household and family. Yet Freud reserves his highest praise for her intuitive understanding of a young man's needs—both intellectual and emotional. "Other mothers," Freud states, not shrinking from including his own, "care only for the physical well-being of their sons; when it comes to their intellectual development the control is out of their hands" (17). Frau Fluss shows her tact in countless ways, sparing Freud embarrassment when he passes out from alcohol taken for a raging toothache, then ministering to him tenderly when he falls violently ill in reaction. But most of all one senses that Freud is grateful for her sensitivity to his shyness and for the delicate way she has of putting him at ease. "She fully appreciates that I need encouragement before I speak or bestir myself," Freud confides, "and she never fails to give it. That's how superiority shows itself: as she directs so I speak and come out of my shell" (18).

In contrast with the "half-naïve, half-cultured" Gisela, who is so oblivious of Freud's feelings that she plays a joke on him, Frau Fluss offers a warm and affectionate sympathy, precisely what he evidently finds missing from that most intimate of family ties, his relationship with his own mother. In his praise of Frau Fluss, Freud all but declares that his mother did not understand him; his experience of falling in love (first with Gisela, then her mother) brings this painful recognition to light.[21]

In his encounters with the Fluss women, mother and daughter, Freud experienced both the risks and the rewards of intimacy. His ambivalence about making himself vulnerable in this way manifests itself in his friendship with Silberstein, first in his efforts to control the course of the relationship (by advising, admonishing, and setting rules), and later in his anxiety over the prospect of Silberstein himself falling in love.

Awkward, diffident, and unsure of himself, Freud idealizes his friend's ease in society and in particular his attractiveness to women. Yet he sees danger in these same qualities. When Silberstein becomes romantically involved with a woman somewhat younger than himself, Freud responds with concern that he may be leading her astray. Passion is unpredictable, he warns, and besides women are easily seduced. "Whereas a thinking man is his own legislator, confessor, and absolver ... a woman, let alone a girl, has no inherent ethical standard; she can act correctly only if she keeps within the bounds of convention" (92). Silberstein must eschew both "rendezvous and secret correspondence" if he wishes to preserve his own honor and that of the young lady in question.

Freud's severity of tone may derive in part from a sense of personal betrayal, from an awareness of having been displaced from his position as privileged correspondent. Later, as the affair dissolves, the eagerness with which he seizes on Silberstein's annoyance with the girl's mother points to another level of anxiety. In Freud's crude fantasy-interpretation, mother and daughter have been in cahoots all along, scheming to entrap Silberstein into marriage.

> The old girl is a shrewd woman, or thinks that she is; she knows that beauty and youth alone cannot support her daughter, but that a wealth of coquetry is needed to vaunt these advantages and to captivate men with social graces. Her daughter may have shown few signs of this so far, which is why she sends her to dancing school, makes sure that she is in male company, and does her utmost to bring out the innate but latent coquetry of the sixteen-year-old daughter of Eve. In that she quickly succeeds, the child takes to the game, and with the obvious pleasure that you are taking notice of her small attentions, and this explains the apparent collusion of mother and daughter. In short, your part in the whole business was that of a dressmaker's dummy *masculini generis* that is, of a tailor's dummy. (96)

There is no question of love here. Silberstein has merely been played for a fool by a particularly unscrupulous mother–daughter pair. Whereas previously Freud had warned his friend against the danger of corrupting a young girl's innocence, the roles are now reversed. Mother and daughter appear in Freud's scenario as sexually knowledgeable, almost rapacious, little better than a prostitute and her madam.

Freud's anxieties about intimacy manifest themselves first in his difficulty expressing his desires (his acknowledged shyness) and then in his fear of being manipulated or betrayed once they are known, hence his multiple injunctions to the somewhat wayward

Silberstein and also his suppression of his attraction to the indifferent Gisela in favor of her openly responsive mother. Yet not all mothers are so gratifying. Freud's reference to his own mother's deficiencies of understanding, in conjunction with his portrayal of maternal interference in the Silberstein affair, points in the direction of unresolved conflicts likely to affect his adult love relations with women. Some of the more puzzling features of Freud's relationship to his fiancée Martha Bernays make sense in this light.

Commencing within a few days of their engagement on June 17, 1882, Freud's correspondence with his fiancée spans a period of four years, stopping just short of their marriage in September 1886 (E. Freud 1975).[22] A year after the engagement, Martha's mother moved with her daughters to Wandsbek, an obvious source of frustration to her future son-in-law, who opposed this decision, but also an occasion for extensive letter writing. While Freud had opportunities to visit Martha during this period, his impecunious circumstances prevented frequent travel. Hence, much of his relationship with his fiancée was negotiated by mail.

Freud seems to have fallen in love in a rather precipitous way, pursuing Martha with passionate determination until she agreed to an engagement barely two months after they met. It was in the wake of this momentous decision that they began the arduous process of coming to terms with the differences in their personalities. Among the many ups and downs Freud experienced during this time, one emotional dynamic in particular stands out.

Of the two lovers, Freud appears to be the more effusive—at least that is how he regards himself. Unlike Frau Fluss who responded to the adolescent Freud with a ready sympathy, Martha not only resisted his initial efforts at courtship but she evidently continued to display a certain coolness or reserve well into their engagement. While frequently expressing a desire for total communication, in which neither holds anything back, Freud just as frequently chides Martha for falling short of his ideal. "Please don't be taciturn or reticent with me" (25), he pleads with her on one occasion, sounding a plaintive note that runs throughout the correspondence.

Yet Freud praises Martha for precisely those aspects of her character that he finds most troublesome. "I have always respected you highly for the very reticence of which I have so often complained," he confesses, offering the explanation that "I could never trust the love that readily responds to the first call and dismisses the right to grow and unfold with time and experience." Here Freud's desire for intimate communication, as expressed in his next statement, "Then I will tell you everything and you will understand me better," comes up against an equally powerful counter-drive to achieve a sense of well-being by overcoming resistance. "You know, after all, how from the moment I first saw you," he reminds Martha, "I was determined—no, I was compelled—to woo you, and how I persisted, despite all the warnings of common sense, and how immeasurably happy I have been ever since, how I regained my confidence and so on" (153).

Freud's need to triumph over obstacles is so urgent, in fact, that it takes on the character of what he would later call a repetition compulsion. Once having won Martha, Freud seems to go out of his way to quarrel with her, provoking new outbursts of resistance, which he must then overcome. Letters in which he bares his soul to his fiancée, confiding his anxieties, his ambitions, and his love, alternate with ones in which he adopts an unaccountably hostile or angry tone. These in turn are followed by apologies and expressions of remorse. "My beloved Marty," one such letter begins, "I dare to say my beloved although I do occasionally have bad thoughts and write so angrily. If I have offended you again, please put it down on the list with the others and think of my longing, my loneliness, my impatient struggle and the shackles that are imposed on me" (70).

So consistent is this pattern of quarreling and reconciliation that Freud himself begins to comment on it. Two years into their engagement, he writes:

> I am so glad for quite a while now there has been no mention in our letters of any mutual indisposition, also that this time we have skipped our little monthly squabble which used to appear with such impressive regularity at the end of every first week, so that by the seventeenth we both had a chance to forgive each other. (84–85)

Six months later, he returns to this theme, expanding it into a meditation on the course of their relationship as a whole, including its inauspicious beginnings.

In a mood of somber self-reflection, Freud writes, "I really think I have always loved you much more than you me, or more correctly: until we separated you hadn't surmounted the *primum falsum* of our love—as a logician would call it—i.e., that I forced myself upon you and you accepted me without any great affection" (117). Prior to their first lengthy separation, nothing in the relationship seems to have warranted the extraordinary degree of Freud's emotional investment. Full of painful recollection, Freud reminds Martha of their bitter quarrels, rooted, he believes, in her native reserve and self-possession.

> Do you remember how you often used to tell me that I had a talent for repeatedly provoking your resistance? How we were always fighting, and you would never give in to me? We were two people who diverged in every detail of life and who were yet determined to love each other. And then, after no hard words had been exchanged between us for a long time, I had to admit to myself that you were indeed my beloved, but so seldom took my side that no one would have realized from your behavior that you were preparing to share my life; and you admitted that I had no influence over you. I found you so fully matured and every corner in you occupied, and you were hard and reserved and I had no power over you. This resistance of yours only made you the more precious to me, but at the same time I was very unhappy, and when at the corner of Alser Strasse we said goodbye for thirteen months, my hopes were very low, and I walked away like a soldier who knows he is defending a lost position. (117–18)

This description is so negative that one cannot help wondering why Freud would fall in love with a woman so obviously cool toward him, then insist on making her his lifetime partner. Freud himself, in this letter, expresses doubts about his and Martha's future. Acknowledging the problems inherent in their long-term separation, Freud muses:

> if at the moment you love so fondly the me whom you haven't seen for such a long time and then you see me again, see the gesture, hear the voice and the opinions which invariably used to arouse your defiance, won't you discover that your fondness was directed at an idea that you made for yourself, and not at the living person who perhaps will have upon you the same effect he did a year or two ago? (118)

The lucidity of Freud's analysis in this instance did not prevent him from further antagonizing his fiancée. "I just couldn't accept what you wanted to do," Freud admits, on another occasion, "without making serious objections," this in spite of the fact that he realizes "how one can offend by love the person one loves most" (161). Evidently helpless against his own impulses in this regard, Freud pleads for forgiveness: "Do you remember how once, after we had parted in anger, I soon came back to you, and you said you would never forget? In the same way I am not ashamed to come back to you now and ask once more for a kind word, a friendly glance" (161). Freud's need to quarrel and reconcile emerges so powerfully in his letters that it begs for interpretation. How can one account for this?

The letters themselves, I believe, offer clues to this emotional riddle. Toward the end of their long engagement, Freud humbly confesses, "I am dearly happy that you have forgiven me; the idea that you were not thinking of me as affectionately as usual gave me a strange feeling of forlornness, a feeling I couldn't have stood for long, the less so because I had no one but myself to blame" (97). Having alienated Martha, Freud feels anxious and bereft, a condition of inner desolation from which only she can rescue him. Yet Freud wants more than this; he wants not only the assurance that Martha still loves him but that she loves him even more than before. "You have forgiven me, and I am deeply grateful," Freud continues gloomily, "yet I am not quite satisfied, for I believe that when one has quarreled one ought to love the other more than ever, otherwise the relationship is no longer what it was" (197–98). It seems that Freud needed to keep testing Martha's affections, almost deliberately pushing her away in order to experience the gratification of her return. The very abuse of Martha's love, in this scenario, guarantees its authenticity. A less loving, less faithful, less truehearted woman would simply not come back.

There is a highly charged and coded reference to this process in Freud's choice of a nickname for Martha: Cordelia. Within a month of Martha's removal to Wandsbek, he writes to her as his "Cordelia-Marty," evidently a matter of recent inspiration, as he immediately adds, "Why Cordelia? This will be explained later" (40). The letter then describes a visit with Josef Breuer, which includes a bath, a leisurely meal, and an intimate conversation, culminating in a moment of a personal revelation. The two men discuss a number of medical matters, "moral insanity and nervous diseases, and strange case histories," gradually moving into areas of mutual confidence: "and then we became rather personal and very intimate and he told me a number of things about his wife and children and asked me to repeat what he had said only 'after you are married to Martha'" (41). Stung by the notion that he and his fiancée keep any kind of secrets, Freud is quick to reply: "This same Martha who at the moment has a sore throat in Düstenbrook, is in reality a sweet Cordelia, and we are already on terms of the closest intimacy and can say anything to each other" (41).

Cordelia, of course, is the youngest, most seemingly intractable, and most deeply loved of King Lear's three daughters. She alone, among her sisters, refuses her father's demand to say how much she loves him and when pressed will admit only to loving "according to [her] bond" (I, i, 94). What can Freud mean by describing Martha as his "sweet Cordelia," with whom he feels he can talk about anything? Evidently what he has in mind is not the silent and unbending Cordelia of the beginning of Shakespeare's play but the devotedly affectionate daughter of its conclusion. The "terms of closest intimacy" that Freud claims to enjoy with his fiancée suggest as much. Yet the choice of the name "Cordelia" is not without ambivalence, as Freud's next comments reveal. Breuer too, he confides to Martha, "calls his wife by that name because she is incapable of displaying affection to others, even including her own father" (41). Far from "sweet," Breuer's Cordelia seems rather cold and unresponsive.

Given what we know about Martha's resistance to Freud's courtship and the fundamental reserve of her nature, it seems odd that Freud should see his own Cordelia as different from Breuer's. Perhaps what is at issue here is not a contrast between two women but an oscillation within the image of a single woman, or even more suggestively a fantasy structure that Freud imposed on his relationship with Martha. Evidence for the latter may be adduced from the fact that Freud kept the image of Cordelia alive well into middle age and beyond, transferred, however, to the youngest and most devoted of his own three daughters, Anna Freud.[23]

Critics of Shakespeare's *King Lear* have commented on the transformation in Cordelia's character after her return from exile and the corresponding difficulty of reconciling her knowing self-surrender with her earlier resistance.[24] Yet the emotional focus of the play lies elsewhere, with Lear himself, his rage, his madness, and his grief. What matters to Lear is not whether his daughter's behavior is consistent but whether it ultimately obeys his need. Viewed from this perspective, Cordelia's character does not have to make sense in its own terms. It simply has to further the aims of the plot, which admittedly revolves around Lear. Similarly, Freud did not have to "make sense" of his inconsistently held views of Martha as long as they did not interfere with the unfolding of his internal drama. What was the nature of that drama? On the basis of my reading of Freud's letters to Martha, I would suggest the following: that behind resistance, Freud fantasized the reward of unconditional love, that repeated validation of this fantasy was required through a cycle of quarrelling and reconciliation, and that this process in turn served as a means of mastering a trauma of separation or loss.

Freud wrestled with bouts of despondency and self-doubt during his engagement, often confiding his anxieties to Martha and appealing for her sympathy. It is clear from these letters what he expects of her, a love that transcends the specifics of his character or achievements, that accepts him simply as he is. "You will not judge me according to the success I do or do not achieve, but according to my intentions and my honesty," Freud explains, in an elaborately spun fantasy of his and Martha's married life, adding somewhat wistfully, "You will be able to read me like an open book, it will make us so happy to understand and support each other" (71). Taking Martha to task on another occasion, Freud complains that she ascribes to him "a measure of kindliness, decency, and I don't know what, which I have never possessed" (89). Fearful that she will be disillusioned, he instructs her once again how she ought to respond. "I don't want you to love me for qualities you assume in me, in fact not for any qualities; you must love me as irrationally as other people love, just because I love you, and you don't have to be ashamed of it" (89).

In keeping with his ideal of total communication, Freud seems to have held a fantasy of unconditional love. The strength of this fantasy may be gauged by the effects of its absence or refusal as represented in the strange object lesson of his friend Nathan Weiss. Freud interrupts the normal flow of his correspondence to Martha to dilate on the story of Nathan's suicide, which, as he admits, has left him "deeply shattered" (59). So intense is Freud's response to this event that he is moved to construct a full explanatory narrative, bearing all the earmarks of one of his later case histories.

Nathan's death, in Freud's view, is the direct result of his unfortunate marriage. In almost a parody of Freud himself, he insisted on courting a woman who was cold toward him. Though "considered intelligent and sensible" she was "a real Brünnhilde, a reserved, not very yielding, extremely demanding creature," a young woman who "didn't seem to feel any need for love" (63). Unable to accept no for an answer, Weiss persisted, almost hounding her into marriage. Freud himself, convinced "that she did not like him," advised his friend to think twice. "But he just could not bear the thought that a girl could refuse him, and he sacrificed everything recklessly with the single object of not having to face the world as a failure" (64). On his return from his honeymoon Weiss hanged himself. Freud's interpretation of the suicide strikes one as particularly urgent and impassioned.

> I believe that the realization of an enormous failure, the rage caused by rejected passion, the fury at having sacrificed his whole scientific career, his entire fortune, for a domestic disaster, perhaps also the annoyance at having been done out of the promised dowry, as well as the inability to face the world and confess it all—I believe that all this, following a number of scenes which opened his eyes to his situation, may have brought the madly vain man (who in any case was given to serious emotional upheavals) to the brink of despair. (65)

In the light of Freud's own situation, it is difficult not to read some degree of personal investment in this story. What is even more striking is the context in which he tells it—to his fiancée, as if to warn her beforehand of the potential for disaster in her not reciprocating his love. Read more from Martha's point of view, this whole episode sounds quite threatening; it seems to represent Freud's worst fantasy of his own love life. "The realization of an enormous failure, the rage caused by rejected passion, the fury at having sacrificed his whole scientific career, his entire fortune for a domestic disaster": these are all concerns (albeit muted in expression) that surface at one time or another in Freud's correspondence with Martha.

In courting a woman who was cool toward him, was Freud himself making a mistake? It is hard not to imagine some such thought passing through his mind as he considered his friend's fate. If so, he seems to be conveying an important message here: that he himself would feel, perhaps even act, like Nathan under similar circumstances. As if to reassure himself otherwise, Freud concludes his letter with a knock-on-wood type of remark, not without its own nervous "what if" quality: "Well, lucky the man who is tied to life by a sweet darling" (66).

Too much seems to depend on Martha's devotion, so much that one wonders what other needs may have been served by Freud's falling in love with her. In choosing her, in fantasy at least, Freud seems to unite aspects of his first two adolescent loves: the indifferent Gisela Fluss and her intuitively responsive mother, themselves representative of the two faces of Cordelia now joined in the single person of Martha. Yet the convergence is not perfect, nor does Freud himself appear to desire such consummation. Instead he oscillates between states of anxiety and enjoyment, anger and reconciliation, acting out a paradigm of separation and reunion, very suggestive of the little spool game played by his grandson Ernst which later in life he describes and attributes to the trauma of mother loss.

Both Freud and his grandson, it seems, play a push-pull game of "disappearance and return" as a means of coping with difficult emotions. The little boy, as Freud describes him in *Beyond the Pleasure Principle* (1920), has the habit of throwing a reel with a string attached to it over the side of his cot to the accompaniment of an expressive "o-o-o-o" sound, which Freud interprets to mean "fort" (gone), and then pulling it back with a corresponding "da" (there). This, Freud states, "was related to the child's great cultural achievement—the instinctual renunciation (that is, the renunciation of instinctual satisfaction) which he had made in allowing his mother to go away without protesting. He compensated himself for this, as it were, by staging the disappearance and return of the objects within his reach" (15). By compulsively reenacting the drama of his mother's departure and return, the child overcomes his feelings of helplessness, anxiety, and (presumably) loss. "At the outset," Freud explains, "he was in a *passive* situation—he was overpowered by the experience: but by repeating it, unpleasurable though it was, as a game, he took on an *active* part" (16).

Freud's emphasis on what he calls the boy's "cultural achievement," that is his self-control, obscures to some extent the initial condition for the game, a feeling of powerlessness or deprivation, which persists through repetition. Whereas Freud interprets the game as a sign of mastery, one might just as easily read it in opposite terms, as a failure to work through (in the sense of letting go of) the painful feelings surrounding separation or loss. That Freud's description of the game occurs as a digression from the subject of the traumatic effects of war injuries lends support to this interpretation; far from mastering their oppressive memories, the victims of war neuroses merely suffer from their recurrence. "Now dreams occurring in traumatic neuroses," as Freud points out, "have the characteristic of repeatedly bringing the patient back into the situation of his accident, a situation from which he wakes up in another fright" (13). Such a person, he concludes, is "fixated to his trauma" (13).

Tempering Freud's optimism about the effects of "instinctual renunciation," one might say that his grandson Ernst, though fixated on the problem of his mother's departure, attempted to come to terms with it through his obsessive play. That other feelings than mastery were involved becomes evident, moreover, through Freud's continuing analysis of the game. By "playing gone" with his mother, the child may have been giving vent to his anger. "In that case," Freud states, the boy's actions "would have a defiant meaning: 'All right, then, go away! I don't need you. I'm sending you away myself'" (16).

The more Freud writes about this incident, the less of a "cultural achievement" it appears. Instead of mastering his feelings, the child merely displaces them by "throwing away objects instead of persons" (16). Even more disturbing than this observation, however, is Freud's footnote concerning it. "When this child was five and three-quarters," he states coolly, "his mother died. Now that she was really 'gone' ('o-o-o'), the little boy showed no signs of grief" (16). "It is true," he adds in a stunning *non sequitur*, "that in the interval a second child had been born and had roused him to violent jealousy" (16). The information we have today that the boy's mother was Freud's Sunday child, his most cherished daughter Sophie, only adds to the psychological density and involution of this comment.

What I am suggesting here is that Freud's description of the fort/da game acts as a delayed form of self-observation, offering clues to his own emotional economy. Thus, through the child Ernst we may catch a glimpse of Freud's own strategies for coping with loss—through anger, denial, displacement, and compulsively repetitive behavior, all rationalized in the name of "cultural achievement." Missing from this scenario is any acknowledgment of grief. Little Ernst not only does not seem to mind his mother's temporary departure, but (more disturbingly) he shows no sign of distress at her death, an oddity that Freud makes only a feeble attempt to explain. Finally, the analogy between Freud's relations with his fiancée Martha and little Ernst's game of disappearance and return points to the possible maternal origins of Freud's difficulty in dealing with loss.

Read in the context of his letters to Silberstein, Freud's correspondence with Martha suggests some of the ways he negotiated his intimate emotional life. What Freud wanted from his friendship with Silberstein was not unlike what he sought in his relationship with his fiancée: a selfless and undemanding love, grounded in intuitive understanding, something approximating the ideal of responsive care that he describes in the ministrations of Frau Fluss. That Freud explicitly contrasted Frau Fluss with Amalia Freud in this regard would seem to indicate that Freud's own mother did not provide the model for his search. More likely, he was looking for something that was missing from this relationship.

Yet the idiosyncrasies of Freud's courtship of Martha bear the marks of transference, a repetition, rather than a transcendence of an earlier emotional bond. Read this way, several of the more problematic features of this relationship fall into place. In pursuing a woman whose resistance he had to overcome, a drama endlessly recreated through the process of quarrelling and reconciliation, Freud offers us clues to his childhood disappointments. Like the repetitive play of his grandson Ernst, his actions speak symptomatically. To what event or set of circumstances can this possibly refer?

Leaving aside the issue, interesting in itself, of Amalia Freud's personality, I would like to look again at Freud's rather bizarre comment on his grandson's lack of response to his mother's death. Freud's footnote occurs in the context of a discussion of hostility. Little Ernst's throwing of his spool, Freud tells us, might be considered as a specifically *angry* gesture. "Throwing away the object so that it was 'gone' might satisfy an impulse of the child's, which was suppressed in his actual life, to revenge himself on his mother for going away from him" (16). Amplifying this comment, Freud adds,

> A year later, the same boy whom I had observed at his first game used to take a toy, if he was angry with it, and throw it on the floor, exclaiming: "Go to the Fwont!" He had heard at that

time that his absent father was "at the front," and was far from regretting his absence; on the contrary he made it quite clear that he had no desire to be disturbed in his sole possession of his mother. (16)

Freud's footnote continues this train of thought, connecting the fact that the child showed "no signs of grief" to the prior interruption of his blissful dyadic relationship due to the birth of a sibling. Yet there is a step missing. Why should the boy's "violent jealousy" of his younger brother result in a failure to mourn his mother's death? Surely Freud does not mean to suggest that his mother's turning her attention to the second child deprived her permanent turning away of any meaning. It makes more sense, I think, in following Freud's buried train of thought, to look at anger.

Imagine, for a moment, that Ernst responds not only with a "violent jealousy" directed at his intrusive sibling but also with anger toward his mother for the loss of her attention. Is this not akin to her physical acts of departure to which the boy responds by symbolically throwing her away? Then imagine her permanent disappearance. Would it not make sense for the boy to experience an even more frustrating and debilitating anger? Yet Freud stops short of saying this. Why?

Perhaps because it was too close to his own experience. Freud, too, found his privileged relationship to his mother interrupted by the birth of a sibling. In a letter to Wilhelm Fliess, Freud confesses that "I greeted my one-year-younger brother (who died after a few months) with adverse wishes and genuine childhood jealousy," adding that "his death left the germ of [self-] reproaches in me" (Masson 1985, 268). The step that is missing in Freud's analysis of little Ernst's reaction to his mother's death is similarly missing here. Whereas Freud can admit to feeling hostility toward his infant rival (even blaming himself for his permanent removal) he cannot, or will not, acknowledge any such reaction toward his mother. As a result, only two sides of this relational triangle (Freud–Julius–Amalia) are emotionally cathected.

In the place of response, there is an absence, as in the case of little Ernst. Once more, what this mirror situation suggests is a contraction or inhibition of Freud's ability to deal with maternal loss. The closest he can get to the complex of emotions surrounding this issue is to posit anger, displaced either into obsessive rituals or onto an unwanted sibling. Such an interpretation would seem to call for a serious revision of both the standard biographical understanding of Freud's relationship with his mother and his theoretical pronouncements concerning mother–son relations.

There is evidence to suggest that both are overly idealized.[25] Instead of providing the "most perfect, the most free from ambivalence of all human relationships," as Freud states in "Femininity" (1933), it seems more likely that Freud's own mother, while cherishing her first born son and expecting him to accomplish great things, did not provide the kind of unconditional love that Freud (judging from his correspondence with Silberstein and Martha) most fervently desired (133). The very fact that she gave birth to eight children (one of whom died in infancy) in the space of ten years would suggest the practical impossibility of any single child receiving her undistracted attention, much less her undivided love. Further, I would argue that Freud's need to overcome resistance in his love relations with Martha points to an earlier structure of frustration, one that I would describe as a loss Freud failed to recognize as such and hence was unable to mourn.[26]

One does not have to suffer the death of a parent in order to experience a profound sense of absence or loss. Hence it is at least possible that the death of Freud's father did not provide him with his first occasion for mourning. In any event, grief does not figure prominently in the ostensible product of this mourning: the oedipal construct that underpins virtually all of Freud's future theorizing. Rather, oedipal theory performs the function of acknowledging anger toward the deceased (murderous wishes directed toward the father) while enshrining an idealized memory of maternal love (mother–son incest). Like his grandson Ernst confronting his first overwhelming grief, Freud seems to bypass sorrow in favor of hostility.

The standard biographical portrait of Freud, by using Freud's own self-construction as a means of interpreting his life, serves, in a circular fashion, to validate his image of himself. More importantly, by taking Freud's self-analysis on faith, it insulates the Oedipus complex from inquiry into the process of its formation and hence from challenges to its transcendental status. Whereas the official biographical portrait views the relationship between Freud's life and his theory as mutually transparent and reinforcing, I see it as mediated and problematic. Such a reading, in turn, opens a new set of interpretive possibilities.

Assuming that Freud's self-analysis, while serious and sustained, was in some sense necessarily incomplete offers a way of juxtaposing biographical information with statements about theory in order to gauge their mutual compatibility. This method, while inherently more speculative than the one employed by Freud's standard biographers, permits a simultaneous interrogation of biography and theory, and hence a problematization of both. Freud's difficulty acknowledging feelings of loss, for instance, may be read not only in terms of its impact on his most personal life but also in the way it informed his oedipal construct. Challenging Freud's mastery of his own self-image in this way necessarily challenges the magisterial status of his theory. While some may be troubled by the implications of such a deauthorization of Freud, others will feel compensated by its result: a less mythologized portrait of the man, a more open and questioning stance toward his work.

Notes

1 Joel Whitebook's *Freud: An Intellectual Biography* (2017) offers a welcome alternative to the tradition that I outline here.
2 It is hard to say whether Freud would have appreciated the notion of the "death of the author" as articulated by Roland Barthes (1989) and Michel Foucault (1977). While he might have enjoyed the cloak of anonymity it provides, he would almost certainly have been troubled by its lack of concern with individual achievement. Freud's objections to biography seem less theoretical than practical. While actively discouraging his friends from writing his life, he made it clear what kind of public image he wished to leave behind. His success in this endeavor may be gauged by the status of Ernest Jones's legend-building three-volume biography (1953–57), superseded only by Peter Gay's *Freud: A Life for Our Time* (1988), which continues in the same hagiographic tradition.

Yet no contemporary reader can remain oblivious of the challenges to the practice of biography raised by poststructuralist theory. "Leaving aside the question of language and representation," as Sharon O'Brien succinctly states, "if the self is considered decentered, multiple, or unknowable, how can any genre purport to give us the 'presence,' 'essence,' or meaning of a self?" (1991, 125) Feminist critics, in particular, have been perturbed by these questions, given the centrality of gender (of authors as well as characters) as a category of analysis in women's writing. Contemporary feminist theory, which focuses on the multiple intersections of race, class, ethnic identity, and sexual orientation in women's textual production, recognizes the fractured nature of subjectivity while continuing to acknowledge the relationship (however complexly mediated) between literature and life. "Rather than erasing the author in favor of an abstract textuality," Cheryl Walker writes, "I prefer a critical practice that both expands and limits the role of the author, in my case by finding in the text an author-persona but relating this functionary to psychological, historical, and literary interactions quite beyond the scope of any scriptor's intentions, either conscious or unconscious" (1991, 114). Liz Stanley sees biography, moreover, as a form of writing like any other—that is to say as a construction or interpretive fiction. Biographers, she reminds us, "select, omit, invent a narrative form, direct the reader's interpretation of the subject, interpret, conclude" (1992, 135). Once biography gives up its presumption to truth and absolute authority, it becomes amenable to poststructuralist understanding. See William Epstein (1991) and Stanley Fish (1991) for defenses of biography from this standpoint.

3   Frank Sulloway points to the uniqueness of psychoanalysis (among other intellectual disciplines) in its demand "that its founder's life and intellectual insights obey the same general laws that he was the first to glimpse. Indeed, the myth of Freud's self-analytic path to discovery epitomizes this requirement" (1992, 159). From this perspective, questions of Freud's biography become relevant to considerations of his theory.

4   Sulloway claims that Freud, in stressing his isolation and originality, laid the groundwork for his biographers' recreations of his life in heroic and quasi-mythic terms. Yet, as he demonstrates, "strong opposition was not the initial reaction to Freud's work," nor did his ideas spring from a vacuum (1979, 453). "By 1906," Sulloway avows, "Freud's reputation as a student of neuroanatomy, hysteria, dreams, the pyschopathy of everyday life, and sexuality was worldwide. It is only the later rise of the psychoanalytic movement (together with Freud's destruction of most of the pre-1907 correspondence) that has made this early period seem like a state of heroic isolation" (464). Sulloway sees Jones's biography as a consolidation of the Freud legend and a critical aid in the advancement of the psychoanalytic movement. Yet Freud's own heroic self-portrait continues to circulate despite the best efforts of Sulloway and other like-minded readers. The labor of deconstructing this image, it seems, must come from the margins of the psychoanalytic establishment. For recent examples of such work, see: Marie Balmary (1982), Phyllis Grosskurth (1991), John Kerr (1993), Marianne Krüll (1986), William McGrath (1987), Paul Roazen (1971), Estelle Roith (1987), Carl Schorske (1981), and Peter Swales (1982; 1983).

5 Sulloway's research flatly contradicts this view. He points out, moreover, that "Freud never stopped feeling isolated, no matter how famous he became," hinting at a psychological basis for Freud's self-perception (1979, 78).

6 For fuller treatment of this episode see Robert Byck (1975). E. M. Thornton (1986) covers much of the same ground, alleging further that Freud's invention of psychoanalysis was in part the product of his cocaine use.

7 In case histories published over a period of years, from 1886 to 1893, Janet described hysterical patients achieving relief by bringing subconscious ideas to consciousness and working them through. Freud and Breuer referred favorably to this work in their *Preliminary Communication* (1893) and in their *Studies on Hysteria* (1895). While Janet disagreed with Freud on other points, he publicly claimed priority for the idea of the cathartic cure of neuroses at a meeting of the International Congress of Medicine in 1913. For this, he was vehemently attacked by Freud's followers, who have been successful over time in expunging his name from the psychoanalytic record. Henri Ellenberger, who has excavated the essential outlines of this story, compares Janet's work to "a vast city buried beneath ashes, like Pompeii." And like any buried city, he reminds us, "it may remain buried forever. It may remain concealed while being plundered by marauders. But it may also perhaps be unearthed some day and brought back to life" (1970, 409).

8 Freud's names, as inscribed in the family Bible, were "Sigismund Schlomo," Schlomo being taken from his paternal grandfather. For Peter Gay, all conjecture about the significance of Freud's name change "must remain purely speculative," since Freud himself never commented on it (1988, 5n). Ronald Clark makes the point that Sigmund is merely the German form of Sigismund, yet he also notes "'Sigismund' was Vienna's favorite name for abuse in anti-Semitic jokes" (1982, 36).

9 William McGrath (1987) sees Freud's fascination with great heroes of history as prompted by his disappointment in his father's failure to stand up for himself in the face of Christian insolence. The story, as Freud tells it in *The Interpretation of Dreams*, involves his father's new fur cap being knocked off into the mud, accompanied by the insulting remark: "Jew get off the pavement!" When Freud asked his father what he did in response, he replied simply, "I went into the roadway and picked up my cap" (1900, 197). This incident, McGrath concludes "conflicted sharply with the heroic image Freud had had of his father, undermining it at a crucial moment in the boy's emotional development" (60).

10 Freud's standard biographers have tended to accept Freud's own representation of his family background as more assimilated than religiously orthodox. A number of other studies, however, challenge this view, pointing to his parents' orthodox upbringing, his father's Talmudic studies, and his mother's Yiddish speech as evidence of Freud's specifically Jewish heritage. See, for instance, Emanuel Rice (1990), Marthe Robert (1976), Estelle Roith (1987), and Yosef Yerushalmi (1991). Freud's attitude toward his Jewishness appears more complex and conflicted in these accounts than it does in the work of either Jones (1953) or Gay (1988). While Jones, a gentile, may have wished to downplay Freud's Jewish identification in order to emphasize the universal nature of his discoveries, there are indications that Freud would also have approved of this approach. While never denying his Jewishness, Freud seems, in his avoidance of ritual observance and in his self-characterizations generally, to want to avert speculation about the significance of his Jewish origins in his life and work.

11 Frank Sulloway states, "To Freud, the destruction of history was an essential part of becoming and remaining a hero in the eyes of posterity. He actively cultivated the 'unknowable' about himself in order to set himself apart from the nonheroic component of humanity" (1992, 155).

12 Freud seems close to an awareness of the radical contingency of the analytic process but does not pursue this line of thought. Had he done so, he might have arrived at a position not unlike that of poststructuralist theory, which stresses the differential play of language in the construction of meaning. From this perspective, one might say that the analytic process does not so much lead to the discovery of the truth of the patient's history, but rather to one of the many possible (and hopefully productive) ways of construing it. For Arnold Cooper, this process resembles that of a literary interpretation:

> Analyst and patient work together to create, during the course of the analysis, increasingly complex, coherent, and complete versions of the patient's life story ... Analysis, as Freud describes it in this paper ["Analysis Terminable and Interminable"] as well as literary criticism, generates endless endings; another version or interpretation of the story is always possible, and every rereading will generate additional meanings. (1991, 121)

13 Anna Freud accepted Dorothy Burlingham's two older children, Bob and Mabbie (Mary), into analysis in the fall of 1925. Dorothy, who had begun treatment with Theodor Reik in 1925, switched to analysis with Freud in 1927. In the fall of 1929, she moved into an apartment on the fourth floor at Berggasse 19, where she had a private phone

line installed between her bedroom and that of Anna Freud on the second floor. Burlinghan remained in analysis with Freud until his death in 1939. For accounts of Burlingham's relationship with the Freud family, see Michael Burlingham (1989) and Elisabeth Young-Bruehl (1988).

14 Freud wrote to Sándor Ferenczi referring to his "faithful Antigone-Anna," and to Arnold Zweig describing her as his "devoted Anna-Antigone" (E. Freud 1970, 106; 1975, 382). To Ferenczi, he confided that Anna provided "the subjective condition for the 'Choice of the Three Caskets'" (1975, 301).

15 The idea of the gift of an intaglio seal to be mounted in a ring as a sign of membership in a secret organization was proposed at a meeting of the original Committee (Ferenczi, Rank, Sachs, Jones, and Abraham) on May 25, 1913. According to Phyllis Grosskurth, who chronicles the fortunes of the Committee, "the rings were pledges of eternal union, symbolizing the allegiance of a band of brothers to their symbolic father, Freud the ring-giver" (1991, 57). Conceived as an all-male association in the beginning, the Committee gradually expanded to include some of Freud's privileged women followers, including, of course, his daughter, Anna Freud. By this point, however, the Committee had suffered losses and defections from its original membership, and its function as a clandestine protective organization had been lost.

16 It is interesting to note that Freud had previously made Burlingham the gift of a brooch (an opal set in gold), evidently in acknowledgment of her services as chauffeur on family outings. Burlingham lost the brooch, however, and Freud felt obliged to give her another (Burlingham 1989, 157). Perhaps the reluctance regarding repetition he mentions in "Subtleties" owes something to an anxiety that Burlingham will not value his gift enough not to lose it. Such an anxiety might also attend his feelings about entrusting Burlingham with his daughter's affections.

17 Freud's word for uprooted is *entwurzeltes*. Mark Edmundson comments: "To be uprooted is to be naked, vulnerable, exposed, but also to take up a new position, unburied and unblinded, in a fresh relation to experience" (1990, 43). While Edmundson is undoubtedly right to stress the opportunity latent in this condition, I think it would be a mistake to gloss over the potential for real fear and anxiety as well.

18 Peter Homans sees Freud's mourning process as providing the impetus for his most creative work. In a larger sense, he views psychoanalysis as a product of cultural mourning for a fading nineteenth-century worldview. "As a theory of culture," he states, "analysis authorizes mourning for the abandoned ideals, often unconscious, of the ancient archaic cultural heritage. Both are instances of the ability to mourn. Without mourning there can be

no growth, no historical advance, no value change, no hope—the most valuable of all historical acquisitions, for hopelessness is little more than mourning gone awry" (1989, 104). Mark Edmundson also sees Freud as goaded into creativity by grief. He regards Freud's theorization of the Oedipus complex as a simultaneous act of self-creation and reinvention of cultural subjectivity. Thus "Freud's textual practice suggests ... that the oedipal complex is the negative term in a symbolic drama of private self-recreation, the fruit of which is a new discourse, a new terminological field" (1990, 41). Unlike Homans, however, Edmundson sees the normalizing tendencies in Freud's work as ultimately confining and in need of recreation themselves.

> As affecting as Freud's sojourn in a space of pure possibility during the year in which he grieved for his father was, the turn to the generalized truth of the Oedipal complex that followed was in many ways disheartening. At a certain point Freud could not extemporize freely on his own identity without defending the results by concealing them within a general theory about the basic identity of all men and women everywhere. (1990, 162)

I am indebted to both Homans and Edmundson for their attention to the issue of mourning in Freud's work. Where they stress the productive effects of mourning, however, I want to focus on those areas where Freud was blocked in his personal responses and perhaps also inhibited in his creation of theory. My view of Freud's mourning process is close to that of Kathleen Woodward (1991), who sees Freud as unable to theorize an alternative between crippling melancholia and a total severing of ties with the dead. For another perspective on Freud's difficulty acknowledging dependency needs, see Judith van Herik (1982).

19 Liz Stanley points out that "the past, like the present, is the result of competing negotiated versions of what happened, why it happened, with that consequence" (1992, 7). Recognizing this not only relieves biography of the burden of laying claim to an absolute truth but it also allows for an understanding of the necessary partiality of any biographical view. According to Stanley, "we should ask of biography the question 'who says?' And 'who says' is someone who has produced one more interpretation from among a range of possibilities, and who has produced it from one particular angle rather than any other" (7). By asking "who says" of the standard biographers of Freud, I do not intend to insulate my own interpretations from such inquiry.

20 Neither Jones (1953) nor Gay (1988) is averse to psychological speculation, of course, but both assent to the salient points of Freud's own self-characterization. Others have been more bold, but their

work enjoys neither the prestige nor the currency of the Jones-Gay portrait. See, for instance, Marie Balmary (1982), Marianne Krüll (1986), Paul Roazen (1971), and Estelle Roith (1987).

21 Robert Holt speculates that, in contrast to Freud's mother, Frau Fluss was not narcissistic. "She had the capacity to be directly, warmly affectionate, or as the psychoanalytic jargon has it, to form object relationships of the attachment type. If his own mother had been capable of loving that fully, it seems doubtful that this lad of 16 years would have formed such a crush on a friend's mother" (1992, 9).

22 The release of the full correspondence between Freud and Martha during the period of their engagement will undoubtedly offer a fuller portrait of their relationship, yet the selection offered by Ernst Freud provides a telling glimpse into their intimacy. The first two German language editions of this extensive correspondence are in print (eds. Fichtner, Grubrich-Simitis and Hirschmüller 2011, 2013) with three more to follow.

23 I treat this topic more fully in my book *The Spectral Mother* (1990). That Freud himself was aware of the extent to which Anna (as nurse) took the place of Martha is evident in his comment to Max Eitingon that "in the course of the day [she] separates out into wife and daughter, but through the night will doubtless remain the latter" (Lisa Appignanesi and John Forrester 1992, 281).

24 See, in particular, Janet Adelman (1992), Marianne Novy (1980), and Coppélia Kahn (1986). Both Adelman and Novy make the point that Cordelia's character becomes less fully realized as the play progresses, making her motivations necessarily opaque. Adelman and Kahn speculate on the way in which the play serves Lear's need to recover in Cordelia a mothering presence for which he longs.

25 Not much is known about Amalia Freud, but testimony from her grandchildren suggests that she was a strong-willed woman used to having her own way. See Judith Bernays Heller (1973) and Martin Freud (1957). Robert Holt affirms this characterization and adds that Freud's parents seemed to reverse conventional gender stereotypes in their personalities as well as in their relationship with each other. He also doubts that "Freud felt that his narcissistic mother's love would always be there, regardless of what he did" (1992, 7). Jim Swan's analysis (1974) of Freud's childhood relationship to his nurse offers an explanation of how the young Freud may have arrived at the idealized image of his mother he carried throughout his life. In *The Spectral Mother* I discuss the consequences of this idealization for Freud's later production of theory.

26 Freud describes such a failure to mourn as the mechanism that drives melancholy. Instead of giving up the lost object, the melancholic

identifies with it, turning his feelings of resentment and hatred against himself. Such patients succeed "by the circuitous path of self-punishment, in taking revenge on the original object and in tormenting their loved one through their illness, having resorted to it in order to avoid the need to express their hostility to him openly" (1917, 251). Given Freud's idealization of the mother–son relationship and his consequent inability to theorize hostile feelings of a son toward his mother, I am tempted to speculate that his depiction of melancholy encodes a reaction to maternal loss—a loss caused not by death but by "those situations of being slighted, neglected, or disappointed, which can import feelings of love and hate into the relationship or reinforce an already existing ambivalence" (251). Louis Breger (2000) regards Freud's childhood as traumatic, as do I. He includes "Reading Freud's Life" among his references, stating that he encountered it, along with my book *The Spectral Mother* and the subsequent essay "Mourning Freud," when his own book was nearly concluded. "Of all the works I have read," he states, "her ideas resonate most closely with my own" (386). Needless to say, our interpretations of Freud's early life, though resonant, diverge in the uses that we make of them.

2

Mourning Freud

> *Freud had a way of telling stories—of telling stories about others and of telling others stories about himself—that made history.*
>
> SHOSHANA FELMAN, *JACQUES LACAN AND THE ADVENTURE OF INSIGHT*

Oedipal politics

Suppose, for a moment, that Freud had managed to invent psychoanalysis without reference to Sophocles' *Oedipus Rex*. Or, even more radically, that a woman had created the founding concepts that underlie psychoanalytic theory and practice. How might our discussions of the relationship between psychoanalysis and feminism be different under these circumstances?

I raise these questions heuristically: in order to highlight the centrality of Freud's oedipal construct to his entire theoretical labor, to signal the chief area of difficulty that feminism (on both sides of the Atlantic) has encountered in its critique of psychoanalytic culture, and to raise the possibility that psychoanalysis might have been conceived of differently, if not by a woman, then by Freud himself, pursuing alternative clues in his self-analysis.

An outgrowth of Freud's intense introspection following his father's death in 1896, the oedipal construct acquired its status as the "nuclear complex" of the neuroses when Jung began to challenge Freud's libido theory through a variety of "complexes" of his own invention. Freud first referred to the "Oedipus complex" in his

1910 essay, "A Special Type of Choice of Object Made by Men," where he connects it to the boy's anguish at discovering his mother's sexual activity (and hence unfaithfulness) with his father. Once he had settled on this term, Freud tied it to a more ambitious project, that of explaining the evolution of human civilization. In *Totem and Taboo* (1913b), Freud's rejoinder to Jung's equally ambitious *Transformations and Symbols of the Libido* (1911–12), Freud locates the Oedipus complex at the very origin of human culture.

In Freud's fanciful anthropology, there was once an all-powerful father who not only dominated his sons but also claimed possession of the available women. The sons rose up against this father, killed him, and ate him. Later, filled with remorse for this deed and recognizing the necessity of making alliance with one another, they collectively atoned for their crime by forbidding the killing of a totem animal and renouncing the women they might have possessed. Freud comprehends these "two fundamental taboos of totemism" in terms of the "two repressed wishes of the Oedipus complex" to kill one's father and marry one's mother (1913, 143). What the sons of the primal patriarch accomplished through a voluntary act of renunciation, subsequent generations achieve by acceding to the castration complex, to the prohibition or the "law" of the father. Systems of ethics, religion, and civilization itself, Freud claims, are built on just such a father–son dynamic.

The obvious problem in this fable is the role it accords women—as passive objects of men's fantasies and desires, as nurturers, rather than creators of human culture. Although Freud (following the lead of J.J. Bachofen) struggled to find a place for matriarchy in his scheme, the best he could do was to imagine it as a transitional stage between two father-dominated periods.[1] Freud treats mother-right as regressive, something like a dark age preceding the restoration of father-rule, which for him signals the highest level of social organization. "The family," he claims, was a restoration of the former primal horde and it gave back to fathers a large portion of their former rights. There were once more fathers, but the social achievements of the fraternal clan had not been abandoned; and the gulf between the new fathers of a family and the unrestricted primal father of the horde was wide enough to guarantee the continuance of the religious craving, the persistence of an unappeased longing for the father (1913, 149).

In Freud's rough sketch of patriarchal social organization, mother goddesses, mother-right, even mothers themselves quietly disappear.

One reason for the success of the Oedipus complex as a structural concept is the ease with which it explains the social status quo. From this perspective, many feminists have found in Freud an ally, one who can help to elucidate the social system we hope to transform.[2] To the extent that the Oedipus complex is considered a universal and immutable phenomenon, however, it seems unlikely that any other outcome than the one Freud describes is possible. Certainly, he himself did not imagine such.

While post-Freudian theorists have focused on areas Freud neglected, such as female sexual development and mother–infant relations, few have directly questioned the existence of the Oedipus complex. The preoedipal researches of the early object relations theorists, for instance, were meant to supplement, rather than to displace, Freud's primary oedipal construct. An argument could be made that contemporary psychoanalysis does not depend very heavily on interpretations based on the hypothesis of an Oedipus complex, yet the term remains intact, less as a sign of its intrinsic appeal, perhaps, than as a tribute to the founding father of psychoanalysis himself.[3] Even feminist theory, I believe, has been hampered by its assumption that the Oedipus complex must somehow be gotten around, rather than interrogated at its core. Ingenious arguments have been proposed for situating women differently within this general structure, yet the structure itself does not permit much flexibility.

Feminist psychoanalytic theorists, while displaying considerable verve and ingenuity in manipulating Freud's oedipal construct, have been unable to alter its bedrock implications.[4] As long as the father (or his function) remains identified with the achievement of language and culture, the position of women will be marginal to both. The Oedipus complex guarantees the perpetuation of this system (in theory at least) by requiring the submission of both men and women to its patriarchal logic.

From mourning to Oedipus

I suggest that the Oedipus complex has enjoyed a privileged status in psychoanalytic theory, not because of its self-evident universality but because of its capacity to reflect men's place in the prevailing sex/gender system in a relatively positive, even at times, heroic light.

In formulating the Oedipus complex, Freud put the best possible face on his own position within a social order that served him personally and whose rightness he never questioned. That he first arrived at this hypothesis through a painful labor of introspection should not only alert us to the personal nature of this achievement but also raise the possibility of alternative constructions. What many theorists tend to forget is the specifically autobiographical ground of Freud's foundational concepts, praising him instead for the unprecedented nature of his discoveries.

As I argued in Chapter 1, Freud's standard biographers take his self-analysis at face value, as if to do otherwise would jeopardize his entire life's work.[5] To question Freud's autobiographical effort, Ernest Jones and Peter Gay imply, would raise doubts about the foundations of psychoanalysis itself. Yet this position relies on a strikingly fallible assumption—that Freud had unmediated access to the contents of his own unconscious. Freud alone, in this view, was free of the wish-fulfilling distortions of fantasy and desire. Given that psychoanalysis rests on the supposition of individual blindness in these matters, it seems contradictory, at the very least, to exempt its founder.

It makes more sense, I think, to scrutinize the process by which Freud arrived at his major insights, considering whether other self-representations might have served him (and us) as well. If, for instance, we suspend judgment about the validity of Freud's self-analysis, we may discover new theoretical prospects in the material he brought to light. Specifically, by remaining open to biographical constructions other than the Oedipus complex we may clear the way for a more fruitful alliance between psychoanalysis and feminism.

Contemporary theories of autobiography suggest that self-writing offers a means of shaping an inner world of coherence out of an inherently contradictory and unstable psychic mix.[6] They tell us that we cannot trust solely to memory, which is notoriously unreliable, a creator rather than a transmitter of evidence. Nor can we hope to comprehend the multitude of social factors that comprise our historical moment, giving rise to the particular vocabulary of our self-construction. Whatever narrative we arrive at will of necessity be a product of conscious artifice, partial and self-serving. As a result, the test of an autobiography lies less in its fidelity to truth than in its use value, the extent to which it satisfies our need for meaning in the context of lived experience.

I propose that we read Freud's formulation of the Oedipus complex as autobiography, as an attempt to stabilize an unstable subject in both culturally mediated and personally invested ways.[7] From this perspective we may see how Freud's choice of the Oedipus story as a foundational myth was consonant not only with his culture's values but also with his individual needs.

Freud's fascination with Oedipus (encouraged by the preoccupation of German Romanticism with the culture of ancient Greece) predated his self-analysis, reaching as far back as his adolescence, when he made a careful study of *Oedipus Rex* in preparation for his *Matura* examination.[8] Writing to his friend Emil Fluss at this time, Freud laid out his program of study: "I have a good deal of reading to do on my own account from the Greek and Latin classics, among them Sophocles's *Oedipus Rex*." Evidently, his preparation paid off, as he later reported to Fluss, "The Greek paper, consisting of a thirty-three-verse passage from *Oedipus Rex*, came off better. [I was] the only *good*. This passage I had also read on my own account, and made no secret of it" (E. Freud 1975, 4).

Not long after this, Freud formed a fantasy that he did not reveal until the occasion of his fiftieth birthday, when he was presented with a medallion bearing an image of Oedipus confronting the Sphinx accompanied by the words from Sophocles's play: "Who divined the famed riddle and was a man most mighty." "When Freud read the inscription," Ernest Jones recounts, "he became pale and agitated and in a strangled voice demanded to know who had thought of it. He behaved as if he had encountered a *revenant*, and so he had" (1955: Vol 2, 14). Freud offered the explanation

> that as a young student at the University of Vienna he used to stroll around the great arcaded court inspecting the busts of former famous professors of the institution. He then had the phantasy, not merely of seeing his own bust there in the future, which would not have been anything remarkable in an ambitious student, but of it actually being inscribed with the identical words he now saw on the medallion. (14)

Early in his life, it appears, Freud formed a powerful identification with Oedipus as heroic investigator. Given his attachment to this figure, it is hardly surprising that he should have returned to it during the period of inner turmoil that coincided with his self-analysis. The oedipal analogy was ready to hand, so to speak, available for Freud's creative use.

One might argue that Freud did not so much discover Oedipus in his unconscious as finally acknowledge the extent to which he had already assimilated this figure into his self-image through his daydreams of heroic achievement. Yet the psychodynamic nature of Freud's interpretation remains at issue. On this level, I believe that the Oedipus myth offered Freud a means of mediating the crisis of mourning precipitated by his father's death.

Freud was in the midst of a profound reexamination of his professional and personal identity when Jacob Freud died in 1896. In the preceding year, Freud's last child, Anna, had been born (leading to a decline of sexual relations with his wife Martha); his patient Emma Eckstein had been operated on (with unfortunate consequences) by his friend and correspondent Wilhelm Fliess; and he himself had produced the dream of Irma's injection, the "specimen dream" of psychoanalysis, in which he questioned his efficacy as a physician of nervous diseases. While struggling to theorize the origins of his patients' neuroses, moreover, Freud was actively investigating and combating his own. He suffered variously from headaches, heart palpitations, sinusitis, fatigue, depression, and the occasional episode of impotence. During this time, he, like Emma Eckstein, submitted to nasal surgery at the hands of Fliess, otherwise treating his sinus symptoms with cocaine, while anxiously attempting to calculate his "good" and "bad" periods according to a complex Fliessian mathematics of male and female cycles. Gloomily, he anticipated an early death.

Though fully aware of his father's failing health, Freud appears to have been devastated by his actual death. Writing to Fliess within three days of this event, he first praises his father's dignified acceptance of the inevitable, "He bore himself bravely to the end, just like the altogether unusual man he had been," then admits to his own feelings of depression, "All of it happened in my critical period, and I am really quite down because of it" (Masson 1985, 201). A week later, he writes with greater emotional urgency.

> By one of those dark pathways behind the official consciousness the old man's death has affected me deeply. I valued him highly, understood him very well, and with his peculiar mixture of deep wisdom and fantastic lightheartedness he had a significant effect

on my life. By the time he died, his life had long been over, but in [my] inner self, the whole past has been reawakened by this event. I now feel quite uprooted. (202)

Freud describes a condition of being overwhelmed and exposed: first caught off guard by "one of those dark pathways behind the official consciousness," then flooded by memories "reawakened by this event," and finally left feeling "uprooted." This last statement stands alone, as if to emphasize Freud's sense of isolation. It also seems to mark some limit of his capacity to think along these lines, as he turns in the next paragraph to matters of professional concern.

Toward the end of this letter, Freud returns to the subject of his father's death, in a partially coded way, however, through reference to a dream. "I must tell you about a nice dream I had," Freud states, "the night after the funeral. I was in a place where I read a sign: You are requested to close the eyes."

Freud recognizes the location of the sign as the barbershop he visits every day. "On the day of the funeral," he explains, "I was kept waiting and therefore arrived a little late at the house of mourning. At that time my family was displeased with me because I had arranged for the funeral to be quiet and simple, which they later agreed was quite justified. They were also somewhat offended by my lateness" (202).

The cryptic injunction to close the eyes, Freud claims, has two meanings, both of which carry a reproach, that "one should do one's duty to the dead (an apology as though I had not done it and were in need of leniency), and the actual duty itself" (202). Although Freud effectively chastises himself through his interpretation of this dream, he does not probe more deeply into his motives for his disappointing his family twice, first by arranging a type of ceremony they do not approve of and then by arriving late. Instead, he implies that he had good reasons for both and hence no real need to feel sorry. If there is an "inclination to self-reproach" embedded in this dream, Freud concludes, its meaning may be found in the feeling-state "that regularly sets in among the survivors" (202).

In *The Interpretation of Dreams* (1900), Freud offers a somewhat different analysis of this dream, where he reports it as an example of the divergent meanings contained in alternative verbal constructions. Here, he tells us that the dream occurred the night *before* his father's funeral and that the printed notice took the following form: "You are requested to close the eyes" or "You are requested to close an eye" (317). "Each of these two versions," Freud maintains, "had a meaning of its own and led in a different direction when the dream was interpreted" (318). The meaning that Freud pursues is the one that indicts him for negligence in his management of his father's funeral. "I had chosen the simplest possible ritual for the funeral," he explains, "For I knew my father's own views on such ceremonies. But, some other members of the family were not sympathetic to such a puritanical simplicity and thought we should be disgraced in the eyes of those who attended the funeral. Hence, one of the versions: 'You are requested to close an eye', i.e., to 'wink at' or 'overlook'" (318).

Reading these two dream interpretations in tandem suggests that Freud indeed felt some guilt or remorse at having settled on a simple funeral for his father. It also opens the possibility (assuming that this dream occurred *before* the ceremony) that his lateness was partly intentional, as though he were begging indulgence for an act he had yet to commit. While the "filial duty" Freud mentions in the letter to Fliess may refer to the actual closing of the dead man's eyes, there is a further likelihood that Freud was in some sense closing his own, that is to say, not fully acknowledging his own reactions.

In consciously choosing a less than full ritual, and in (unconsciously perhaps) arriving late, was Freud expressing some reluctance to deal with his own grief? Both acts elicited his family's disapproval, as though he were slighting the occasion. In the preface to the second edition (1908) of *The Interpretation of Dreams*, Freud refers to his father's death as "the most important event, the most poignant loss, of a man's life" (1908, xxvi). Yet his scanting of his father's funeral suggests a more conflicted and evasive response.[9] What might account for this?

Freud's correspondence with Fliess in the aftermath of Jacob Freud's death deals with the symptomatology of his patients (which he continues to attribute to sexual seduction in childhood), his own physical complaints, and his darkening mood. Late in November, he writes: "What I am lacking completely are high spirits and pleasure in living; instead I am busily noting the occasions when I have to occupy myself with the state of affairs after my death." Freud's reference to his own death is somewhat cryptic, as if he had merged his identity with that of his father in the process of disposing of the deceased man's estate. At the very least, it suggests that he is still preoccupied by the thought that he will die young, "a topic," he confesses, that "one should not deal with too extensively if one loves one's friend and only correspondent" (Masson 1985, 204). However discreetly, Freud seems to be acknowledging a death wish.

In subsequent letters, Freud offers evidence from his clinical practice confirming his seduction theory, culminating in the personal observation that "unfortunately, my own father was one of those perverts and is responsible for the hysteria of my brother (all of whose symptoms are identifications) and those of several younger sisters. The frequency of this circumstance often makes me wonder" (231). His entire family, Freud seems to conclude, is sick. We know, of course, that Freud abandoned the idea that every neurosis conceals a history of sexual seduction, overcoming his own nervous depression in the process of defining himself as an oedipal subject. So triumphant, in fact, was Freud's emergence from this period of personal crisis that few have thought to question its dynamics. Yet it is not altogether clear why his formulation of the Oedipus complex should have released him from his physical symptoms, his anxiety, and his deepening melancholy.

In abandoning his seduction theory, Freud foreclosed certain lines of investigation while opening and pursuing others. The most immediate effect of his change of heart was to exonerate his father from the charge of abuse.[10] "Then the surprise," as Freud states to Fliess on this occasion, "that in all cases the father, not excluding my own, had to be accused of being perverse—the realization of the unexpected frequency of hysteria, with precisely the same conditions prevailing in each, whereas surely such widespread perversions against children are not very probable" (264). In a single stroke, Freud dispenses with the "paternal" etiology of his siblings' hysteria—not to mention his own complex of nervous symptoms. From this perspective alone, Freud's expression of relief makes sense. "Here I am again," Freud begins his momentous September 21, 1897, communication to Fliess, "refreshed, cheerful, impoverished, at present without work, and having settled in again, I am writing to you first" (264).

Freud's tone elsewhere in this letter is almost jubilant. Far from being daunted by this newest discovery, he feels relaxed and confident. "If I were depressed, confused, exhausted, such doubts would surely have to be interpreted as signs of weakness," he allows. "Since I am in an opposite state, I must recognize them as the result of honest and vigorous intellectual work and must be proud that after going so deep I am still capable of such criticism." He eagerly anticipates a few days' "idyll for the two of us" in his friend's company, claims that he is "in very good spirits," and concludes that he has "more the feeling of a victory than a defeat" (265).

Freud's evident good humor at encountering this latest stumbling block in his theoretical work suggests that something more than an intellectual conviction is at stake. His upbeat mood signals an emotional shift, as though the process of mourning instigated by his father's death has finally run its course, releasing him from the weight of his depressive feelings. Yet, "cheerful and refreshed" as Freud professes himself to be, he also makes an odd allusion to Hamlet at the moment of the hero's recognition of his impending death. Adapting Hamlet's statement, "The readiness is all," in response to Horatio's warning about Laertes, Freud pronounces "'To be in readiness': to be cheerful is everything!" hence, neutralizing Shakespeare's meaning (265). Even more significantly, Freud ignores the implications of his identification with Hamlet's tragic fate.

In a draft statement included in a letter to Fliess on May 31, 1897, some months before his dismissal of his seduction theory, Freud speculates on a disturbing thought process, evidently discovered in the course of his self-analysis. "Hostile impulses against parents (a wish that they should die)," he offers, "are also an integrating constituent of neuroses." Pursuing this idea further, he links it with a meditation on mourning. "These impulses are repressed," he observes, "at periods when compassion for the parents is aroused—at times of their illness or death. On such occasions it is a manifestation of mourning to reproach oneself for their death (so-called melancholia) or to punish oneself in a hysterical fashion, through the medium of the idea of retribution, with the same states [of illness] that they have had" (250). Freud as much as admits that he wished his father dead, yet in the face of his actual death turns this thought inward, punishing himself for his murderous desires through the medium of his neurotic symptoms and depression. In this way, the idealized image of the father remains intact, while the guilty son gets his due.

It is tempting to speculate that if Freud was unable to sustain a theory of the neuroses that pointed the finger at a "perverse" father, it was at least in part because he could not allow himself such an act of filial impiety in the face of his father's death.[11] Trashing his father's memory in this way would be the equivalent of killing him twice over. Like Hamlet, Freud leaves his father's reputation intact, choosing to vent his hostility elsewhere.

Although Freud's comments on death wishes against parents suggest that they emerged from his observations of his own mourning, he does not pursue this train of thought. His abandonment of the seduction theory, by curtailing the question of his father's complicity in his children's neuroses, also appears to cut off his investigation into the dynamics of the grieving process. As a result, the reasons Freud may have had for wishing his father dead remain largely opaque. By the time Freud chose to theorize them (in his oedipal construct), he had abstracted these impulses beyond the point of individual guilt or reproach.

Freud's dream containing the injunction "You are requested to close the eyes" acquires even greater resonance in this regard. It is as though Freud chose to turn away, at the very moment of his father's death, from the full psychic impact of this event. Emotionally he seems to have come to an impasse until the momentous decision to jettison the troublesome seduction theory, at which point he began to emerge from mourning and to forge a new identity. Yet Freud leaves clues, I believe, to the fate of his grieving process in his interpretation of *Hamlet*, beginning with the piece of revisionary self-help advice, "To be cheerful is everything!"

Perhaps the most striking parallel between Freud and Hamlet is their experience of father loss. If Shakespeare's play is about anything, it is surely about grief. Yet Freud passes over this obvious source of identification, reading the play instead as a disguised version of *Oedipus Rex*. In superimposing the oedipal plot on the Shakespearean text, Freud indicates the extent to which his heroic identification with Oedipus took precedence over his sympathy with the mourning Hamlet.

Near the first anniversary of his father's death, Freud announced his breakthrough discovery to Fliess, "A single idea of general value dawned on me," he states. "I have found, in my own case too, [the phenomenon of] being in love with my mother and jealous of my father, and I now consider it a universal event in early childhood." Immediately the analogy with Oedipus springs to mind. "If this is so," he continues,

> we can understand the gripping power of *Oedipus Rex* ... [T]he Greek legend seizes upon a compulsion which everyone recognizes

because he senses its existence within himself. Everyone in the audience was once a budding Oedipus in fantasy and each recoils in horror from the dream fulfillment here transplanted into reality, with the full quantity of repression which separates his infantile state from his present one. (Masson 1985, 272)

Freud's secondary train of association concerns *Hamlet*, which he interprets as a repressed version of *Oedipus Rex*. Although Shakespeare's plot does not portray father-murder and mother–son incest, Hamlet's actions make sense, Freud maintains, if understood as expressive of his unconscious desire. Hence Freud reads Hamlet's delay in avenging his father's death as the product of "the torment he suffers from the obscure memory that he himself had contemplated the same deed against his father out of passion for his mother," concluding that Hamlet's "conscience is his unconscious sense of guilt" (273).

In his focus on the "unconscious" substratum of the play, Freud deliberately ignores the surface construction of the plot, which is at least as relevant to his situation as the oedipal interpretation he provides. If we look, for instance, at the material from his childhood that Freud was investigating immediately prior to his pronouncement concerning himself and Oedipus, we may discern other lines of identification with *Hamlet* that he was either unable or unwilling to pursue. To have done so, I maintain, would have led him in the direction of a less optimistic construct than that of oedipal desire, which (however much based in tragedy) manages to obviate the question of death.

Shakespeare's Hamlet suffers not only from feelings of loss concerning his father's death but also from resentment at his mother's remarriage, which offends him on multiple grounds. She has chosen the wrong person (her brother-in-law Claudius), at the wrong time (within two months of her husband's death), for the wrong reasons (to satisfy her lust). In Hamlet's eyes, her relationship with Claudius is incestuous, adulterous, and possibly even murderous. So deeply, does he feel the betrayal of his father's memory that he has the Player Queen speak the lines: "A second time I kill my husband dead,/ When second husband kisses me in bed" (II. ii. 194–95), posing a question about Gertrude's complicity in her husband's murder to which the play provides no answer.[12] We, like Hamlet, are left pondering Gertrude's desire, wondering how much she knows.

Among the flood of memories awakened by Freud's grieving process, the most striking ones relate to the period of his earliest childhood. Although Freud separates these figures in his imagination, their images blur around issues of sexuality, betrayal, and loss. These reminiscences seem called to life, moreover, in the absence of a paternal figure, much as Hamlet's torment about his mother's desire is elicited by his father's death. It is as though Freud's present loss speaks to older, deeper wounds. Yet the questions he poses about his early relationship to his mother (and mother-surrogate) are foreclosed in his oedipal construction of family dynamics, which effaces the issue of maternal desire.

The first of Freud's startling discoveries concerns his childhood nurse, whom he refers to as "the 'prime originator'" of his sexuality, "an ugly, elderly, but clever woman who told me a great deal about God Almighty and hell and who instilled in me a high opinion of my own capacities" (Masson 1985, 268). This woman, Freud claims, who washed him in reddish water in which she had previously washed herself and who persuaded him to steal, "was my teacher in sexual matters and complained because I was clumsy and unable to do anything." Freud's recollections of this figure are clearly mixed. Although he associates her with feelings of humiliation and impotence, he also credits her with bolstering his self-esteem. She provided him, he avows, "with the means for living and going on living," so that even now he can feel "the old liking breaking through again" (268).

When Freud asked his mother, Amalia, about this woman, she confirmed his memories of her religious influence on him, correcting him, however, in one particular. Whereas Freud had thought that he was induced by his nurse to steal, it was in fact she who took "shiny new kreuzers and zehners" from him. When this was discovered, Freud's half-brother Phillipp fetched the police, and she was sentenced to ten months in prison. Freud's distortion of memory is based on a dream interpretation. "For the dream picture was a memory of my taking money from the mother of a doctor—that is wrongfully. The correct interpretation is: I = she, and the mother of the doctor equals my mother" (275). At midlife, in his dreams, Freud and his nurse are one.

It seems that Freud's nurse treated him badly on several accounts: by sexually seducing him, casting doubt on his abilities, sexual and otherwise, taking money from him, and finally leaving him. Yet Freud cannot suppress an "old liking," even to the point of identifying with her in his dreams. What might he have felt as a child at her sudden, unexplained departure?[13]

Freud asks himself a similar question: "if the old woman disappeared from my life so suddenly, it must be possible to demonstrate the impression this made on me. Where is it then?" The scene he recalls in response introduces a number of considerations that suggest further parallels between his situation and that of Hamlet.

"My mother," Freud relates, "was nowhere to be found; I was crying in despair. My brother Phillipp (twenty years older than I) unlocked a wardrobe [*Kasten*] for me, and when I did not find my mother inside it either, I cried even more until, slender and beautiful, she came in through the door." The meaning of this puzzling memory fragment now seems clear. "When I missed my mother," Freud explains, "I was afraid that she had vanished from me, just as the old woman had a short time before." Thinking that his mother has been "boxed up [*eingekastelt*]," like his nurse, Freud looks to his brother for help. "The fact that I turned to him in particular," Freud offers, "proves that I was well aware of his share in the disappearance of the nurse" (272).

In a footnote added in 1924, Freud offers a further association to these events. "The wardrobe or cupboard," he now reveals, "was a symbol for him of his mother's insides," hence his insistence on opening the cupboard. "Besides the well-founded suspicion that this brother had had the lost nurse 'boxed up,' there was a further suspicion against him—namely that he had in some way introduced the recently born baby into his mother's inside." Freud's clever brother, who dispatches his nurse and confuses the child with his punning manner of speech, here takes on a more sinister aspect. In the boy's imagination, Phillipp "had taken his father's place" through an illicit liaison with his mother, thus aligning his position with that of Claudius in the analogy with *Hamlet*. Instead of a sexual triangle, moreover, as described by the relations among Oedipus, Laius, and Jocasta, we have something more like a quadrangle composed of an absent (or ineffectual) father, an adulterous couple, and a son who feels both confused and aggrieved.

It appears that in the days and weeks preceding his formulation of the oedipal model, Freud was exploring not his childhood rivalry with his father and desire for his mother, but rather his feelings of being displaced or betrayed in an evolving family dynamic that included a dismissed nanny and a mother whose attention was given elsewhere, if not to the distraction of an affair, at least to the very real demands of pregnancy and confinement. In this field of force, the powerful figures appear to be the seductive nurse, sly brother, and enigmatic mother, rather than the classic forbidding father and libidinous son of oedipal theory.

Just as Hamlet senior's death raises questions in the mind of Hamlet about the bounds of his mother's sexuality, Jacob Freud's death seems to have opened a space for his son to explore the question of Amalia Freud's desire. Did she, in fact, as Freud fantasized, betray his father? If so, how could Freud himself rely on her love? These are the kinds of questions that plague Hamlet, who expresses as much emotion over his mother's misdeeds as he does over his uncle's crime. Yet Freud glosses over these issues in his interpretation of Shakespeare's play, choosing a more convoluted explanation of Hamlet's anger and despair.

The image that torments Hamlet and that finally goads him into action (in killing Polonius) is that of Claudius and Gertrude making love. At the same time, he spends much of the play repressing (or displacing), not his fantasized desire to kill his father but his rage against his mother, an emotion that Freud in his long life never admitted to personally and that he scrupulously avoided discussing in theory. Freud's oedipal construct effectively banishes such an unfilial response. Yet the circumstances of his early life suggest more than one reason why the boy Freud might have felt resentment, if not outright anger, at the failure of maternal care.

Between the ages of one and a half and four, Freud suffered a number of potentially traumatic losses, most of which he alludes to (in condensed form) in his letters to Fliess. The first major shock was the birth, followed quickly by the death, of his brother Julius, whom Freud "greeted ... with adverse wishes and genuine childhood jealousy" and whose death "left the germ of [self] reproaches" in him (Masson 1985, 268). A circumstance, which Freud does not mention and may have complicated his reactions to the death of Julius, is the fact that his mother's brother, also named Julius, had died the preceding month.[14] That Amalia named her second son after her brother suggests some degree of sisterly affection. Although we have no evidence concerning the nature or extent of her grief, it is likely that her second mourning was compounded by the first. Under these circumstances, Freud may well have felt her unavailability or removal.

At the time of Julius's death in the spring of 1858, moreover, Freud's mother was already pregnant with her third child, Anna, who was born in December of that year. The following month, Freud's nanny was caught stealing and dismissed. Then, in August 1859, Freud's family relocated from Freiberg to Leipzig, a move evidently prompted by the failure of Jacob Freud's business. In less than a year, the family was on the road once again, this time to Vienna, where at last they set down roots. The mere chronology of these events suggests a high degree of disruption in Freud's early life: through death, the arrival of unwanted siblings, the departure of his nurse, the breakup of his extended family system, and loss of their Freiberg home. The reawakening of memories from this period is more than likely to have renewed old feelings of distress.

Freud's memories of his early years touch on other significant themes, such as paternal failure (in business), and maternal sexuality (including nursery seduction and adult infidelity), in addition to sudden unexplained loss and death.[15] So powerful are these issues and so various the possibilities for interpretation that no single narrative seems adequate to frame them. If we compare the plots of the two plays Freud offers as analogues of his psychic life, however, the events of *Hamlet* appear to be more resonant. Yet Freud chose *Oedipus Rex* not only as a means of comprehending his own experience but also that of humankind. What purpose could this momentous decision have served?

If we examine Freud's self-analysis in the light of his grieving process, we may achieve a fresh understanding of his oedipal identification. That Freud felt profoundly ambivalent toward his father is clear not only from his handling of the details of his funeral but also from his self-reproach and accompanying death wishes. That he suffered specifically from feelings of sexual rivalry with him in childhood is much less evident. Rather, Freud's early memories chiefly concern the ambiguous and disturbingly seductive behavior of his mother and his nurse. In this confusing environment, moreover, Freud's own needs for love and reassurance appear to have been overlooked. The emotional tone of these memories is primarily one of anxiety, in response to the multiple dislocations of Freud's early life. So painful was Freud's reaction to his family's departure from Freiberg, for instance, that he associated the gas jets at one of the railway stops with his nanny's description of the fires of hell. His lifelong travel anxiety was evidently due to the effects of this trauma.[16]

Freud's "uprooted" feeling in the aftermath of his father's death speaks to the period in his childhood when he was literally uprooted from his familiar family setting and perhaps similarly distraught.[17] The memories that Freud produces from this time suggest, in addition, that his mother was emotionally preoccupied or unavailable, thus compounding his feelings of anxiety and bewilderment. In this way, Freud's current state of mourning appears to have touched on ancient griefs and fears. Yet these issues do not inform his oedipal theory, which posits a passionately desiring son in relation to conventionally gendered, and otherwise idealized, parental figures.

What is missing from this formulation is an awareness of loss. As Freud later (and here implicitly) rewrites *Oedipus Rex*, for instance, no one has to die. The father's authority will prevent the son from enacting his incestuous desire, hence instilling in him the habit of renunciation necessary for participation in culture. If the mother is unavailable, moreover, it is not because of any wayward desire of her own but rather because of the son's deference to his father's authority. In such a scenario, there is no weak, ineffectual, or dying old man to reckon with, no mother capable of enacting her own will.[18] From this perspective, it appears that Freud did less to uncover than to obscure the intimate dynamics of his family life. If anything, he closed the door on the earliest period of his childhood when he chose the figure of Oedipus to represent his psychic life.

The shadow of the object

The cornerstone position of the Oedipus complex in psychoanalytic theory has made it difficult, if not impossible, for subsequent critics to examine its appropriateness to the material from which it springs.[19] Yet if we consider this construct in the light of Freud's mourning process it appears less transparently self-evident than artfully imposed. In recreating himself as an oedipal subject, Freud clearly found relief from his personal crises. Yet the Oedipus complex, in displacing questions of early childhood loss, occludes the most critical issues to emerge in the aftermath of Jacob Freud's death.

Freud's construction of an authoritative "oedipal" father not only prevented him from exploring the multiple trajectories of desire within his family system but it also barred him from conceptualizing maternal eroticism and aggression, while rendering meaningless his childhood anxieties and ambivalences about the adequacy of maternal care. Perhaps most importantly, it created the illusion that social and cultural life begins with a child's recognition of his father's commanding presence in the private sphere of the family, as in the world.

While critical of Freud's reasoning, most feminist psychoanalytic theorists do not seek to dislodge the Oedipus complex per se.[20] Their achievements, as a result, fall short of their radical political aims. A focus on the preoedipal/Imaginary period, however useful in rescuing the figure of the mother from the shadowy background of Freud's theory, does not alter her position within the overall structure that absents her from culture. I believe that feminist theory will remain obstructed by this problem as long as it fails to question the foundational status of the Oedipus complex.

If, however, as I have argued, Freud's oedipal construct serves to displace and occlude a profound crisis of mourning, then we may be free to consider other theoretical prospects in his self-analysis and hence alternate scenarios for the genesis of psychoanalytic theory. We may speculate, for instance, on how psychoanalysis might have developed had Freud chosen to theorize mourning (that is to say, the dynamics of loss), instead of Oedipus.[21] Freud himself offers hints along these lines in his essay "Mourning and Melancholia" (1917a), where he picks up threads of his earlier communications with Fliess.

In "Mourning and Melancholia," Freud returns, so to speak, to the scene of mourning, probing more deeply into its painful dynamics than he was evidently capable of doing in the aftermath of his father's death. As if to signal this awareness, Freud also returns to Hamlet, referring to him this time not as an oedipal subject but as a classic victim of melancholy. Like the melancholic, who suffers from a disturbance of self-regard, Hamlet sees himself as "petty, egoistic, dishonest, lacking in independence, one whose sole aim has been to hide the weaknesses of his own nature" (1917a, 246). Indeed, Freud's whole interest is fixed on this syndrome, which he contrasts with so-called "normal mourning."

Whereas in normal mourning the ego gradually detaches itself from the lost object, releasing affective energy, the melancholic ego, according to Freud, holds on to the loved object through a process of identification.[22] This mechanism derives from the "preliminary stage of object-choice," or the oral phase. "The ego wants to incorporate this object into itself," Freud explains, "and, in accordance with the oral or cannibalistic phase of libidinal development in which it is, it wants to do so by devouring it" (249–50). "By taking flight into the ego," as Freud states poetically, "love escapes extinction" (257).

Yet the love preserved in this way is full of conflict. "The loss of a love-object," Freud allows, "is an excellent opportunity for the ambivalence in love-relationships to make itself effective and come into the open." In melancholia, especially, "the occasions which give rise to the illness extend for the most part beyond the clear case of a loss by death, and include all those situations of being slighted, neglected, or disappointed, which can import opposed feelings of love and hate into the relationship or reinforce an already existing ambivalence." Because the subject has incorporated the loved object, moreover, anger or hatred will be directed against the self. In this way, the melancholic's rage "comes into operation on this substitutive object, abusing it, debasing it, making it suffer and deriving sadistic satisfaction from its suffering" (251).

Freud's understanding of melancholic identification as a psychic mechanism inherited from the oral phase suggests that he is thinking about the earliest stages of love and loss, and hence, the period in his own life when he was most vulnerable to disruptions of maternal care. If this is so, Freud may well have been describing the residue of his childhood reactions to his mother and his nurse, neither of whom died, yet both of whom disappeared temporarily or permanently and evoked ambivalent emotions. While Freud's nurse aroused him, shamed him, and left him, his mother simply (and perhaps of necessity) turned her attentions elsewhere. Although Freud does not directly address the issue of maternal loss, it hovers in the background of his description of melancholia, as a kind of shadow text.

A powerful metaphor, moreover, links Freud's discussion of melancholia with his thoughts on the same subject in 1895, indicating that Freud was preoccupied with this subject *before* his father's death and hence prior to his mourning for that loss. In a draft statement to Fliess (included in an envelope postmarked January 1895), Freud offers a neurological explanation of the dynamics of melancholia.[23] As a result of "a very great loss in the amount of excitation," he states, "there may come about *an indrawing*, as it were, *into the psychic sphere*, which produces an effect of suction upon the adjoining amounts of excitation." This giving up of excitation produces pain. Next, "there sets in, as though through an *internal hemorrhage*, an impoverishment in excitation," which "operates like a *wound*." Comparing this process to neurasthenia, in which excitation runs out, "as it were, through a hole," Freud concludes that "in melancholia the hole is in the psychic sphere" (Masson 1985, 103–4).

Freud's imagery of sucking in anticipates his description of oral incorporation in "Mourning and Melancholia," where the wound metaphor also recurs. Here, he states, "the complex of melancholia behaves like an open wound, drawing into itself cathectic energies ... and emptying the ego until it is totally impoverished" (1917a, 253). This account, while less graphic than his earlier one, portrays the same dynamic. Evidently attached to this idea, Freud repeats it toward the conclusion of his essay where he tries, rather unsuccessfully, to explain how melancholia comes to an end. "The conflict within the ego," he suggests, "which melancholia substitutes for the struggle over the object, must act like a painful wound which calls for an extraordinarily high anti-cathexis" (258). Whereas the mourner gradually accepts the fact that "the object no longer exists," the melancholic must somehow manage to eject it, by "disparaging it, denigrating it, and even as it were killing it," in order to obtain relief (255, 257).

Freud's discomfort with this explanation manifests itself in the abruptness with which he brings his essay to a close. Immediately after invoking the wound metaphor, he admits: "But here once again, it will be well to call a halt ... As we already know, the interdependence of the complicated problems of the mind forces us to break off every enquiry before it is completed—till the outcome of some other enquiry can come to its assistance" (258). The effect of these concluding remarks is to hold the wound metaphor in suspension, as if melancholia itself were an interminable illness.

Freud's investigation into the dynamics of melancholia at least a year and a half before his father's death suggests that more than so-called normal mourning is at issue. Since he (as well as his patients) suffered from depression at this time, it seems likely that his theoretical labor was autobiographically informed from the beginning. Taking these suppositions together with the memories of early childhood loss that emerged in the aftermath of Jacob Freud's death and the specifically oral nature of Freud's description of melancholia in the 1917 essay, one might easily speculate that the "open wound" metaphor he uses to convey the psychic affect of melancholia also gives expression to his feelings about the ruptures and losses of his early life.

What is most striking about the wound metaphor, of course, is its resemblance to Freud's later language about castration, a condition that he attributes literally only to females. While the boy may act to repress his desire for his mother under the threat of castration, only the girl experiences it through her awareness of phallic lack. Whereas the sight of the little girl's genitals arouses a "terrible storm of emotion" in the boy, who feels a "horror of the mutilated creature," as Freud states in "Some Psychical Consequences of the Anatomical Distinction between the Sexes," the girl incurs a "wound to her narcissism" and "develops, like a scar, a sense of inferiority" (1925b, 252–53). Melancholia, in contrast, is not gender marked. Both boys and girls, men and women, may be subject to wounding, internal hemorrhaging, and psychic scars.

Whereas Freud's concept of the castration complex acts to displace and defer the threat of wounding for the boy, his representation of melancholia as a painful hole in the psyche suggests otherwise. For the melancholic, struggling to preserve his or her love objects, castration has always already taken place. Such a construction of lack—as primary loss—not only obviates the gender imbalance of Freud's oedipal construct but it also avoids the problem of positing separation, or the inception of the Symbolic stage, as a function of the father.[24] Only if one imagines an ordinary state of blissful mother–infant union, moreover, does such a step become necessary.[25]

When Freud looked back to his early childhood, what he remembered was not a paradisal condition of oneness with his mother but rather multiple contexts of pain, disappointment, and loss. Although he invented psychoanalysis under the sign of mourning—for his father Jacob Freud and for the child he once was—he chose to theorize from a text that offered him more consoling images. Out of the tragic material of *Oedipus Rex*, Freud forged a hopeful, if sober, psychic construct. Perhaps more importantly, he fashioned a family he could live with—one that revolved around a vigorous and commanding father, an ideally loving mother, and a lively, upstart son. Having taken this momentous step, he rarely looked back. As if in response to the dream request to close the eyes, Freud appears to have averted his gaze from the scene of mourning, effectively deferring the question of his own grief. Yet Freud's image of pathological mourning as an open wound attests to the hold of this issue over his imagination, in addition to its status as an ongoing theoretical problem. Given Freud's own depression both before and after Jacob Freud's death, one might say that psychoanalysis, insofar as it originated in his self-analysis, begins not with Oedipus but with the wound. One might even say that for Freud, being *in* psychoanalysis (founding it, laboring within it) was like being *in* mourning.[26]

For Freud, loss is not a foundational concept. Being in mourning, like being "uprooted," was perhaps too painful a position for him to contemplate as a basis for psychoanalytic theory as a whole. From the perspective of feminism, however, it may offer a more useful starting point than the Oedipus construct, which decides one's sexual and cultural destiny with a single phallic stroke.

Notes

1 J.J. Bachofen, in *Myth, Religion and Mother Right* (1861, 1967), postulates an early matriarchal stage of the family in which women exercised power. At the same time, he considers the emergence of the patriarchal family as a definite advance in human civilization. Many other nineteenth-century theorists accept the idea of a matrilineal phase in human history, while rejecting Bachofen's concept of matriarchy per se. Freud, while reluctant to posit an *initial* matriarchal phase, nevertheless tried to incorporate the notion of matriarchy as a transitional moment in the evolution from an original father-dominated primal horde to the modern form of the patriarchal family. His discomfort with the very idea of matriarchy, however, manifests itself in the confused accounts he gives of this process in *Totem and Taboo* (1913b) and in *Moses and Monotheism* (1939). I treat this subject (including the complicating factor of Freud's rivalry with Jung) at greater length in *The Spectral Mother* (1990, 86–119).

2 Juliet Mitchell, in *Psychoanalysis and Feminism* (1974), makes a case for reading Freud in a descriptive, rather than a prescriptive sense. In this way, she argues, we may better comprehend the unconscious structure of patriarchy, as a necessary first step in dismantling it. While Mitchell reads Freud through the lens of Lacanian theory,

Nancy Chodorow offers an object relations approach. In her enormously influential book *The Reproduction of Mothering* (1978), she analyzes the development of masculinity and femininity within the confines of the patriarchal nuclear family. Paradoxically, however, the very success of her exposition has proved an obstacle to envisioning social change, as many feminists have found her description of feminine development within patriarchy more attractive than otherwise.

3 Stephen Mitchell, in *Hope and Dread in Psychoanalysis* (1993), gives a lucid account of the developments in psychoanalytic theory since Freud that have combined to displace his drive theory model of interpretation in favor of a more interactive approach, one that recognizes the subjective situation of both analyst and analysand in the construction of meaning. Psychoanalysis, he believes, participates in the shift toward perspectivist explanation that characterizes contemporary philosophy and science. "For Freud," he observes,

> psychoanalysis was embedded in the broad, invigorating, reassuring, scaffolding of the scientific worldview... That scaffolding does not sustain us in the same way it did for Freud and his contemporaries, cannot sustain us; this fact has, in some sense, stranded psychoanalysis, unmoored it from the context that gave it its original meaning. Those who think of analysis in ways similar to our analytic ancestors seem to most of us today more like cultists than scientists. (21)

4 Feminists who take psychoanalysis seriously, at one point or another, come up against the Oedipus complex. For a while during the 1970s, it seemed that an emphasis on the preoedipal period might offer a theoretical avenue of escape from the imposition of oedipal authority. The *a priori* definition of this phase as standing somewhere outside of the Symbolic order, however, limits the possibilities for the liberation of female (and maternal) subjectivity. More recently, feminists have focused either on locating the mother–infant relationship within the Symbolic order or on redefining the Oedipus complex in such a way as to soften its patriarchal implications. Kaja Silverman offers an example of the former strategy in *The Acoustic Mirror* (1988), where she proposes a new reading of the mother–daughter relationship. "To situate the daughter's passion for the mother within the Oedipus complex," she argues, "is to make it an effect of language and loss, and so to contextualize both it and the sexuality it implies firmly within the symbolic" (123). Jessica Benjamin, rather than accepting the presymbolic/symbolic dichotomy (and hence the location of men and women on opposite sides of the cultural divide), offers a redefinition of the Oedipus complex from the standpoint

of intersubjective theory. "The three pillars of oedipal theory," she concludes,

> the primacy of the wish for oneness, the mother's embodiment of this regressive force, and the necessity of paternal intervention—all combine to create the paradox that the only liberation is paternal domination ... By going beyond Oedipus we can envisage a direct struggle for recognition between a man and a woman, free of the shadow of the father that falls between them. (1988, 181)

5   Ernest Jones, until recently Freud's most eminent biographer, considers Freud's self-analysis as "his most heroic feat." Far from questioning Freud's (or anyone's) capacity to carry out such a task, he valorizes its achievement. "It is hard for us nowadays," he states, "to imagine how momentous this achievement was, that difficulty being the fate of most pioneering exploits. Yet the uniqueness of the feat remains. Once done it is done forever. For no one again can be the first to explore those depths" (1953: Vol. 1, 319). Peter Gay, who brings Jones's work up to date, admits that "self-analysis would seem to be a contradiction in terms," yet he excuses Freud on the grounds that he had "no teachers but had to invent rules for it as he went along" and he does not question its results (1988, 96, 98).

6   See, for instance, Liz Stanley's *The Auto/biographical I* (1992), which summarizes the developments in Foucaultian and poststructuralist theory that give rise to these assumptions. See also William Epstein's *Contesting the Subject* (1991a) for reflections on how contemporary views of the self affect the writing of biography.

7   Mark Edmundson, whose argument parallels mine in certain respects, sees Freud's invention of the Oedipus complex as an act of self-creation. "Freud's textual practice," he states, "suggests ... that the Oedipal complex is the negative term in a symbolic drama of private self-recreation, the fruit of which is a new discourse, a new terminological field" (1990, 41). Edmundson regards Freud's oedipal narrative as confining and recommends a skeptical stance toward this aspect of his achievement.

8   I am indebted to Peter Rudnytsky's *Freud and Oedipus* (1987) for this account.

9   This behavior recurred, in a more extreme form, at Freud's mother's death in 1930. Freud not only did not attend her funeral but he also seems to have experienced more relief than grief. Given that Amalia died at the age of 95 and that her son was himself 74 at the time, it may not be surprising that Freud felt no active pain. Yet the parallel with his earlier avoidance behavior around his father's funeral suggests otherwise. Herbert Lehmann (1983) speculates that Freud's very identification with his mother from an early age made it difficult

for him to acknowledge the reality of her loss. Harry Hardin, who sees Freud's relationship with his mother as profoundly ambivalent, offers the explanation that he sent his daughter Anna as a "mourner by proxy" because she "could grieve without the constraints her father experienced because of his lifelong alienation from her grandmother" (1988a, 85). Peter Homans observes that in Freud's "unconscious his anxiety about his own death and his anxiety about his mother's death were probably linked, condensed, maybe even interchangeable." He connects Freud's "psychological sense of his own death" in later life with this profound identification (1989, 98).

10 Marianne Krüll makes this point in a different way. She reads the dream injunction "to close the eyes" as Freud's warning to himself against exploring his father's tendencies toward perversity, among which she includes his (presumed) habit of masturbation. She concludes that "the two central threads running through Freud's entire theoretical and therapeutic work—the subject of sexuality, which was to become the pivot of his theory of human behavior, and the subject of guilt of the sons toward the father ... were the very areas in which Jacob Freud himself felt beset with guilt" (1986, 101). Jeffrey Masson (1984) emphasizes Freud's conflict of allegiance between his patient Emma Eckstein and his friend Wilhelm Fliess (over the matter of Fliess's bungled operation on her nose), arguing that Freud chose to side with Fliess rather than with Eckstein when he abandoned the seduction theory. For Samuel Slipp, the most important factor in Freud's repudiation of the seduction theory is his problematic relationship with his mother. He speculates that "Freud abandoned the Seduction theory as an attempt to deny the traumatic impact of others, since he could not deal with a pre-Oedipal conflict with his mother" (1988, 155). Larry Wolff (1988) locates the discussion of Freud's seduction theory in the context of several well-publicized trials involving child abuse at the turn of the century in Vienna, making the point that Freud would have had deliberately to ignore the questions raised by these scandals in order to relinquish his own theory.

11 Marianne Krüll believes that Jacob Freud conveyed an unspoken mandate to his son, that he "was expected to turn his back on tradition but not on one of its most central tenets, that of filial piety on which, ultimately, the entire Jewish tradition is based" (1986, 178). In the face of his father's death, Freud was unable to resist this mandate, and hence, "dutiful son that he was, took the guilt upon his own shoulders with the help of his Oedipus theory" (179). Although I do not agree with every point of Krüll's argument concerning Jacob Freud's transgressions, I believe that her reading of Freud's inability to point the finger of blame at his father after his death is accurate.

12 In one of Shakespeare's sources, Geruth (Gertrude) betrays her husband before his death with his brother Fengon (Claudius), thus raising the suspicion "that she had been the causer of the murther, thereby to live in her adultery without controle" (Belleforest 1992, 136). See Janet Adelman's *Suffocating Mothers* (1992, 25–26) for a lucid exposition of the fantasy content of the Player's Queen's lines.
13 In a series of essays on Freud's early mothering, Harry Hardin (1987, 1988a,b) argues that a child's loss of a surrogate mother is fully as traumatic as the loss of a biological mother. He believes that Freud experienced some alienation from his actual mother as a result of his having had a nanny, but that he could not admit to these feelings.
14 Samuel Slipp provides this information. He believes that Amalia Freud's unhappiness made it difficult for her to respond fully to the needs of her first-born son. After listing the multiple disappointments of her early marriage, he concludes that by the time the family left Freiberg, "not only may she have felt disillusioned and trapped in her marriage, but in all likelihood she was in mourning for her dead brother and son" (1988, 158). Joel Whitebook believes that "there is good reason to assume that Amalia became depressed, withdrawn, and psychologically unavailable to Freud" after the death of her son Julius "and may even have spent some time away from him in Roznau, a spa to which she regularly retreated" (2017, 38). He sees Amalia as an example of André Green's "dead mother," that is to say "*a mother who remains alive and physically present but who is, so to speak psychologically dead in the eyes of the young child in her care*" (quoted by Whitebook, 38; italics supplied by him).
15 There is general agreement that Freud's father was mild-tempered and nonauthoritarian in manner, and that his easy-going nature stood in contrast to that of his wife. Robert Holt (1992) and Estelle Roith (1987) explore the reversal of conventional gender roles in Freud's family as it affected his construction of theory. William McGrath (1987) believes that Jacob Freud's lack of resistance to anti-Semitic insult meant that he could not provide a masculine model for his son, while Samuel Slipp (1988) sees Jacob's failure in business as possibly contributing to Amalia Freud's disappointment with him as a husband.
16 Freud himself makes the connection between the sight of the gas jets and his travel phobia (Masson 1985, 285).
17 Freud's word for uprooted is *entwurzeltes*. Mark Edmundson notes: "To be uprooted is to be naked, vulnerable, exposed, but also to take up a new position, unburied and unblinded, in a fresh relation to experience" (1990, 43). I am inclined to lay the emphasis on Freud's sense of vulnerability and exposure.

18 Kathleen Woodward comments astutely: *The Interpretation of Dreams* may be read as a son's book of mourning for his father, albeit a strange one. But, I also want to insist that to the extent the figure of the dead father dominates the book in the abstract, the figure of the infirm and aged father haunts it. It is aging, not death, which castrates the father ... The infirm father is all too literally present as painfully weak. (1991, 33)

19 Didier Anzieu's treatment of Freud's articulation of the Oedipus complex, though somewhat hyperbolical, is typical of the way most readers approach the subject. He writes: "in the course of his discovery of the Oedipus myth, Freud completes the threefold process—at once subjective, objective, and self-representing—which began to get under way at the start of his self-analysis. It is the discovery of a universal truth; the discovery of himself; and the discovery of itself, by which I mean the correlative discovery of the very process through which the main discovery is made." (1986, 244)

20 One might argue that reformulating the Oedipus complex in such a way as to dissolve its primary impact constitutes an effort to abolish it, yet those whose work might be construed in this way do not make this claim. Shoshana Felman, for instance, so thoroughly rewrites the Oedipus complex in her essay "Beyond Oedipus" (1987, 99–159) that one might wonder how much of Freud's concept remains. At the same time, she does not propose changing Freud's nomenclature.

21 A case could be made that Melanie Klein's (1935) concept of the depressive position works a transformation of this sort. Yet she herself does not make this claim, and her allegiance to the Oedipus complex, however reworked in her system of thought, stands in the way of a full break from Freud. Julia Kristeva's *Black Sun* (1989) comes close to such a break by emphasizing loss as the point of departure for the subject's entry into language. However, Kristeva adheres to Lacan's assumption of the necessity of third-party intervention (the function of the father) in order for this development to take place, hence invoking the phallus as a privileged signifier. Peter Homans (1989) sees the invention of psychoanalysis as a work of personal and cultural mourning, but he does not critique the outcome of this process.

22 Kathleen Woodward comments on the inadequacy of Freud's account of "normal mourning." "In this unequivocal distinction [between mourning and melancholia]," she observes, "I find a peculiar kind of piety, an almost ethical injunction to kill the dead and to adjust ourselves to 'reality.' In 'Mourning and Melancholia' Freud leaves us no theoretical room for another place, one between a crippling melancholia and the end of mourning" (1991, 116). I am very much indebted to this insight.

23 Freud later abandoned the attempt to blend psychology with neurology. For a full discussion of the impact of Freud's neurological training on his psychoanalytic constructs, see Frank Sulloway's *Freud: Biologist of the Mind* (1979).
24 I have argued this position more extensively in *The Spectral Mother* (1990), where I make a case for regarding the ego as an "elegiac construct."
25 According to Daniel Stern, contemporary observations of mother–infant interactions reveal that there is no such thing as a period of mother–infant symbiosis. He states, "infants begin to experience a sense of self from birth. They are predesigned to be aware of self-organizing processes. They never experience a period of total self/other undifferentiation. There is no confusion between self and other in the beginning or at any point during infancy" (1985, 10).
26 Peter Homans (1989), who regards psychoanalysis as the result of Freud's "ability" to mourn, emphasizes the success of this process. My focus, in contrast, is on the inhibited or failed aspects of Freud's mourning and his consequent "inability" to acknowledge the full impact of loss.

3

Freud, Irma, and the Dream of Psychoanalysis

> As in no other discipline, psychoanalysis has been blessed and burdened by its creation by one person. Psychoanalysis is not psychoanalysis without Freud, though psychoanalysis continues to evolve beyond Freud and the pioneer analysis.
> HAROLD P. BLUM, "A PSYCHOANALYTIC ODYSSEY"

Psychoanalysis was Freud's dream—in every sense of the word. A validation of his creative powers and a worldly achievement he considered on a par with the conquests of military leaders, such as Alexander the Great, Cromwell, or Napoleon. A dreamboat of an idea. But it was initially something he literally dreamed, night after night, and transcribed by day in convoluted structures of imagery and word play—a product of his sleeping, unconscious mind and, as such, resistant to full elucidation. Unavoidably, Freud's own interpretations seem incomplete, leading one to speculate about lines of association that he either fails to recognize or deliberately avoids; the richer the dream, the more opportunity it offers for further analysis.

Such is the case with the dream of Irma's injection, which Freud referred to as his "specimen dream," the centerpiece of his new theory of interpretation. Freud's insistence that the dream represents his wish to exonerate himself from blame for Irma's physical complaints fails to satisfy most contemporary readers, who make use of Freud's own hermeneutic methods to arrive at a variety of different conclusions. The line of interpretation I wish to pursue builds on the work of Max Schur (1966), Erik Erikson (1954), and Jim Swan (1974), all of whom emphasize Freud's latent identification with his patient, an association that Freud himself assiduously avoids, preferring instead to focus on his role as conscientious physician.[1]

Freud's insistence that the dream represents his wish not to be held responsible for Irma's condition reveals his preoccupation with issues of mastery and competence, both "masculine" or phallic concerns. Aspects of the dream that associate him with Irma herself, however, emphasize vulnerability and helplessness, traits Freud consistently regarded as "feminine." Irma's mouth, both the sign of her "femininity" and the dream's imagistic center, offers a point of departure for an oral (as opposed to phallic) interpretation. Such an implicitly "feminine" reading, in turn, subverts the normative and prescriptive Oedipus complex, while revealing a concern with the oral fixations and traumas of infantile life that Freud hints at elsewhere in his work but does not fully theorize. These issues, which find expression in images of oral violation, point to a preoccupation on Freud's part with traumatic loss.

Ironically, the latent content I plan to excavate in Freud's Irma dream became manifest in his life. The oral cancer diagnosed in 1923 that led to Freud's death in 1939 literalizes his dream imagery, while compelling him to act the part of Irma.[2] In this sense, Freud's body bears the burden of his dream—as its uncanny container and conduit. Irma's mouth is Freud's mouth, offering silent testimony to the legacy of trauma embedded in the dream of psychoanalysis.

Freud's Irma dream occurred on the night of July 23, 1895. The text is as follows:

> A large hall—numerous guests, whom we were receiving. Among them was Irma. I at once took her on one side, as though to answer her letter and to reproach her for not having accepted my "solution" yet. I said to her: "If you still get pains, it's really only your fault." She replied: "If only you knew what pains I've got now in my throat and stomach and abdomen—it's choking me"—I was alarmed and looked at her. She looked pale and puffy. I thought to myself that after all I must be missing some organic trouble. I took her to the window and looked down her throat, and she showed signs of recalcitrance, like women with artificial dentures. I thought to myself that there was really no need for

her to do that. She then opened her mouth properly and on the right I found a big white patch; at another place I saw extensive whitish grey scabs upon some remarkable curly structures which were evidently molded on the turbinal bones of the nose. I at once called in Dr. M, and he repeated the examination and confirmed it ... Dr. M. looked quite different from usual; he was very pale, he walked with a limp and his chin was clean-shaven .... My friend Otto was now standing beside her as well, and my friend Leopold was percussing her through her bodice and saying: "She has a dull area low down on left." He also indicated that a portion of the skin on the left shoulder was infiltrated. (I noticed this, just as he did, in spite of her dress.) ... M. said: "There's no doubt it's an infection, but no matter; dysentery will supervene and the toxin will be eliminated." ... We were directly aware, too, of the origin of the infection. Not long before, when she was feeling unwell, my friend Otto had given her an injection of a preparation of propyl, propyls ... propionic acid ... trimethylamin (and I saw before me the formula for this printed in heavy type) .... Injections of this sort ought not to be made so thoughtlessly .... And probably the syringe had not been clean. (1900, 107; all ellipses in original)

Freud's lengthy analysis of this dream leads him to conclude that the dream encodes his wish to disclaim responsibility for Irma's continuing symptoms and to avenge himself against his physician friends by casting blame for Irma's condition on them instead. The meaning of the dream, Freud states categorically, "was that I was not responsible for the persistence of Irma's pains, but that Otto was. Otto had in fact annoyed me by his remarks about Irma's incomplete cure, and the dream gave me my revenge by throwing the reproach on to him" (118).

Yet Freud himself calls attention to the speciousness of this position. "The whole idea," he confesses,

> reminded one vividly of the defense put forward by the man who was charged by one of his neighbors with having given him back a borrowed kettle in a damaged condition. The defendant asserted first, that he had given it back undamaged; secondly, that the kettle had a hole in it when he borrowed it; and thirdly, that he had never borrowed a kettle from his neighbor at all. (120)

Although Freud clearly offers this anecdote as an illustration of the irrationality of dream logic, he also (inadvertently) alludes to the bad faith of his own interpretation. Something in it, he senses, does not ring true; the joke masks his uneasiness.

The profusion of Freud's associations to his dream, combined with his willingness to confess to the motive of revenge, seems designed to disarm the reader. Yet if we follow Freud's own train of thought, while attending to the lines of association opened by subsequent biographical research, we arrive at a wholly different interpretation, one that displaces Freud's emphasis on his role as a physician in favor of a more troubled and anxious identification with the figure of Irma as hysterical patient. Viewed in this light, Freud's insistence that his dream gives expression to a dual wish for exoneration and revenge is misleading.

Freud tells us just enough to pique our curiosity, inviting us to probe further. In offering this dream as a prime example of the workings of his own unconscious mind, he simultaneously offers himself as a subject for future analysis. Given the richness and multiplicity of his associations specifically along sexual lines, which Freud himself fails to interpret, he would even seem to be soliciting our involvement in his labor of self-analysis—this collaboration or complicity being perhaps his most hidden and disguised wish.

Freud analyzes his dream, phrase by phrase and line by line, dutifully reporting his thoughts and reactions. Read in this scattershot way, his associations do not reveal an underlying coherence or organization, thus lending a superficial credence to Freud's own interpretation. If we gather his associations into two clusters, however, one surrounding Irma, the other accruing to the men who try to diagnose her, another structure of meaning begins to emerge.

Irma brings the following women to mind: Freud's wife Martha, who is bashful and suffers from thrombosis during her pregnancies; a governess who has false teeth; two friends of Irma's, one of whom is reserved, the other of whom would have yielded to examination, "open[ing] her mouth properly"; Freud's daughter Mathilde; a patient named Mathilde who died of a drug overdose; women patients in general, who must be examined through their clothes; an 82-year-old woman whom Freud injected with morphine; another patient of Freud's (Emma Eckstein), who "developed an extensive necrosis of the nasal mucous membrane" (1900, 111).

What binds this series of women is a train of thought including the following: illness and need to the point of addiction, combined with a reluctance to submit to medical examination suggestive of sexual inhibition.

Freud's associations to male physicians include: his wish for an organic diagnosis; his rheumatic shoulder, nasal affliction, and cocaine use; the death of his friend (Fleischl von Marxow) from an overdose of cocaine; his half-brother, who rejects a suggestion he makes; two physicians, Dr. M (Josef Breuer) and Otto (Oscar Rie), who also reject his suggestions; a patient with difficulty defecating who subsequently developed dysentery; his friend's (Willhelm Fliess's) theories concerning trymethyamin and the turbinal bones of the nose. Freud focuses his interpretive energy on these male figures, confessing to feelings of anxiety regarding his own medical competence and a desire to avenge himself against those who reject his treatment of hysteria.

There are two points at which Freud calls a halt to his train of association. The first concerns Irma's friend, who "would have been wiser, that is to say she would have yielded [to his interpretation] sooner. She would then have *opened her mouth properly*, and have told me more than Irma" (1900, 111; italics in original). In a footnote to this passage, Freud calls attention to his inability to sustain this line of thought. "I had a feeling that the interpretation of this part of the dream was not carried far enough to make it possible to follow the whole of its concealed meaning," he says. "If I had pursued comparison between the three women, it would have taken me far afield." The three women in question are: Irma, her friend, and Freud's wife Martha, whom he has already described as "bashful in my presence" (110) and as likely to resist "treatment" as Irma. Irma's friend, though also reserved, would surely submit to him, Freud feels, by accepting his "solution" of her hysterical problem, opening her mouth fully and divulging her inner secrets.

More than one reader has noted the sexual implications of this dream imagery, which Freud underscores with his own associations.[3] Yet this is precisely the moment at which he chooses to break off. "There is at least one spot in every dream," he claims, "At which it is unplumbable—a navel, as it were, that is its point of contact with the unknown" (1900, 111–12). In his attempt to extricate himself from his interpretive dilemma, Freud only digs himself in deeper. Both Irma and Martha have suffered from pains in the abdomen, the anatomical region of the navel, to which Freud refers. Freud's use of "navel" focuses our attention on the very area of the female body from which he tries to avert his eyes. Freud invites us to make this connection, while refusing to admit it to himself. Such a strategy of doublethink informs his interpretation of the dream as a whole, allowing him simultaneously to reveal and to conceal his disavowed train of thought.

The second point at which Freud stops himself from pursuing a line of association concerns the way that women in his day submitted to medical examination. When he arrives at the image of Irma's infiltration, Freud pauses briefly on the phrase "in spite of her dress," which he describes as "in any case only an interpolation." Yet this phrase calls to mind the fact that standards of modesty require women to be examined through their clothes. "Further than this," Freud says, as if literally impeded by the female garments in question, "I could not see." To press this issue would seem to involve him in an act of mental undressing. "Frankly," Freud reassures us, "I had no desire to penetrate more deeply at this point" (1900, 113). Looking more closely, like following his own line of association regarding Irma's complaint, seems to elicit forbidden fantasies and desires.

Having dropped the issues of female modesty and male intrusiveness, presumably because of the sexual thoughts to which they give rise, Freud nevertheless returns to the question of sexuality in his treatment of the word "trimethylamin." A friend, "who had for many years been familiar with all my writings," Freud confides, had once "mentioned among other things that he believed that one of the products of sexual metabolism was trimethylamin" (1900, 116).[4] The thought of his friend (Wilhelm Fliess) leads Freud to expand this line of association. "Trimethylamin," he asserts,

> was an allusion not only to the immensely powerful factor of sexuality, but also to a person whose agreement I recalled with satisfaction whenever I felt isolated in my opinions. Surely this friend who played so large a part in my life must appear again elsewhere in these trains of thought. Yes. For he had a special knowledge of the consequences of affections of the nose and its accessory cavities; and he had drawn scientific attention to some very remarkable connections between the turbinal bones and the female organs of sex. (Cf. the three curly structures in Irma's throat). (117)

By a circuitous route, Freud has returned to the oral-vaginal nexus that he earlier shied away from. His invocation of Fliess serves not only to embolden him but also to legitimize this connection—as if to say "I'm not alone in holding this view, and it was Fliess's idea in the first place."

Having come this far, however, Freud can go no further. His associations to the next phrase, "Injections of that sort ought not to be made so thoughtlessly ... and probably the syringe had not been clean" (1900, 107), focus on the issue of medical conscientiousness in administering drug injections, neatly steering clear of the notion of sexual contamination. With an air of satisfaction, Freud then declares summarily, "I have now completed the interpretation of the dream" (1900, 118). Having led us to contemplate the "navel" of the dream, as it were, Freud breaks off. Why?

Over the course of the last century, a great deal of information has come to light regarding Freud's life. Scholars may consult two monumental biographies (Jones 1953–57; Gay 1988), in addition to numerous books about specific issues or periods in his life and several fat volumes of correspondence between Freud and various of his followers. More documentary material, including many more volumes of intimate correspondence, waits in the wings in the Freud Archives. In the meantime, the data we have at our disposal provide a compelling subtext to Freud's published work. It is now impossible to read him without reference to this rich (and growing) body of biographical research.

What we now know about Freud's life in the period 1895–1900 indicates that it was a time of profound turmoil, crisis, and transition. The dream of Irma's injection touches on every aspect of this crisis, which included his relationship with his wife, his patients, his intimate friend Fliess, and the professional medical community. At issue was Freud's identity in all these spheres, which he resolved in a fashion that not only set the course of his future theorizing but also defined the shape of his personal life.

By July of 1895, Martha was pregnant with her sixth and last child Anna, who was born the following December. She had been nearly continuously pregnant since her marriage to Freud in 1886, putting a strain not only on her health but also on their meager family income. Obviously, Martha was fertile yet one cannot help wondering why the Freuds were unable to space their children more widely. The answer seems to lie in Freud's opposition to contraception—through any of the means available to him in his day, including sexual practices that did not involve ejaculation in the vagina. Freud's theory of the "actual neuroses" held that anything less than full vaginal intercourse was psychologically harmful for both partners. While men fell prey to anxiety, he believed, women would succumb to hysteria. Freud frowned equally on the use of condoms, vaginal sponges, cervical barriers, oral and anal sex, masturbation, and *coitus interruptus*. With so few options, it is no wonder that Martha kept getting pregnant. Ultimately, Freud resolved his procreative dilemma by choosing abstinence. Evidently, he and Martha rarely enjoyed sexual relations after the birth of Anna.[5]

Freud's relationship with Fliess was also in transition, on both personal and intellectual grounds. Begun a few months after Freud's marriage in 1886, this attachment, which involved frequent exchanges of letters punctuated by occasional meetings termed "congresses," quickly developed a degree of emotional intensity that Freud never again achieved or even attempted with a male friend. Fliess was his confidant, the person with whom Freud shared his nascent ideas, to whom he confessed his doubts and uncertainties, and whose advice he sought for numerous physical complaints. Both men suffered from migraine headaches and sinusitis. In addition, Freud worried over cardiac symptoms and depression. While he was engaged in working out his own theories of the neuroses, he seriously entertained Fliess's ideas concerning periodicity (based on a twenty-eight-day female and a twenty-three-day male cycle) and the intimate link between afflictions of the nose and those of the sexual organs. The latter, identified as the "nasal reflex neurosis," led Freud to submit to nasal surgery at the hands Fliess, while also recommending this course to his patients.

One young woman suffered grievously as a result, Sometime in January or February of 1895, Fliess operated on Emma Eckstein's nasal cavity to remove her turbinate bone. He left behind some gauze packing, which subsequently putrefied, causing infection. When the packing was removed by another physician, Eckstein hemorrhaged with such force that she nearly bled to death. Freud, who was present at this scene, was distressed to the point of fainting.

Details of this episode came to light with the publication of the complete correspondence between Freud and Fliess. Jeffrey Moussaieff Masson (1985), the editor and translator of these letters, had previously published a book (1984) in which he maintained that Freud abandoned his so-called "seduction theory" of neurosis as a result of his need to exonerate Fliess from the charge of malpractice. According to Masson, Freud, who had once believed that adult neuroses could be traced to incidents of sexual trauma in childhood, embraced the notion that patients "cause" their own emotional difficulties as a result of their sexual fantasies. The sexual fantasy theory allowed him to convince himself that Eckstein was responsible for her own bleeding.

As convoluted as this line of reasoning appears to be, it makes a certain kind of sense. Freud was clearly unnerved by the spectacle of Eckstein's bleeding, which he witnessed on more than one occasion, and hastened to assure his friend that he was not at fault. As Eckstein's health improved, Freud began to focus on the content of her sexual fantasies and to link them to her repeated bleeding episodes, referring to them as "hysterical." Freud's thinking about the significance of sexual abuse in childhood was obviously undergoing revision at this point in time, a process to which the Eckstein incident appears to have contributed. Two years later, in a well-known letter to Fliess dated September 21, 1897, Freud declared that he no longer believed in his seduction theory.

I have argued elsewhere (1990) that Freud's traumatized response to Eckstein's bleeding caused him to dissociate from her suffering, a reaction that enhanced his alliance with Fliess, along with his desire to exonerate him from charges of wrongdoing and his need to believe that Eckstein's hemorrhages were hysterically motivated. This response effectively masked his identification with Eckstein, the sight of whose bleeding nose literally made him feel "sick." Freud's fateful choice to side with Fliess later smoothed the path for his elaboration of the Oedipus complex, with its emphasis on the rewards of masculinity and concomitant devaluation of femininity.

Freud had reason to feel anxious about Eckstein's position vis-à-vis Fliess, given that he himself had submitted to nasal surgery at his hands in January of the same year. It is hard to imagine Freud witnessing Eckstein's near-death from hemorrhage without experiencing concern for himself. Though we will never know what flashed through his mind in that instant, we do know its effect. He temporarily lost consciousness. What was it that he could not tolerate?

Freud's squeamishness at the sight of blood had earlier motivated him to pursue a career in medical research, as opposed to patient care, and no doubt, this disposition played a role in his faint. Yet the freshness of his own surgical experience seems more immediately relevant, adding a supercharge to Freud's admitted vulnerability. If, for a moment, Freud could not distinguish between Eckstein's nose and his own, what meanings might we attribute to such a realization?

Surely if Eckstein could die as a result of Fliess's bungling operation, so could he. Both patients had permitted Fliess access to an intimate bodily opening—Eckstein because of her neurotic symptoms, Freud presumably because of his persistent sinusitis. Yet even here, the distinction is difficult to maintain, given Fliess's conviction regarding the connection between the turbinate bone and the female sexual organs. Freud had submitted to Fliess's medical intervention on the same terms as Eckstein. Was he hoping to cure his own neurotic symptoms? Did he fantasize himself in the "feminine" attitude of submission toward Fliess? Was he aware (at this point in time) of the homoerotic aspect of his friendship? If so, how might he have interpreted Eckstein's bleeding?

Wayne Koestenbaum (1988) has argued that Freud associated male creativity with the anus (as opposed to the uterus, the organ of procreation) and that his response to Eckstein's hemorrhage represented his anxiety about anal penetration while also evidencing his homophobia. Koestenbaum is right, I think, that Freud's dissociation from Irma was motivated, in large measure, by homosexual anxiety. To identify the nose solely with the anus, however, seems too restrictive an interpretation. The Irma dream abounds with references to bodily points of entry—including mouth, throat, navel, vagina, and uterus, in addition to the anus, Each of these orifices, I suggest, represents a site of vulnerability and potential violation. Irma is, after all, infected due to an unclean injection. While Freud's dream no doubt performs the surface labor he describes, hence exonerating him from the charge of having mistreated his patient, it works simultaneously on a subterranean level to negate this achievement by effacing the distinction between himself and Irma.

By confessing to a lesser sin—his desire to defend himself (as well as the unnamed Fliess) against the charge of malpractice—Freud obscures what is for him the more troubling issue, his likeness to Irma. For Freud, the meaning of the dream is: "I didn't hurt Irma; it's someone else's fault." Rather, I believe, the dream is saying:

"Both Irma and I have been hurt by Fliess." Freud's interpretation, I maintain, is defensive, designed to divert both his and our attention from the dream's most powerful spectacle—its scene of oral violation.

If Irma is Emma, with whom Freud himself identifies, the dream offers a line of interpretation that Freud deliberately avoided, one in which he occupies a position of helpless passivity, regarded as "feminine." Both the dream figure of Irma and her real-life counterpart Emma suffer from contamination of the orifice associated with their sexual organs. Freud's interpretation stresses his role as anxious male physician over his role as sexually victimized patient. This line of interpretation, in turn, facilitated the later development of his theory of aggressive oedipal desire and female castration. Above all, Freud resisted acknowledging his likeness to Irma/Emma, infected, bleeding, traumatized to the point of death.

Over the course of the next three years, Freud gradually detached from Fliess, both as friend and professional colleague, later attributing this move to a successful triumph over his homosexual impulses. The seduction theory, which required Freud to posit a childhood history of violation at the hands of his own father, succumbed to a less scandalous (and more normative) hypothesis that children harbor active sexual wishes toward their parents. Each of these moves contributed to Freud's elaboration of a phallic self-image while acting to suppress the orally violated "feminine" identification that runs, like a flashing subliminal message, through his dream.

With a vicious irony and fatality, Freud's disavowed identity with Irma returned to plague him in later life. Many of the circumstances surrounding the diagnosis and treatment of the oral cancer that led to his death recall specific elements of his Irma dream. It is almost as if Freud's choice of this dream to launch his new method of dream interpretation elevated it to premonitory status.

By 1923, when the malignant growth in his mouth was first discovered, Freud was no longer suffering the crises of self-confidence evident in his letters to Fliess. Psychoanalysis had won acceptance, having taken root not only among medical professionals in Vienna but also among a group of wealthy, intellectual patrons. In addition, Freud had weathered a series of early defections—by Stekel, Adler,

Jung—and had emerged the apparent victor. The First World War had ended, facilitating travel across national borders and the exchange of ideas so dear to him, while a growing number of young people embraced his concepts, especially ones that seemed to liberate them from Victorian and Edwardian habits of sexual constraint. Freud's practice was thriving; his family was stable, and he had no immediate financial concerns. In the midst of the professional success he had only dared to fantasize in the vexed period of the 1890s, Freud, not unlike his hero Oedipus, was struck down. Not for the sin of incest, or even the confession of such a forbidden, phallic wish, but for an oral compulsion, his addiction to cigars.

There is no question that the lesion discovered in 1923 by Felix Deutsch, Freud's family physician, had been induced by his lifelong habit of smoking.[6] Although the link between smoking and oral cancer may not have been apparent in the 1890s when Freud attempted to give it up, he *was* aware of a possible connection between his nicotine habit and the troubling cardiac symptoms he was experiencing at that time. Freud tried and failed, then, to give up smoking. Evidently, he never again considered relinquishing this habit, which, he was convinced, focused his thinking and helped him to write.

As if in denial of the gravity of his condition in 1923, Freud arranged for an operation on what he considered to be a leukoplakia (a precancerous alteration) at an outpatient clinic, with the surgery to be performed by a nonspecialist. This experience, not unlike that of Eckstein over twenty-five years earlier, proved traumatic. Freud hemorrhaged and nearly bled to death. Deutsch, who had colluded with Freud in minimizing the significance of the malignant growth in his mouth, reports this incident as follows:

> We drove to the hospital together, with the understanding that he would be home immediately after the operation. But he lost more blood than it was foreseen and as an emergency had to rest on a cot in a tiny room on a ward of the hospital, since no other room was available, with another patient who, by tragicomic coincidence, I might say, was an imbecile dwarf. (Schur 1972, 351)

Deutsch did not stay for the surgery, nor had Freud informed any member of his family of his operation. Although Martha and Anna were later summoned to bring articles Freud needed for an overnight stay, they were sent away again over the lunch hour, As a result, Freud was alone with the dwarf when he began to bleed again. When Martha and Anna returned, as Ernest Jones (1957) reports:

> they learned that he had had an attack of profuse bleeding, and to get help had rung the bell, which was, however out of order; he himself could neither speak nor call out. The friendly dwarf, however, had rushed for help and after some difficulty the bleeding was stopped; perhaps his action saved Freud's life. Anna then refused to leave again and spent the night sitting by her father's side. He was weak from loss of blood, was half-drugged from the medicines, and was in great pain. (90)

Freud hemorrhaged on yet another frightening occasion, before submitting to the radical oral surgery necessitated by his malignancy. He and Anna were traveling together to Rome, when, once again, he began to bleed from the mouth. As Jones reports, "A grim episode in the train ... took place during breakfast. Suddenly a stream of blood spurted from Freud's mouth, a hard crust having evidently loosened a piece of tissue. There was no doubt of its significance in either of their minds" (1957, 93–94).

While Freud may have suspected the true nature of his illness, none of his medical consultants confirmed it for him. Deutsch had considered it a kindness not to deliver the news of the pathology report until Freud's return from Rome at the end of the summer. In the meantime, he made arrangements for Freud's second surgery. At last, on October 4, 1923, Freud underwent this mutilating operation, described by Max Schur, who succeeded Deutsch as Freud's personal physician, as a "resection of the major part of the right maxilla, a considerable part of the mandible, the right soft palate, and the buccal (cheek) and lingual (tongue) and mucous membranes" (1972, 362). Such extensive surgery required the construction of a prosthesis to separate the oral and nasal cavities, which Freud wore for the remainder of his life. "The result," according to Schur "was a life of endless torture" (364). Schur continues:

> Eating, smoking, talking could be carried on only with great effort and pain. If the prosthesis was just right for proper occlusion and separation between the oral and nasal cavities, this resulted in

sores, pressure upon the mandibular joint, and often intolerable pain. If some of the prosthesis was removed, speech, eating, and smoking became much more difficult ... the prosthesis could be taken out only for cleaning purposes—to avoid shrinkage. To take it out and reinsert it required an intricate technique. (364)

Like Irma, Freud suffered from an affliction of the mouth. Like Eckstein, he bled profusely as a result of a botched operation. His second surgery introduced the necessity for a prosthesis, which made it difficult to open his mouth, yet he was subject to repeated oral examination for the purpose of detecting suspicious tissue changes. Over the course of the next sixteen years, Freud suffered more than thirty operations to treat what Schur describes as "an endless cycle of leukoplakia, proliferation, precancerous lesions" (1972, 364), all of which seem to have been induced by Freud's smoking habit. It is as though Freud's dream had turned to nightmare, one in which he was condemned to play the role of Irma until he died.

Freud was evidently able to give up sex but he was not able to give up smoking—an oral form of gratification with analogies to other kinds of erotic pleasure, such as sucking at a woman's nipple or a man's penis. In his Dora case history, Freud speculated that Dora fantasizes fellatio with her father. It is Frau K, he assumes, who must have offered such service to him (given his presumed impotence) and Dora who must have incorporated such an awareness into her oedipal desire for her invalid father. Many readers have taken issue with Freud's interpretation on this count.[7] Why assume that gratifying sex for a woman ministering to an impotent man would take the form of fellatio? Unless the interpreter saw himself, not in the position of his female patient, but in that of her ailing parent?

In defending his attribution of the fellatio phantasy to Dora, Freud points to the "innocent" analogies of thumb-sucking and breast-feeding. "It needs very little creative power," he maintains,

> to substitute the sexual object of the moment (the penis) for the original object (the nipple) or for the finger which does duty for it, and to place the current sexual object in the situation in which gratification was originally obtained. So, we see that this excessively repulsive and perverted phantasy of sucking at a penis has the most innocent origin. It is a new version of what may be described as a prehistoric impression of sucking the mother's or a

nurse's breast—an impression which has usually been revived by contact with children who are being nursed. In most instances, a cow's udder has aptly played the part of an image intermediate between a nipple and a penis. (1905, 52)

Freud reiterates this analogy, some years later, in his analysis of Little Hans as a way of explaining the boy's difficulty differentiating between the penis and the nipple (both of which Little Hans refers to as "widdlers"). For Little Hans, whose primary attachment and identification is with his mother, the sight of a cow being milked elicits the exclamation "Oh, look! ... there's milk coming out of its widdler." "I once put forward the view," Freud writes coolly,

> that there was no need to be too much horrified at finding in a woman the idea of sucking at a male organ. This repellent impulse, I argued, had a most innocent origin, since it was derived from sucking at the mother's breast; and in this connection, I went on, a cow's udder plays an apt part as an intermediate image, being in its nature a *mamma* and in its shape and position a penis. (1909, 7)

If a penis can be regarded as interchangeable with a nipple or a *mamma*, what other meanings may we attribute to fellatio?

As if fascinated by his deconstruction of penis into nipple, Freud elaborates on it further in his treatise on Leonardo, where he makes a crucial series of connections, linking the fantasy of fellatio with the mother's (phallic) nipple and the baby's wounded mouth. Freud begins by analyzing a childhood memory reported by Leonardo of lying in a cradle when "a vulture came down to me, and opened my mouth with its tail, and struck me many times with its tail against my lips" (1910b, 82).[8] Almost immediately, Freud translates the word tail (coda) into penis, maintaining that "the situation in the phantasy, of a vulture opening the child's mouth and beating about inside it vigorously with its tail, corresponds to the idea of an act of *fellatio*, a sexual act in which the penis is put into the mouth of the person involved," hastening to add that "this phantasy ... resembles certain dreams and phantasies found in women or passive homosexuals (who play the part of women in sexual relations)" (1910b, 86; italics in original).

Anticipating his readers' objection to such an interpretation, Freud argues that "the inclination to take a man's sexual organ into the mouth and suck at it, which in respectable society is considered a loathsome sexual perversion, is nevertheless found with great frequency among women today—and of earlier times as well, as ancient sculptures show." Besides which, he adds, "in the state of being in love it appears completely to lose its repulsive character" (86). Having safely projected the desire for fellatio onto women who seem to "find no difficulty in producing this kind of wishful phantasy spontaneously," Freud presses further. The desire for fellatio, he confides, "may be traced to an origin of the most innocent kind. It only repeats in a different form a situation in which we all once felt comfortable—when we were still in our suckling days ... and took our mother's (or wet nurse's) nipple into our mouth and sucked at it" (87).

The path of interpretation is, by now, familiar. "The organic impression of this experience," Freud confidently relates, "doubtless remains indelibly imprinted on us; and when at a later date the child becomes familiar with the cow's udder whose function is that of a nipple, but whose shape and position under the belly make it resemble a penis, the preliminary stage has been reached which will later enable him to form the repellent sexual phantasy" (87). Nothing new here. In what follows, however, Freud ventures into uncharted territory—equating mother with vulture with Egyptian mother goddess, with the boy child's fantasies of the maternal phallus and corresponding fears of castration not through the agency of an authoritative father but through that of a sensual and capricious mother.

Having equated the vulture's tail with the mother's nipple (by way of the fellatio fantasy and the cow's udder), Freud then asks how a mother could possibly be endowed with such an obvious mark of masculinity. The answer lies in "the vulture headed Egyptian goddess Mut" (93), who was often portrayed by the Egyptians as possessing a phallus. The addition of a phallus to the female body, he goes on to explain, was no doubt designed to represent the "primal creative force of nature" (94). Yet women do not possess such a prized organ, as little boys inevitably discover, leading them to conclude that "little girls too had a penis, but it was cut off and in its place left a wound" (95). No doubt the infant Leonardo himself thought as much of his mother—that she once possessed a phallus, which she has since lost. Yet the process of disillusionment that Freud ascribes to Leonardo has less to do with a discovery of his mother's lack of a penis than with her callous abandonment of him. First, he imagines, the poor Caterina must have lavished affection on her child, suckling and kissing him in ways that felt oppressive to him. Leonardo, he claims, "stresses, the intensity of the erotic relations between mother and child," from which linking "of his mother's (the vulture's) activity with the prominence of the mouth zone it is not difficult to guess that a second memory is contained in the phantasy ... My mother pressed innumerable passionate kisses on my mouth" (107). It is not too far-fetched to say here that Freud imagines Leonardo as being orally violated by his mother's nipple.

Not only, Freud presumes, was Leonardo subject to maternal seduction (in the form of aggressive kissing and breast-feeding) but he was also subsequently abandoned through his mother's relinquishment of her rights in him to those of his aristocratic father. Having been overly stimulated by his mother's unsatisfied desire for a husband, Leonardo was then abruptly dropped, leaving him with an abiding sense of maternal attraction, power, and unreliability. Hence, his adult fascination with the "Mona Lisa" smile, which contains at once "the promise of unbounded tenderness and at the same time sinister menace" (1910b, 115). Out of such a matrix of historical document, inductive reasoning, and fantasy, Freud arrives at an explanation of Leonardo's homosexual disposition. It is not only women who fantasize sucking at the male organ.

Sometimes a cigar is more than a cigar.

We know (from a letter to Fliess) that Freud regarded smoking as a substitute for the "single great habit, the 'primal addiction'" (Masson 1985, 287), masturbation. How curious that he did not make the more obvious connection between sucking on a cigar and sucking at either a man's penis or a woman's nipple. When faced with a confession of his own sexual fantasies, Freud seemed more comfortable admitting to a desire for phallic gratification than the expression of an oral wish.

I suggest that Freud's difficulty acknowledging his own oral desires stems from two sources: his lifelong inability to examine his relationship with his mother and his corresponding failure to theorize the preoedipal period. Both seemed to confront him with issues he wished to suppress or evade—memories of his own disappointments and losses as a child, along with the feelings of helplessness they entailed.

Freud's obviously idealized portrait of the mother–son relationship in his essay on "Femininity" as "altogether the most perfect, the most free from ambivalence of all human relationships" (1933, 133) masks the troubled conditions of his own early relationship with his mother and his nurse, which I have described in Chapters 1 and 2 as including the following: the introduction of a rival for his mother's attention through the birth of his brother Julius; his mother's mourning the subsequent death of this child, whom she had named after her recently deceased brother; the seductive behavior of Freud's nanny, followed by her abrupt dismissal for stealing; the family's bankruptcy and departure from Freiburg to Leipzig and later Vienna. Although Freud alludes to these events in his correspondence with Fliess and in his dream interpretations, he does not explore their psychological meanings in terms of the child's relationship to its first love object, the mother. To have done so, I believe, would have led Freud to consider more closely his own thwarted oral impulses, which in turn might have facilitated a recognition of his likeness to Irma/Emma. Instead, he recoiled from such an identification, stressing the anatomical difference between men and women as a sign of their divergent social roles and psychological destinies.

By choosing the penis to represent the mark of gender difference, Freud simultaneously theorized femininity as lack, a condition that lends itself to fantasies of female wounding and castration. For the male child, Freud maintains, the sight of female genitals "arouses a terrible storm of emotion in him and forces him to believe in the reality of the threat which he has hitherto laughed at." Fear of castration, in turn, inspires either "horror of the mutilated creature or triumphant contempt for her" (1925b, 252). Although these passages refer to imagined responses of a small boy, Freud elsewhere refers to female castration as a given, a fact. To be a woman, Freud implies, is to be wounded, bleeding, emasculated—a theorization of femininity that mirrors his response to the sight of Eckstein's nasal hemorrhage. Freud's insistence on the specifically phallic mark of masculinity protected him from the collapse of gender identity threatened by his Irma dream.

This repudiated identity returned to haunt him not only in terms of his oral cancer but also, in a persistent subliminal way, on the level of theory. When Freud first began to speculate about the dynamics of mourning, as I pointed out in Chapter 2, he likened the process to that of a hemorrhage. He described melancholia as a loss of excitation, which causes "an in-drawing, as it were, into the psychic sphere, which produces an effect of suction upon the adjoining amounts of excitation." Such a loss of stimulation produces pain, which Freud images as a form of internal bleeding that "operates like a wound" (Masson 1985, 103–4). Freud goes on to compare this process to that of neurasthenia in which excitation drains away "as it were through a hole." We know that Freud considered himself neurasthenic during the 1890s and that he suffered specifically from depression, which he relieved with regular applications of cocaine to his nose. Was he describing his own psychic life when he theorized melancholia as a bleeding wound?

When Freud re-engaged this subject in his essay "Mourning and Melancholia," he revived the wound metaphor. Building on my argument in Chapter 2, I want to emphasize the persistence of Freud's thinking about melancholia in terms of the primitive dynamics of loss and its connection to the earliest phases of life.

In "Mourning and Melancholia," Freud returns to the notion of sucking in of excitation, arguing that "the complex of melancholia behaves like an open wound, drawing to itself cathectic energies ... and emptying the ego until it is totally impoverished" (1917a, 253). In pathological mourning, the attempt to preserve the object, through incorporation of it into one's own psyche, creates a hole that acts both like a voracious mouth and like an unhealed wound. Frued underscores his attachment to this imagery by repeating it toward the end of his essay, emphasizing that the melancholic's inner struggle over containing or relinquishing the lost object "must act like a painful wound" (258). The melancholic's refusal to relinquish the lost object functions like a vortex, a self-perpetuating cycle of need and pain—not unlike an addiction.

In pathological mourning, Freud speculates, the ego identifies with the abandoned object. Such a narcissistic type of identification corresponds to "the first stage of object choice," presumably, the kind an infant might form in relation to its mother. "The ego," he states, at this stage, "wants to incorporate this object into itself, and in accordance with the oral or cannibalistic phase of libidinal development in which it is, it wants to do so by devouring it" (1917a, 250).[9] The breast-feeding baby, it would seem, wants to eat its mother. The frustration of such a wish may lead to the kind of self-punishment Freud ascribes to the condition of melancholia, in which object loss is "transformed into ego-loss" (249), leading to the characteristic self-denigration of depression.

On a barely theorized (and mostly imagistic) level, Freud adumbrates the following scenario: a primitive relationship of mutual gratification and intensity abruptly terminated, succeeded by an infant form of melancholia in which the child's loss is translated into a metaphorics of oral violation and addiction—the perpetual dissatisfaction and endlessly renewed need of a wounded, bleeding mouth. That Freud ascribes such an early history to Leonardo thinly disguises his own investment in it.

We may easily graph this scenario, as I suggest in Chapter 1, onto the narrative of Freud's early life, which included the drama of his attachment to his young mother and progressive loss of her to the rapid succession of siblings, not to mention her own mourning for her brother and dead child, both named Julius. Freud's entire preoedipal history was marked by loss—of his mother's exclusive attention, his nanny, his initial extended family, and Freiburg family home. The most powerful, and unnamed, loss of Freud's life was that of his mother, who (however devoted to him as her singular, first-born son) could not offer him her undivided care or love. Freud's lifelong idealization of the mother–son relationship helped him to obscure, deny, and repress this awareness. In the place of such a realization, he theorized little boys who give up their naughty desires for their mothers as a result of powerful male authority, while little girls suffer from a self-denigrating and incurable wound.

Freud's theorization of femininity, like his dream of Irma's injection, very nicely describes his own dilemma. That he himself did not make this connection is not surprising. As the inventor of psychoanalysis, he was, after all, pulling himself up by his own bootstraps, at the same time that he subscribed to most of the conventional prescriptions for heterosexual masculinity of his time. Yet his dream life partially liberated him from such anxiety and constraint. In dreams, he states, it is all right to regress.

In "A Metapsychological Supplement to the Theory of Dreams" (1917b), published in the same year as "Mourning and Melancholia," Freud elaborates on an idea he had earlier expressed in *The Interpretation of Dreams*, where he traces the ability to distinguish between internal psychic states and external reality to the child's frustration in experiencing the unavailability of the mother's breast. "At the beginning of our mental life," Freud states in the later text, we hallucinated "the satisfying object when we felt the need for it. But in such a situation satisfaction did not occur, and this failure must very soon have moved us to create some contrivance with the help of which it was possible to distinguish such wishful perceptions from a real fulfillment and to avoid them for the future." The dream state, in contrast, restores the conditions for "hallucinatory wishful psychosis," hence "re-establishing the old mode of satisfaction" (231). In dreams, Freud seems to say, we can fashion the world according to our own desires. Whereas in life we experience conflict and frustration, in dreams we feel relief from these pressures; we can have our own way. Yet, the dreams that Freud reports, including the dream of Irma's injection, do not support this view. Freud's conclusion that every dream represents the fulfillment of a wish requires a labor of interpretation that often strikes the reader as counterintuitive.

I have been arguing such a case for his analysis of the dream of Irma's injection, where Freud imposes a phallic interpretation on material that is rife with oral implications. Freud's inability to explore the possible meanings of Irma's oral violation stems, in turn, from his anxiety regarding his likeness to Irma, the consideration of which would have led him to examine more closely the homoerotic nature of his relationship with Fliess as well as the multiple losses of his early life, including his frustrated desire for his mother's exclusive attention. The residue of this anxiety may be detected in the manner in which Freud theorized sexual difference. It also took symptomatic form in his lifelong addiction to smoking, culminating in the debilitating, and ultimately fatal, cancer of his mouth and jaw.

If we consider Freud's cigar habit as representative of an unacknowledged (and hence unresolved) oral need, we may understand not only his reluctance to identify with the unfortunate Emma Eckstein and her dream avatar Irma but also his preference for phallic forms of interpretation, including insistence on the Oedipus complex as the means by which a boy severs his infantile attachment to his mother. It is not that the boy's mother abandons *him*. Rather, he abandons *her*. Yet Freud's Irma dream suggests otherwise. Instead of offering a safe haven of regression to a condition of primary narcissism where all wishes are gratified, sleep presented him with a more complex state of affairs.

Perhaps Freud's monumental labor in *The Interpretation of Dreams* functioned to allay the kinds of anxieties that his dream-life elicited. In any case, we know how he chose to die—by lethal morphine injection—as if to return to the "intrauterine" state of infantile wish fulfillment he attributed to dreams. "Sleep," Freud lyrically observes in "A Metapsychological Supplement to the Theory of Dreams," "is a reactivation of intrauterine existence, fulfilling as it does the conditions of repose, warmth and exclusion of stimulus; indeed, in sleep many resume the foetal posture" (1917b, 222). Perhaps, at long last, Freud sought to restore such a primal state of being—to induce (and insure) a dreamless sleep.

Notes

1 Carl Jung called Freud's attention to his resemblance to his patient Irma in a letter dated December 3, 1912: "As for this bit of neurosis, may I draw your attention to the fact that you open *The Interpretation of Dreams* with the mournful admission of your own neurosis—the dream of Irma's injection—identification with the neurotic in need of treatment" (1974, 526). Max Schur (1966) was the first to make the connection between Irma and Emma Eckstein, pointing to the parallel between Freud's and Emma's respective nose operations at the hands of Wilhelm Fliess. Others follow Didier Anzieu (1959) in assuming that Irma represents Anna Hammerschlag Lictheim, a young widow and friend of Freud's family. Erik Erikson (1954), who is not too concerned with the real life counterpart of Irma, nevertheless focuses on the specifically "feminine" aspects of Freud's identification with Irma. Jim Swan's (1974) argument is perhaps the most far-reaching of these in its emphasis on Freud's resistance to his identification with Irma as a factor in his construction of the Oedipus complex. I am especially indebted to Swan's essay, which informs the reading I offer here.
2 The only reader to have made the connection between Freud's Irma dream and his subsequent cancer of the mouth appears to be Thomas Hersh (1995), who takes this uncanny condition as evidence that dreams may warn us of underlying physical states. Had Freud been aware of this possibility, he argues, he might have been spared much bodily suffering. Peter Rudnytsky points out that Freud's contemporary Georg Groddeck believed that physical illness has a psychic component, "recognizing the inseparability of the somatic from the psychic and endorsing the principle that even a 'physical event' can represent unconscious 'emotional needs'" (2002, 158). Rudnytsky wonders whether Freud may

have intuited his fateful encounter with cancer when he wrote to Fliess in 1901 regarding his (only partly joking) analysis of his choice of the number 2467 as the sum of possible errors in *The Interpretation of Dreams*. Freud's wish for another twenty-four years of work (bringing him to the age of 67) corresponds to the span of time separating him from his cancer diagnosis. During the years of his self-analysis, Freud had tried and repeatedly failed to end his smoking habit. It is tempting, under these circumstances, to conclude that he understood (at least subliminally) the danger that his cigar-smoking posed—yet chose to ignore it. I would add that Freud's inability to analyze the sources of his oral need contributed to this psychic disposition.

3 Karl Abraham may have been the first to comment on the sexual content of Freud's dream. In a letter dated January 8, 1908, he queries Freud: "I should like to know whether the incomplete interpretation of the paradigm dream in the *Interpretation of Dreams* is on purpose. I think that trimethylamin leads to the most important part, to sexual allusions, that become more distinct in the last lines. Surely, everything does point to the suspicion of syphilitic infection in the patient?" (Falzeder ed. 2002, 19). Freud's response was evasive: "In the paradigm dream there is no mentioning of syphilis," he claims. "Sexual megalomania is hidden behind it; the three women—Mathilde, Sophie, and Anna—are the three god-mothers of my daughters, and I have them all! There would be one therapy for widowhood. All sorts of intimate things, naturally" (21). One senses that Freud deliberately chose not to pursue lines of association that might have led to personal embarrassment—at least in print. To what extent he explored them privately is not clear. A recent reader, however, finds that "the sexual reading ... forces itself on the reader immediately. The scenario presented by Freud is one where four men gaze on and probe the body of a reluctant young woman—which scenario suggests, of course, sexual violation, even a gang rape" (Anspaugh 1995, 430). Sexual violation is at issue, I believe, but in a less specific way than that of rape.

4 Frank Hartman notes that

> The formula for Irma's injection ... may contain an allusion to the condom. While the first latex condom was commercially introduced in England in 1890, most condoms in 1895 were still made from fish bladders that had to be preserved in salt, or sheep intestines that had to be kept moist in a preservative solution of denatured (mixed with propyl) alcohol or isopropyl alcohol and reusable ... Proprionic acid can also serve this purpose. It was introduced in 1889 as a treatment for vulvo-vaginal moniliasis. It

is still in use today, especially during pregnancy. Trimethylamin's smell of rotting fish should be remembered. (1983, 578)

5. In a letter dated November 6, 1911, where Emma Jung tries to mediate the growing conflict between her husband and Professor Freud, she alludes to Freud's comment to her about his marriage as having "long been amortized," so that "now there was nothing more to do except—die" (McGuire 1974, 456). Peter Gay (1988, 163) cites Freud's distaste for all known methods of birth control as the primary factor in his decision to restrict his sexual activity with Martha.

6. Schur remarks that "Freud knew full well that smoking was an irritant to his mucous membrane, but would never agree to give up smoking because of this, although he was advised to do so in no uncertain terms" (1972, 411). Gay quotes Freud's comment to Jones after his first medical consultation concerning the lesion in his mouth as follows: "My own diagnosis had been epithelioma, but was not accepted. Smoking is accused as the etiology of this tissue-rebellion" (1988, 419). Although Felix Deutsch, Freud's personal physician at the time, failed to tell him the truth of his condition, Freud himself divined it—as well as its cause. Paul Stepansky notes, interestingly, that Freud's use of surgical metaphors to describe the therapeutic aspect of psychoanalysis waned in almost direct proportion to his subjection to surgical procedures for his cancer, suggesting perhaps Freud's unwillingness to associate his oral difficulties with his psychological state (1999, 134).

7. See, in particular, Neil Hertz (1983), Toril Moi (1981), and Sharon Willis (1983). For a fuller consideration of this issue, see also my essay on Dora (1985).

8. Due to a mistaken translation in the German text he used, Freud thought that the bird in question was a vulture (*Geier*), rather than a kite (*nibbio*). His subsequent line of argument (including the figure of the Egyptian mother goddess) depends on this error of attribution. I am not concerned with the inaccuracy of the translation, but rather with the line of association that stems from it.

9. Melanie Klein (1935) builds on the suggestiveness of this statement in her essay "A Contribution to the Psychogenesis of Manic-Depressive States."

PART TWO

Transitions

4

Undoing Incest

When we think about the family, what we have is never anything that can rightly be identified as "the family" so much as a discourse about such a construction.
LYNDA E. BOOSE AND BETTY S. FLOWERS, *DAUGHTERS AND FATHERS*

In speaking to one of the editors of *Daughters and Fathers* at a professional conference, I made a crucial slip. I had seen a notice of the book and asked whether it was in print, referring to it by what I thought was its title: *Fathers and Daughters*. When the editor graciously corrected me, I realized the significance of my error. In placing fathers before daughters, I was contributing to the very phenomenon the book seeks to examine—the subordination and effacement of the daughter within Western family structures and traditions. By reversing the terms of this relationship, the editors hope not only to highlight the position of the daughter within it but also to assist a process of cultural transformation, with the aim of altering the network of systems that ensure the ideological reproduction of the family.[1] This is an ambitious project, fittingly served by the large design and ample proportions of the collection of essays gathered in its name.

It would be an impossible task to comment on the entire contents of this book, so I will concentrate on what I take to be its most consistent concerns as well as its overall impact on me as a reader. I feel invited to do this by the editors themselves, who in their introduction state that their book is meant to evoke a process of reflection in which each reader will question her own socialization process and "think beyond even the collection itself... [to] the numerous essays, literary, historical, or even autobiographical, that are not—but might have been—included in *Daughters and Fathers*" (1989, 8–9).

Although each of the three sections of *Daughters and Fathers* stresses one aspect of the topic—its theoretical rationale in psychoanalysis and structural anthropology, the daughter's traditional role as exemplified by literature and biography, and the female artist's struggle to free herself of her negative paternal legacy—I am most struck by the consistency of the portrait of daughter–father relations that emerges from the collection as a whole. This is due, no doubt, to the editors' focus on the Anglo-American literary tradition, which in turn is undergirded by the "closed, hierarchical, patronymic, and patriarchal" nuclear family structure (4). The news, as might be expected, is not good.

While the theoretical essays perform an elegant (and pessimistic) analysis of the Western patriarchal family, the literary and biographical essays assess its toll on daughters, none of whom (in fiction or in life) seems to escape unscathed. Only one historical subject, Queen Elizabeth I, offers a wholly positive model of female accomplishment, yet the circumstances of her birth and achievement are so obviously anomalous that they have little or no relevance to the lives of ordinary women (Leah S. Marcus). Despite (or perhaps because of) the excellence of the essays in this collection, I could not help feeling disheartened by their conclusions. I was also provoked, as the editors urge, to further thought.

What, on the whole, do these essays reveal about the primary determinants of the daughter's oppression and the means by which it might be alleviated? Again and again, it seems to me, the authors indict the dynamics of the nuclear family as anatomized and rationalized by Freud. Yet the problem may reside less in the Oedipus complex itself than in its troubling corollaries or subtexts: the exchange of women and father–daughter incest. So many of the chapters in this volume deal directly or indirectly with these topics that they come to constitute a thematic focus, one that ultimately calls into question the universalizing tendency of psychoanalysis as well as the way in which it has served to sustain the cultural status quo.

The typical Western drama of coming-of-age female is dismal at best. Lynda Boose traces this drama through Freud's account of female castration to Lévi-Strauss's depiction of the incest taboo as constitutive of the exchange of women and hence as the linchpin of social order. She problematizes Lévi-Strauss's overly optimistic account, however, by signaling the conflict at the heart of the exchange system between the father's wish to retain his daughter's love for himself and his desire to give her in marriage to a husband of his choosing. Reflecting on the function of marriage in creating political ties in *Beowulf*, for instance, Boose points out that the object of exchange, far from stabilizing alliances, becomes an agent of disruption, uncovering "a violent text of desire and competition, not one of mutual cooperation" (29). At the core of Lévi-Strauss's elegant explanation of social harmony guaranteed by the exchange of women, Boose finds the dark trope of father–daughter incest.

Literary and sociological evidence both suggest that the taboo on incest, however it might inhibit sexual contact between mothers and sons, is often weak or ineffective in the sphere of father–daughter relations. Boose astutely points out that the typical oedipalized daughter–father relationship "has no effective internal mechanisms for negotiating its dissolution" (46). Most of the chapters in this collection corroborate this view. While several contributors (Evan Carton, Elizabeth Cullingford, Katherine Hill-Miller, and Dianne Sadoff) analyze relationships between actual fathers and their daughters (Brontë, Evans, Freud, Hawthorne, Thackeray, and Yeats) as implicitly incestuous, other contributors (Joanne Diehl, Christine Froula, Judith Gardiner, Sandra Gilbert, Janice Haney-Peritz, and Hortense Spillers) identify father–daughter incest as the central drama of women's (and sometimes men's) literary production. A third and partially overlapping group (Cullingford, Gardiner, Haney-Peritz, and Spillers) seeks to uncover the ideological apparatus at work in the mechanism of the Oedipus complex and the daughter–father relationship it inscribes, in order to reveal the discursive and material conditions of its reproduction. I find this third effort the most interesting and useful because it alone seems to offer hope for change. Here I will be focusing on only one aspect of this multifaceted analysis—the evolution of the psychoanalytic paradigm of the nuclear family romance—because it seems to go directly to the heart of the problem with daughters and fathers.

Collectively, these chapters indict the Oedipus complex as a screen for the exchange of women and for father–daughter incest. Freud's focus on the incest taboo as the site of cultural production is one-sided, they imply. In directing his attention to the paternal prohibition on sexual relations between mother and son, Freud not only deliberately averted his gaze from the issue of father–daughter incest on which he had based his original theory of hysterical neurosis but he also elaborated a theory that tacitly encourages such abuse. Freud's conception of the incest taboo does not allow for a mother's prohibition, for example, of sexual relations between father and daughter, nor does it offer a rationale (corresponding to the son's renunciation of the mother) for the daughter's relinquishment of the father as love-object in preparation for her choice of a future husband or lover. Only Lévi-Strauss includes the daughter and sister along with the mother in the incest taboo, yet even here, as Boose points out, the prohibition is only partially successful. The exchange of women on which Lévi-Strauss bases his view of social relations relies less on an externally enforced law than on a voluntary act, on the father's willingness to give up his daughter. The father may, and often does, act as his own law in this regard. Given the existence of a social order that allows him to dispose of his daughter as he chooses, moreover, he may at one time decide to retain her and at another to let her go, so that the exchange of women, while in tension with father–daughter incest, is not always incompatible with it. At the very least, however, a daughter's eventual departure from her father's house provides no guarantee that she has not experienced incest.

Several contributors locate a dynamic within the Oedipus complex that may help to explain the phenomenon of father–daughter incest. The father's desire for his daughter, they argue, may represent a displacement of the oedipal boy's frustrated desire for his mother (Cullingford, Gardiner, Gilbert, and Hill-Miller). Sandra Gilbert makes a presumptive case by pointing out that on the eve of abandoning his seduction theory Freud reported a dream in which he felt erotic urges toward his daughter Matilde, but then based his oedipal construct on the son's desire for his mother. "Why," asks Gilbert, "assume that Freud's dream of paternal desire 'screens' a consciousness of *daughterly* eroticism towards the *father?* Is it not possible that paternal desire and the son's Oedipal wishes are inextricably linked, each a manifestation of the other?" (272). Gilbert sees the boy's oedipal wish for his mother played out in the adult male's fantasies of father–daughter incest, which allow him "both to have and to humble the mother" (272). Could it be that the Oedipus complex itself is contaminated by the very desire it silences and repudiates in its rejection of the seduction theory? While it has been proposed before that the father who desires his daughter as love object seeks a mother surrogate, I have never seen the argument carried so far, into the internal construction of the Oedipus complex itself. To do so challenges the cultural hegemony of Freud's theory and hence releases its near-stranglehold on a feminism that seeks to redefine or to reconfigure the daughter–father relationship. I want to pursue some of the implications of this line of speculative argument.

Freud's traffic in women

What exactly is prohibited in Freud's taboo on incest (meaning, primarily, the son's desire for his mother)? How likely, after all, is it that a preadolescent boy would be able to actualize his fantasies of incest with his mother? Surely, such a relationship could only occur in the context of the mother's active desire for or seduction of her son. Yet Freud, despite numerous allusions to maternal seductiveness in his work, never developed a theoretical model that acknowledged such a possibility. He was, in fact, notoriously unable to theorize maternal desire, or to put it another way (with apologies to Virginia Woolf), he could not "think back through his mother."[2]

In the absence of desire for her son, the mother herself would hardly require the threat of paternal castration in order to discourage unwanted advances. Freud's Oedipus complex, modeled on Sophocles's representation of the actions of a grown man, obscures the point that constitutes the greatest challenge to its credibility: the young boy's relative helplessness, weakness, and sexual incapacity. From the child's perspective, both parents are likely to appear strong and possibly threatening. Given women's historic domination of early child-rearing, moreover, it may be the mother who is initially the more awe-inspiring figure of the two.[3]

Evidence that suggests this was the case in Freud's own family offers us a means of reevaluating the subjective grounds for Freud's choice of Oedipus as the analogue of his self-analysis, as well as his lifelong application of this model in thinking about the evolution of human culture. This line of speculative argument, moreover, permits reassessment of the standardized Freudian biography, which generally takes Freud at his word regarding the oedipal construction of his own early life. If, however, we now appraise Freud's formulation of the Oedipus complex as an obscuration of the signifying possibilities of the mother's agency and desire, then we can also observe both how it sustains the exchange of women by men and how it serves to screen father–daughter incest, not only in theoretical terms but also in the context of Freud's life.

Although many have noted Freud's obvious idealization of his mother, few have commented on its consequences within his theory.[4] Nor have they seriously challenged Freud's portrayal of his mother as completely loving and devoted to his needs. Even the small biographical evidence that we have, as I argue in Chapters 1 and 2, suggests a more painful construction. Members of Freud's own family have described Amalia Freud as an energetic but domineering woman who was subject to fits of temper. In the eyes of one of her grandchildren, she was quite simply "a tyrant and a selfish one."[5] Unquestionably, she had high expectations of her first-born son Sigismund, whom she was fond of referring to as her "goldener Sigi," yet the young Freud may have experienced this belief in his future achievements as a potential source of anxiety: whether as a demand that he realize his mother's wishes for his future or, even, as an implicit statement about how to earn her approval.[6] That his mother's love was conditional, or at least divided, might well have been brought home to him by the birth of two siblings in rapid succession, Julius and Anna. Freud's report of his infantile jealousy of Julius and his dislike for Anna (assigning her the status of his least favorite sister) suggest his sensitivity to being unable to command his mother's full affection or even attention. The unusual circumstance of his father's being twenty years older than his mother and of Freud's having half-brothers who were his mother's age contributed to the complexity of this family constellation.

In *The Psychopathology of Everyday Life* (1901, 51n), Freud confesses that he held his mother and his half-brother Phillipp responsible for the appearance of one of his siblings—a linkage that casts suspicion (if only in fantasy) on Amalia's fidelity to her husband, who, from all accounts, was an easy-going, kindly, but somewhat ineffectual man. Interestingly, in this scenario it is the mother's rather than the son's desire that is problematic and illicit, while the father, far from acting as an agent of prohibition, occupies the humiliating position of cuckold. When we add to these dynamics Freud's accounts of his childhood nurse, who aroused and shamed him sexually and who later stole from him, we may begin to discern a family configuration that not only problematizes but also inverts the familiar terms of the Oedipus complex. Here women (read, mothers) actively seduce and betray, while fathers and sons are helplessly acted upon. Whereas the Oedipus complex requires a mother whose erotic impulses are unthreateningly centered on her male child and otherwise relatively inert, Freud's family structure evinces a female desire that is mobile, autonomous, and subversive of male control. Looked at this way, the Oedipus complex reads less as the unmediated product of Freud's self-analysis than as a highly compromised and disguised reaction to the circumstances of his birth and early life. We might even say that it represents the theoretical outcome of a flight from the problematics of maternal desire.

Stressing the son's erotic agency and subsequent submission to paternal authority, which Freud describes as a cultural achievement, the account of the Oedipus complex constitutes a heroic narrative celebrating masculine initiative and power. Read from the perspective of the father–daughter relationship, however, this story yields a quite different set of meanings. *Oedipus at Colonus,* in Lynda Boose's reading, "dramatizes the father's seduction of his daughter as embedded within the attempt to reconstruct his lost union with the mother, an adult reversion to infantile dependency and a state of helplessness to which women—and, in particular, daughters—are expected to respond." Boose interprets this strategy as the adult male's attempt to undo the "defeat that as an infant he suffered from his own father" (41), but we might also see it as a means of satisfying the desire for unconditional love that he felt missing in his relationship with his actual mother. If mothers cannot be coerced, daughters can. The power accruing to adult men in Western patriarchal society sets the stage not only for the phenomenon known as the exchange of women but also for the indulgence of fantasized need represented by father–daughter incest. The outlines of both emotional strategies may be discerned in the circumstances of Freud's later life.

Further evidence suggests that Freud himself in his intimate relations participated in the economy of exchange that Lévi-Strauss (1989) has characterized as the outcome of the incest taboo and

Gayle Rubin (1975) bluntly refers to as "the traffic in women." That Freud's relationships with men were often mediated by a significant female figure has been remarked by a number of critics. Peter Rudnytsky (1987), for instance, discerns such a structure in Freud's relationship with his friend Wilhelm Fliess in responding to the bungled surgery performed on Emma Eckstein, tracing this pattern back to a childhood incident described in "Screen Memories" in which Freud joins with his playmate John (the son of his older half-brother Emanuel) in attacking and humiliating John's sister Pauline. Others have drawn the inevitable connection between Freud's treatment of Eckstein and his attitude toward his patient Dora, whom he encourages to submit to the implicit pact between her father and Herr K.[7] In each of these instances, Freud consolidates an alliance with other males by subjecting a female figure to a sexually charged experience of a shameful or degrading nature.

Biographers of Freud have documented other examples of Freud's complexly mediated relationships with his male followers, although they have tended not to observe or to interpret the structure I am describing. Aldo Carotenuto (1982), for instance, illuminates the role that Sabina Spielrein played in the dissolution of Freud's friendship with Jung.[8] Spielrein, a patient of Jung's who had fallen in love with him and believed her feelings reciprocated, appealed to Freud to help her escape a situation which could only prove painful or compromising to a young woman romantically involved with a married man. Freud, reluctant to believe that his chosen heir to the psychoanalytic movement could have behaved less than honorably under the circumstances, at first responded coldly but, on learning from Jung himself of the truth of her claims, he took another tack.

This incident coincided with a general cooling off of Freud's friendship with Jung, who was beginning to articulate ideas that Freud found heretical. The correspondence from this period between the two men reveals the extent to which each expressed his discontent with the other by reacting to Spielrein, who was by now delivering papers (influenced by her former mentor Jung) to Freud's Wednesday circle in Vienna. Stepping between Freud and Jung at a critical moment in their relationship, Spielrein acted as the charged conduit for some of the disagreements between the two men. I would also suggest that, for Freud, Spielrein's apparent defection from Jung, manifested in her physical flight from Zurich to Vienna, may have acted as a consolation for the loss of his male follower. If Freud could not triumph over his rival Jung in theoretical terms, he could at least win over Jung's former lover. While I am not suggesting that Freud wished to acquire Spielrein as his actual mistress, I cannot imagine how his acceptance of her into his inner coterie could have been devoid of sexual import.

Another story, with a similar structure of rivalry, emerges in connection with Lou Andreas-Salomé, the former lover of Freud's brilliant and unruly disciple Victor Tausk. While Freud maintained extremely cordial, even flirtatious relations with Andreas-Salomé, he gradually edged Tausk out of the circle of his favor.[9] While frequently engaging Andreas-Salomé in intimate conversation, for instance, he refused to analyze Tausk, whom he considered too independent a thinker with the additional uncanny knack of anticipating his own ideas. Instead Freud recommended that Tausk see Helene Deutsch, herself in analysis with Freud and someone whom Tausk might rightly consider his peer rather than his superior in analytic training. Nevertheless Tausk acquiesced, with the result that much of Deutsch's own analysis with Freud became occupied with her concerns about treating Tausk.

At a certain point in this deeply entangled state of affairs, Freud delivered an ultimatum: if Deutsch wished to continue her analysis with him, she would have to terminate Tausk. In a perhaps predictable decision under the circumstances, Deutsch chose to remain with Freud. Not long thereafter, Tausk committed suicide. While Tausk's unstable disposition may have determined his fate, it seems likely that he registered Freud's pointed message at this particular juncture, that he was persona non grata within Freud's analytic circle. Once again, Freud emerged in possession of the field, both erotically, as the intimate of the beautiful and worldly Andreas-Salomé, and professionally, as the survivor of the theoretical arena of conflict between himself and Tausk.

In his relationships with his half-nephew John, his friend Fliess, the father of his patient Dora, and Herr K., Freud's efforts seem designed to sustain male bonds at the expense of a suffering woman. A different structure emerges in his friendships with Jung and Tausk, Here Freud exploits an erotically charged relationship with a woman in order to defeat a male rival. Both configurations stress the woman's role as a mediator of male alliances and hence fit under the general heading of a "traffic in women," which I, along with Lévi-Strauss, Gayle Rubin, and many of the contributors to *Daughters and Fathers*, see as a corollary of the Oedipus complex. But I have also been claiming that Freud's life offers evidence of an even more troubling disposition—toward father–daughter incest. One final, intricately extended story involving Freud's friendship with his biographer Ernest Jones, his treatment of Jones's mistress Loe Kann, and Jones's subsequent courtship of Anna Freud, who later nursed her father (much as Dora nursed hers) through his sixteen-year illness with cancer, interweaves these two motifs in such a way as to render them inseparable.

An otherwise favorable biography of Ernest Jones by Vincent Brome (1983) offers a rather unflattering story, reminiscent of Dora's case history, about Jones's separation from the beautiful and wealthy, but morphine-addicted mistress, Loe Kann.[10] Toward the end of a seven-year relationship, in which Jones often represented Kann as his wife though they were never legally married, Jones approached Freud about the possibility of his taking Kann into analysis. Correspondence between Jones and Freud from this time indicates that Jones was weary of Kann and wished to be rid of her, while Kann herself (perhaps intuiting his intent) was wary of psychoanalysis. Freud, who must also have understood the terms of this bargain, was nevertheless agreeable, and eventually even Kann was persuaded to undergo analysis.

Through this period Jones and Freud continued to correspond and exchange information on Kann's treatment, neither showing any concern to protect her privacy. Whereas Freud took a rosy view of her progress, Jones's reports, based directly on Kann's letters to him, told a different story. Much like Dora, Kann complained of being manipulated and misunderstood. Freud twisted her words, she claimed, and disbelieved her. She was unhappy in analysis and considered leaving it.

From this point, events took a distinct turn for the worse. Jones, who had, on the advice of Freud, been living apart from Kann in Berlin, returned to Vienna for a visit and managed to seduce Kann's companion and maid, a woman named Lina. When confronted by Freud with this dereliction, of which Kann was also aware, Jones defended himself lamely by saying that he had only resumed a previous affair with the woman, thus betraying a new level of callousness in his relations with Kann. Kann, exasperated by this state of affairs in which she saw Freud and Jones allied against her, appears to have acted next as Jones secretly intended, withdrawing from him by contracting a new relationship, ironically with another man named Jones. Evidently unperturbed, Jones the First, as he jokingly referred to himself thereafter, resumed his relationship with Lina.

It is easy to see how Kann might have felt herself a pawn in a game, where the very men who solicited her confidence calculated her moves in advance. But the story does not end here. While Kann succeeded in removing herself from this unsavory triangle, it reconstituted itself for a perilous moment around an even more vulnerable figure, Freud's daughter Anna.

Not long after Jones ended his relationship with Kann, he returned to England, from whence he offered to escort Anna Freud on her first visit to that country. Loe Kann, suspecting Jones of designs on Anna, warned Freud against such a course of action. Both Kann and Freud, moreover, were aware of charges of sexual molestation that had been brought against Jones in the past by three female patients, two of whom were underage. While Jones had never been convicted of wrongdoing, his medical reputation suffered enough to make him drop his practice in England and emigrate for a time to Canada. Kann may have had reason to fear more than a conventional romantic interest on Jones's part toward the relatively inexperienced 18-year-old Anna.

Evidently alarmed, Freud nevertheless permitted the trip to proceed as planned, choosing to express his concern through letters to both Anna and Jones.[11] To his daughter, he delicately suggested that she was too young to think of marriage, implying that Jones as an experienced man had needs that she could not be expected to fulfill, surely an understatement, given Freud's intimate knowledge of Jones's affairs. To Jones, he stressed Anna's unworldliness and lack of interest in men, a not-so-veiled hint, according to Peter Gay, "that for Jones to put his hands on Anna would be equivalent to child abuse" (1988, 434).

Anna Freud, who rather disliked Jones, later stated that she felt he was only interested in her as a conduit to her father, an astute assessment of her status as an object of exchange (Young-Bruehl 1988, 66). Freud suspected Jones of an even less attractive motive. At the height of his anxiety about Anna's safety, he wrote to Ferenczi, who was Jones's analyst, that he did not want to "lose the dear child to an obvious act of revenge—one opposing any rationality that speaks against it" (quoted in Young-Bruehl 1988, 67). Freud evidently feared that Jones would attempt to seduce his daughter to retaliate for the loss of his mistress Loe. While never absolutely forbidding Anna to see Jones, Freud consoled himself with the thought that Loe would "keep watch [over her] like a dragon" (quoted in Young-Bruehl 1988, 67).

Freud's letter to Ferenczi registers an implicit rivalry with Jones for the affections of Loe Kann as well as Anna's position between them as a contested sexual object. With his knowledge of Jones's character, is it possible that he had no distrust until alerted by Loe? Did Freud mean to test his daughter's virtue and filial obedience? What would have happened if Jones had overstepped the bounds of propriety, a not entirely unlikely possibility? Freud's gesture in sending his daughter to England, almost literally into the arms of an acknowledged rival, was either extraordinarily innocent or else heavily overdetermined.

This incident illustrates, as clearly as any literary example, the tension that Lynda Boose finds at the heart of the exchange of women. Structurally, Anna stepped into the position vacated by Loe Kann, yet Freud sanctioned her visit to England, where she was sure to be welcomed, if not actually squired, by Jones. Almost simultaneously, Freud marked his daughter with the unmistakable sign of his possession, putting his rival on notice not to touch. While Freud's actions read from Jones's perspective might suggest mediation of male bonds through Anna's marriageable status, Freud's words attest a need to retain her for himself. Such a situation, problematic at best, would no doubt be difficult to sustain. Indeed, subsequent events indicate a shift away from the triangulated relationship characteristic of the exchange of women and toward the dual structure of father–daughter incest.

It is well known that Freud analyzed his daughter Anna and that she was his closest companion as well as nurse during his declining years. Tellingly, Freud identified her not only with Antigone, the mainstay of her father (and brother) Oedipus in his old age, but also with Cordelia on whose "kind nursery" King Lear wishes to depend in his dotage. Analyzing what she terms the Antigone model of daughterly conduct, Boose identifies this structure as incestuous (40–41), as does David Willbern in his overview of the father–daughter relationship in Freudian theory (91–92). Carolyn Heilbrun's afterword goes one step further by suggesting that, on the basis of what we already know, it is not impossible to conceive of actual incest between Freud and his daughter (419). Even so careful a historian as Peter Gay (1988), who never discusses the possibility of literal incest, evidences discomfort on this topic. In his biography, he describes Freud as "helplessly entangled" in his relationship to his daughter, the "emotional costs" of which, he says, "have never been calculated" (441).[12]

Freud's attitude toward his daughter, if not literally incestuous, was extremely possessive. He was known to say that his attachment to her was as powerful as his need for cigars—that is to say, an addiction (Gay 1988, 441). Moreover, there is evidence of the role reversal that Boose and others detect in the situation of incest. Aging, ill, and dependent, Freud turned to his daughter for the kind of care most often associated with mothers. While serving him professionally in a variety of ways, she also tended to his most intimate personal needs, examining his oral cavity, for instance, for signs of cancer and helping him to insert and remove his cumbersome mouthpiece. That Anna Freud loved her father is apparent; that Freud did little or nothing to discourage this attachment or to promote other sexual or emotional ties is equally self-evident.[13]

Certain features of Freud's relationship to his daughter in the latter half of his life, moreover, are reminiscent of Dora's case history, which hinges on the analyst's attempts to convince a young girl of her desire for fellatio with her ailing parent. Juxtaposing Freud's comment about Anna being as indispensable to him as his cigars with his statement that smoking substitutes for masturbation, one can perhaps discern the outlines of a secret wish: that his daughter gratify him sexually in the way that he imagines Dora ministering to her father. If Freud was unable early in his career to sustain the notion of father–daughter incest as central to the etiology of neurosis, toward the end of his career he was equally unable to perceive the extent to which his own needs and desires might be characterized as incestuous.

Undoing Oedipus

As the example of Freud's own life suggests, the oedipalized patriarchal family structure may act both to produce and to screen the exchange of women and father–daughter incest. Such, at least, appears to be the overall message of *Daughters and Fathers*. But how are we to interpret what I take to be the other main perception of this collection, that the structure of father–daughter incest obscures a more primitive attempt to satisfy needs deriving from infantile dependency? If, as Boose suggests, such needs result from the frustrations induced in the son by the father's prohibition of incest, then it is difficult, short of lifting the taboo itself, to imagine a way of alleviating its consequences for girls and women. If, however, one assumes that Freud's notion of the castration complex may be traced not to his conviction of his father's authority but to his perception of his mother's remoteness or unreliability, then it also becomes possible to propose an intervention with the hope of altering the most negative implications of this structure.

Throughout his work, Freud's insistence on a mother's totally fulfilling and unambivalent love for her male offspring strikes a false note. Instead these statements appear to mask a feeling of absence or loss that Freud was unable to attribute to the agency of the mother herself. Rather than tarnish his maternal ideal, Freud chose to point the finger at his father, holding him responsible for frustration that may have originated in his mother's character and the difficult circumstances of her life. The love he desired was unavailable, he rationalized, not because his mother would or could not satisfy this demand but because his father forbade it. Instead of recognizing his disappointment and coming to terms with it as such, Freud elaborated a theory that would authorize his adult desire to have women fulfill his fantasy needs.

Reading Freud's theory in this way, as the compromised product of his insufficiently analyzed life history, opens new possibilities for understanding the problem of father–daughter incest. If, for instance, we can read Freud's monopoly on his daughter Anna's affections as a delayed and rationalized attempt to obtain the tenderness he felt he missed in his early life, then we may begin to examine the role of failed nurturance (including the inability to come to terms with it in a mature way) in the incidence of father–daughter abuse. In support of this view, I will offer a brief reading of the incest motif in Toni Morrison's novel, *The Bluest Eye* (1972).

Among Morrison's many achievements as a writer, one of her bravest, to my mind, is her characterization of Cholly Breedlove, who rapes and impregnates his barely adolescent daughter Pecola.

While a lesser writer might have concentrated solely on Pecola's plight, which is achingly grim, Morrison chooses to enter into Cholly's mentality in such a way that we cannot help perceiving this father–daughter tragedy as mutual.

Cholly's story begins with abandonment. "When Cholly was four days old, his mother wrapped him in two blankets and one newspaper and placed him on a junk heap by the railroad" (105). Cholly's mother, who leaves town when her transgression is discovered, cares so little for her baby that she even fails to name him. His father has long since disappeared. Raised comfortably though somewhat eccentrically by his great-aunt Jimmy, Cholly finds himself orphaned for a second time in early adolescence. This event, which precipitates his first experience of intercourse, also becomes the occasion of sexual and racial humiliation when he is surprised by a group of white men who symbolically rape him by forcing him to perform for their amusement. Thus an act that begins in mutual pleasure turns into one of violence and hatred. Unable to vent his fury on men who hold every form of power over him, physical, racial, and economic, Cholly turns his rage against his equally victimized partner.

> Cholly, moving faster, looked at Darlene. He hated her. He almost wished he could do it—hard, long, and painfully, he hated her so much. The flashlight wormed its way into his guts and turned the sweet taste of muscadine into rotten fetid bile. He stared at Darlene's hands covering her face in the moon and lamplight. They looked like baby claws. (117)

As a result of this experience, Cholly becomes what Morrison calls a "free man"—not one who feels autonomous or self-authorized but one who is unmoored, free to veer this way or that. "Abandoned in a junk heap by his mother, rejected for a crap game by his father, there was nothing more to lose. He was alone with his own perceptions and appetites and they alone interested him" (126). Cholly, who cannot get even a fraction of what he needs from the desperate world he is born into, finally turns to his daughter out of a confused longing for what is missing from his life. It is not primarily sexual comfort that he seeks (a comfort which in any case he can no longer obtain from his soured marriage), but something deeper, something if not actually childlike then reminiscent of childhood in all its seeming innocence and vulnerability. Pecola reminds him perhaps of a lost or buried self, one who is deserving of love.

Most remarkable (and even shocking) in Morrison's description of the rape scene is her use of the word "tenderness" to characterize the process of Cholly's sexual arousal. When a simple gesture of Pecola's suddenly reminds him of his first encounter with his wife, Cholly attempts a reenactment of that earlier moment:

> The tenderness welled up in him, and he sank to his knees, his eyes on the foot of his daughter. Crawling on all fours toward her, he raised his hand and caught the foot in an upward stroke. Pecola lost her balance and was about to careen to the floor. Cholly raised his other hand to her hips to save her from falling. He put his head down and nibbled at the back of her leg. His mouth trembled at the firm sweetness of the flesh. He closed his eyes, letting his fingers dig into her waist. (128)

Even after he feels Pecola's resistance, he wishes to sustain this illusion of loving contact. "Surrounding all of this lust was a border of politeness. He wanted to fuck her—tenderly. But the tenderness would not hold." This scene, which begins in a gentle reminiscence—"it was such a small and simple gesture, but it filled him then with a wondering softness,"—ends in physical and spiritual violation (128). What Pecola receives from her father is nothing like tenderness; instead she gains his legacy of self-hatred and despair. Radically unnurtured himself and unable to comprehend the social determinants of his deprivation, Cholly radically unnurtures his child.

In her afterword to *Daughters and Fathers*, Carolyn Heilbrun firmly states that "only in a world freed from the organization of the Freudian or Biblical nuclear family" is a "non-power driven relationship between women and men ... possible" (418). She reminds us that Queen Elizabeth, the obvious exception among the oppressed daughters in this collection, "did *not* grow up in an Oedipal or nuclear family position; she achieved power and esteem in her job because the usual daughter–father relationship did not, in her case, apply" (422). Heilbrun also observes that the absent-father situation prevalent among black families in poverty may actually serve to promote the daughter's aspirations, although she concedes that this is "not a conclusion likely to be granted by many" (421). One significant alternative she does not mention is that of the lesbian, who may draw sufficient support from her mother or other female role models to subvert the paternalistic influence of her actual father or the culture at large. Heilbrun is clear in her assertion, however, that "the family will have to be redefined, enlarged, extended, totally undone in those aspects that make it Oedipal in order for daughters to thrive" (420).

While Heilbrun's conclusions develop pragmatically rather than theoretically, they can be extended along some of the lines I have been arguing. We have, I believe, outgrown our embrace of Freud's oedipal construct, especially when we consider its ostensible origins—as a defense against certain realizations about the autonomy of women's desire and the corresponding pain of coming to terms with the actual (as opposed to the ideal) nature of maternal love. Whatever failures of nurturance Freud may have experienced, his need to sustain an ideal of maternal plenitude falsified that experience and perpetuated an unrealistic fantasy of unconditional love, which in turn shaped his adult relations with women. For Freud, the Oedipus complex seems to have rationalized a need simultaneously to control women's mobility (the exchange of women) and to command the domestic display of their affections (father–daughter incest). When we begin to examine the subjective bases of Freud's theoretical formulations, we also begin to neutralize their hold over our imagination.

Yet I remain interested in the psychological springs of Freud's oedipal model for what they can tell us about the etiology of father–daughter abuse. If, as Morrison implies, a radical failure of nurturance (adding cultural to parental deficits) plays a role in the creation of this problem, then we could promote family and societal conditions (and theories of these conditions) that might ameliorate the failure. Heilbrun offers a step in this direction when, in the name of a new conception of daughter–father love, she issues a call:

> For affection for the father that does not deprive the mother, or scorn or fear her; for a love from the father that desires neither the daughter herself nor the use of her to relate to other men; for a fatherly devotion that does not, as in Shakespeare, serve only to redeem the father morally and socially, without the

daughter's undergoing any moral change. Above all, [this call] is for a fondness between the daughter and father that allows for the interplay of other affections, that threatens her neither with control nor desertion, and that in no way reflects the father's unique power. (420)

Surely such love has existed historically but it has never, as far as I know, achieved the status of theory nor been publicly celebrated.[14] Yet it is precisely this kind of love, rooted in the capacity for caregiving, which seems counterindicative to father–daughter incest. As Lynda Boose notes, "The fathers who seemed least inclined to become incestuous were those whose relations with their daughters had been defined from birth by active participation in a physically and maternally nurturing role" (36).

There is a moment in *Daughters and Fathers* that invokes such a father–daughter relationship; this, if not specifically nurturing, suggests at least a peaceful transfer of power. I want to close with this evocation from the Sumerian myth of Inanna, not in order to endorse a return to a mythical past but, rather, in the spirit of a toast—to celebrate the blessing of fathers conferred on daughters who will succeed them in years as in the exercise of authority. In this passage, Lynda Boose explains, Inanna "acquires the *me,* or all the powers possible by defeating Enki, her sky-god father of wisdom, in a beer-drinking contest" (34).

> Enki and Inanna drank beer together.
> They drank more beer together.
> They drank more and more beer together.
> With their bronze vessels filled to overflowing,
> With the vessels of Urash, Mother of the Earth,
> They toasted each other; they challenged each other.
> Enki, swaying with drink, toasted Inanna:
>> In the name of my holy power! In the name of my holy shrine!
>> To my daughter Inanna I shall give
>> The high priesthood! Godship!
>> The noble, enduring crown! The throne of kingship!
>> Inanna replied: "I take them!" (299)

Notes

1. I have adopted the theoretical strategy that Boose and Flowers propose when referring to the daughter–father relationship except in those instances where incest is at issue. In such cases it seems to me that the reversal of terms ascribes an agency to the daughter that is untrue to the circumstances.
2. See my book *The Spectral Mother* (1990).
3. See Nancy Chodorow (1978) and Dorothy Dinnerstein (1976).
4. Jim Swan's essay "Mater and Nannie: Freud's Two Mothers and the Discovery of the Oedipus Complex" (1974) is an obvious and important exception to the rule. More recently, Estelle Roith (1987) has argued that Freud's inability to come to terms with his mother's domineering personality is reflected in his theoretical activity, specifically in his construction of the Oedipus complex. Joel Whitebook (2017), following in part my argument in *The Spectral Mother*, also traces the impact on Freud's thinking of his idealization of his mother.
5. Judith Bernays Heller (1973).
6. Robert Holt argues something similar in "Freud's Paternal Identification as a Source of Some Contradictions Within Psychoanalysis" (1992). Holt sees Freud's parents as having reversed, in their personalities, the conventional gender stereotypes of the day. He speculates that conflicts within the psychoanalytic establishment between values of nurturance and authoritarianism stem from Freud's having absorbed (and transformed) aspects of both his parents' dispositions in his character. Phyllis Grosskurth (1991) argues further that since Freud "had apparently received little tenderness from the stern Amalie Freud, his ability to empathize was frozen" (201).
7. See Lawrence Frank, "Freud and Dora: Blindness and Insight" (1989, 32–38). For parallels between the situation of Dora and that of Emma Eckstein, see also Rudnytsky (1987) and Jeffrey Moussaieff Masson (1984).
8. John Launer offers an in-depth account of Spielrein's involvement with Jung and with Freud, with an emphasis on the development of her own ideas in *Sex Vs. Survival: The Life and Ideas of Sabina Spielrein* (2015).
9. See Roazen, *Brother Animal* (1969) and *Freud and His Followers* (1971).
10. Vincent Brome, *Ernest Jones* (1983).
11. See Gay (1988) and Young-Bruehl (1988).
12. Gay (1988). This topic receives perhaps its definitive treatment in Patrick Mahony's essay "Freud, Family Therapist," in *Freud and the History of Psychoanalysis* (1992).

13 If anything, there is evidence that Freud wished to supervise or control his daughter's emotional life. Not content with analyzing Anna herself, he undertook to analyze her close companion Dorothy Burlingham when it became evident that the two women were becoming especially intimate. For an account of the early stages of this relationship, see Young-Bruehl (1988, 65–139).

14 Bebe Moore Campbell's memoir *Sweet Summer: Growing Up with and Without My Dad* (1989), which describes a loving and supportive father–daughter relationship, offers a wonderful exception to this general rule. Campbell's tribute to her disabled father's ability to "raise her right," despite the fact that he was divorced from her mother and hence in contact with her for only a part of the year, also calls into question the supposed dysfunction of the so-called black matriarchal family.

5

Freud as Memoirist

> *It may indeed be questioned whether we have any memories at all from our childhood: memories relating to our childhood may be all that we possess.*
> SIGMUND FREUD, "SCREEN MEMORIES"

At a time when Freud was deeply engaged in the labor of self-analysis that led to the publication of *The Interpretation of Dreams* (1900), the groundwork for much of his subsequent theorizing, he was also concerned with the dynamics of memory itself—the raw material of his own analysis, as well as the basis for the discipline of psychoanalysis. In an essay titled "Screen Memories" (1899), he makes the startling claim that memories from childhood vividly recalled in adult life bear no specific relationship to what happened in the past. Rather, they are composite formations—elements of childhood experience as represented through the distorting lens of adult wishes, fantasies, and desires. Although Freud did not pursue the full implications of such a view of memory, it has proved to be prescient, resonating with two contemporary phenomena: the neural network theory of memory formation and retrieval, and the elevation of memoir writing to premier literary status. These two developments, in turn, pose questions about psychoanalysis as a memory-based discipline. A reading of "Screen Memories" that focuses on the memoiristic aspects of Freud's writing offers a useful point of departure for exploring this issue.

Freud as a literary writer

Freud, who began his career as a neurologist, then as a medical practitioner treating patients suffering from neurological diseases, regarded himself primarily as a scientist, even when he turned his attention to matters of mind that could not directly be observed and were not susceptible to laboratory testing or experimentation. Interpretation of mental distress for Freud became a matter of decoding the obscure symbols and representations offered by the dreaming (or fantasizing) mind and by the disguised symptomatics of the body. In *The Interpretation of Dreams*, Freud outlined his method by describing the dreaming mind's strategies of repression, displacement, and condensation that serve simultaneously to conceal and to reveal the expression of a wish. Freud attributed these mental dynamics to the activity of the unconscious, a part of the mind that we cannot directly know but can infer from its ceaseless productivity. Cognitive activity, no matter how sophisticated, can never fully capture the workings of the unconscious, which by its very nature eludes representation.

For this reason, Freud's writings have struck many of his readers as more literary than scientific.[1] How, after all, can one prove the existence of the Oedipus complex? That Freud uncovered a wish in his own fantasy life to displace his father in order to enjoy his mother's undivided love and attention seems reasonable enough, but it is less clear that every male child—across history and culture—shares this wish. It is even less apparent that Sophocles's drama *Oedipus Rex* validates Freud's hypothesis that every boy wants to murder his father in order to have sex with his mother. Freud's interpretation, however ingenious, is just that—an interpretation.[2]

Nor does widespread assent to Freud's incest/murder scheme demonstrate its validity. The fact that others find personal meaning in Freud's hypothesis does not in itself indicate its universal truth. Assent may be a condition of discipleship, of professional status (especially in the formative stages of psychoanalysis as a discipline), of shared cultural experience, of a desire for group identity, of pleasure in espousing an unorthodox concept, or of a tendency toward credulity. Assent in itself proves nothing except perhaps the power of an idea to shape cultural understanding. In the absence of a means of confirming Freud's hypotheses (apart from a sense of intuitive rightness or their capacity to provide meaning to cultural experiences specific to the twentieth and twenty-first centuries), it is more useful, I believe, to regard Freud as a literary writer whose persuasive rhetoric has exercised a profound influence over Western habits of mind.[3] That Freud received the Goethe (rather than the Nobel) Prize for distinguished achievement, moreover, gives evidence of how at least some of his contemporaries regarded his work. Indeed Freud's writings, which (by his own admission) often read more like personal essays or short stories than dry scientific texts, virtually invite us to read him through the lens of literary analysis.[4]

Self-analysis as autobiography

As I have argued in Chapters 1 and 2, Freud's self-analysis—elements of which may be discerned in his dream book (since he drew amply from his own dreams to illustrate his theories of dream interpretation) and in his intensely personal correspondence with Wilhelm Fliess—constitutes a unique form of autobiography.[5] Freud was his own most intimate, most immediate, and best subject. Understanding his mental processes and their roots in the so-called unconscious lay at the heart of his creation of psychoanalysis. Prior to undertaking this monumental (and largely unprecedented) effort, Freud suffered from symptoms that he considered hysterical. Taking up and then abandoning material theories of neurosis, e.g., Fliess's notion that neurotic symptoms could be cured by nasal surgery or his own briefly entertained idea that neuroses could be traced to incidents of childhood sexual abuse, Freud finally turned inward for an explanation of adult physical and sexual malaise. What he discovered in the recesses of his own mind were forbidden, hence repressed, wishes, which led him to the articulation of childhood sexuality and ultimately to the construction of the Oedipus complex. These discoveries, in turn, relieved him of his symptoms, elevated his self-esteem, and provided him with a new professional identity. Just as Anna O benefited from what she termed the "talking cure," Freud seems to have benefited from a form of bibliotherapy, or "writing cure."

Freud's construction of himself as an oedipal subject—a libidinous, ambitious, and even aggressive son—appears to have liberated him from the doldrums of his faltering medical practice while dissolving his array of neurotic symptoms, thereby resolving his identity crisis on both personal and professional levels. Through his self-analysis and the concepts it produced, Freud performed an act of self-reinvention that gave purpose and meaning to his life and sustained him over a long and productive career.

It is the function of autobiography to give shape to the chaos of everyday life as well as to offer a compelling narrative or storyline. Freud made use of self-writing in an even deeper way: to provide the basis of theory.[6] Most readers are aware of how Freud's musings on his reactions to his father's death sparked his formulation of the Oedipus complex. Fewer may be aware of how Freud's reflections on his own life experiences continued over time to inform his thinking.[7] Freud's essay "Screen Memories," composed during the same period of time that he was writing his dream book, offers a vivid illustration of the way Freud made use of his own memories to theorize about the functioning of memory itself.

Screen memories

On January 3, 1899, Freud reported a significant finding in a letter to Fliess. "In the first place," he states, "a small bit of my self-analysis has forced its way through and confirmed that fantasies are products of later periods and are projected back from what was then the present into earliest childhood, the manner in which this also occurs also emerged, once again by a verbal link." Such projections call into question the possibility of a pure, or uncontaminated childhood memory. Freud implies as much when he goes on to say, "To the question 'What happened in earliest childhood?' the answer is 'Nothing, but the germ of sexual impulse existed.' The thing would be easy and a pleasure to tell you, but writing it out would take half a sheet so [I shall keep it] for our congress at Easter, together with other elucidations of the story of my early years" (Masson 1985, 338). At the outset of his new career path—as the founder of psychoanalysis—Freud in effect states that there is no such thing as verbatim memory, at least insofar as it relates to childhood. Rather, memory is a product of wishful distortion, based on adult needs and desires.

It is perhaps not surprising that Freud's conception of memory bears a family resemblance to his understanding of dream work, given his preoccupation with this subject at the time. In any event, his elucidation of childhood memory formation, as represented by his "Screen Memories," reads, in many respects, like the analysis of a dream. Like a dream, moreover, it presents itself to the reader in disguised form.

Freud begins his essay with a general observation about the fragmentary nature of memories from earliest childhood and the seeming paradox that the most significant events from that time (such as the death of a parent or sibling) may appear only in displaced form. He cites the work of V. and C. Henri, who conducted an extensive questionnaire on early memory retention, to demonstrate this point, summarizing his own views on the subject as follows:

> We must first enquire why it should be that precisely what is important is suppressed and what is indifferent retained; and we shall not find an explanation of this until we have investigated the mechanism of these processes more deeply. We shall then form a notion that two psychical forces are concerned in bringing about memories of this sort. One of these forces takes the importance of the experience as a motive for seeking to remember it, while the other—a resistance—tries to prevent any such preference from being shown. These two opposing forces do not cancel each other out, nor does one of them (whether with or without loss to itself) overpower the other. Instead, a compromise is brought about, somewhat on the analogy of the resultant in a parallelogram of forces. And the compromise is this. What is recorded as a mnemic image is not the relevant experience itself—in this respect the resistance gets its way; what is recorded is another psychical element closely associated with the objectionable one—and in this respect the first principle shows its strength, the principle which endeavors to fix important impressions by establishing reproducible mnemic images. The result of the conflict is therefore that, instead of the mnemic image which would have been justified by the original event, another is produced which has been to some degree associatively displaced from the former one. (306–7)

Up to this point, Freud's essay reads as a work of nonfiction, citing previous research and offering a general hypothesis to explain an otherwise puzzling phenomenon. At this point, however, it takes an autobiographical turn—one that is not presented as such but rather as an extended illustration of the concept Freud has just put forward. Here, Freud focuses on an individual example drawn from his own experience but offered as one taken from "a considerable number" (309) of such instances encountered in the course of his medical practice. In taking this rhetorical step, Freud abandons the field of nonfiction for that of memoir. Given his deliberate deception of the reader in making this move, he also enters the realm of fiction.

The subject of his observation, Freud claims, "is a man of university education, aged thirty-eight," someone who "has taken an interest in psychological questions ever since I was able to relieve him of a slight phobia by means of psycho-analysis." At the same time, Freud portrays his subject as relatively normal, "not at all or only slightly neurotic" (309). His close acquaintance with this psychologically attuned subject facilitates the flow of intimate disclosure and interpretation that follows. Given that Freud's agreeable and eminently persuadable interlocutor is none other than himself, the ensuing dialogue reads not only like memoir and self-analysis but also like a sophisticated form of short fiction.

Freud's subject begins with an overview of his early memories, which date from his second and third years and which he groups into categories of scenes recounted to him by his parents and fragmentary memories of the railway journey that removed him from his small-town birthplace to a much larger town. Other, more important, incidents—the birth of a younger sister and an injury to his chin—which he cannot recollect—cause him to reflect that the scenes he does recall "are displaced memories from which the essential element has for the most part been omitted" (310), a position that Freud had earlier articulated in his correspondence with Fliess. This speculation leads, in turn, to the heart of the essay: an extended treatment of a vividly recalled childhood memory that the subject can make neither heads nor tails of.

The scene, recounted in the first-person, has a dream-like quality.

> I see a rectangular, rather steeply sloping piece of meadow-land, green and thickly grown; in the green there are a great number of yellow flowers—evidently common dandelions. At the top end of the meadow there is a cottage and in front of the cottage door two women are standing chatting busily, a peasant-woman with

a handkerchief on her head and a children's nurse. Three children are playing in the grass. One of them is myself (between the age of two and three); the two others are my boy cousin, who is a year older than me, and his sister, who is almost exactly the same age as I am. We are picking the yellow flowers and each of us is holding a bunch of flowers we have already picked. The little girl has the best bunch; and, as though by mutual agreement, we—the two boys—fall on her and snatch away her flowers. She runs up the meadow in tears and as a consolation the peasant-woman gives her a big piece of black bread. Hardly have we seen this than we throw the flowers away, hurry to the cottage and ask to be given some bread too. And we are in fact given some; the peasant-woman cuts the loaf with a long knife. In my memory the bread tastes quite delicious—and at that point the scene breaks off. (311)

What accounts for the intensity of this scene, elements of which seem "exaggerated in an almost hallucinatory fashion?" Freud's subject asks in bewilderment. In response, Freud slyly inquires whether this memory was actually produced in childhood or at a later date. Freud's subject readily concedes, "Now that you have raised the question, it seems to be almost a certainty that this childhood memory never occurred to me at all in my earlier years" (312). Abandoning the field of true childhood memory, he then avers that it was at the age of 17 that this scene surfaced, along with "many other recollections of my earliest childhood" (312).

Having established his point that it is impossible faithfully to reproduce memories from childhood, Freud moves to the next stage of his argument—that adult fantasies give retrospective shape to memories we attribute to childhood. His subject obliges with another reminiscence, this time from his adolescent years. "When I was seventeen," he begins, "and at my secondary school, I returned for the first time to my birthplace for the holidays, to stay with a family who had been our friends ever since that remote date. I know quite well what a wealth of impressions overwhelmed me at that time" (312). What follows is a condensed version of Freud's own early history, accompanied by a description of his first love for the fifteen-year-old daughter of the family he visited.[8]

So listen. I was the child of people who were originally well-to-do and who, I fancy, lived comfortably enough in that little corner of the provinces. When I was about three, the branch of industry in which my father was concerned met with a catastrophe. He lost all his means and we were forced to leave the place and move to a large town. Long and difficult years followed, of which, as it seems to me, nothing was worth remembering. I never felt really comfortable in the town. I believe now that I was never free from a longing for the beautiful woods near our home, in which (as one of my memories from those days tells me) I used to run off from my father, almost before I had learnt to walk ... But it is no use evading the subject any longer; I must admit that there was something else that excited me powerfully. I was seventeen, and in the family where I was staying there was a daughter of fifteen, with whom I immediately fell in love. It was my first calf-love and sufficiently intense, but I kept it completely secret. After a few days the girl went off to her school (from which she too was home for the holidays) and it was this separation after such a short acquaintance that brought my longings to a really high pitch ... I passed many hours in solitary walks through the lovely woods that I had found once more and spent my time building castles in the air. These, strangely enough, were not concerned with the future but sought to improve the past. If only the smash had not occurred! If only I had stopped at home and grown up in the country and grown as strong as the young men in the house, the brothers of my love! And then if only I had followed my father's profession and if I had finally married her... A strange thing. For when I see her now from time to time—she happens to have married someone here—she is quite exceptionally indifferent to me. Yet I can remember quite well for what a long time afterwards I was affected by the yellow colour of the dress she was wearing when we first met, whenever I saw the same colour anywhere else. (312–13)

Freud easily relates the color of the young girl's dress to that of the flowers in the previous dreamlike scene. From this point forward, however, his reasoning becomes more convoluted, as he induces his alter ego to yield yet another young adult memory, this time related to visiting his uncle and cousins—the "same two cousins, the boy a year older than I am and the girl of the same age as myself, who appear in the childhood scene with the dandelions"—in a "far-distant city," in fact Manchester, England, to which Freud's uncle had emigrated some years before (315). On this occasion he becomes aware of a plan concocted between his father and uncle that he should marry his cousin, a plan that does not transpire. This association, however, leads Freud to fuse aspects of his subject's childhood scene with his two adult memories in a manner reminiscent of dream work. He concludes, on behalf of his subject, that "the childhood scene we are considering emerged at this time, when you were struggling for your daily bread—provided, that is, that you can confirm my idea that it was during this same period that you first made the acquaintance of the Alps" (315). Once again, his subject concurs: "Yes that is so ... But I still cannot grasp your point" (315). Here "Freud" unfolds the train of association that links the two adult memories with the childhood scene. While the bread that tastes so delicious represents the fantasy of a comfortable life his subject might have enjoyed had he stayed in the country and married the girl in the yellow dress (or his cousin), the throwing away of the flowers signifies his giving up his "unpractical ideals" in favor of a "'bread and butter' occupation" (315). His subject not only assents but also provides the next step in Freud's hermeneutic process.

> It seems then that I amalgamated the two sets of phantasies of how my life could have been more comfortable—the "yellow" and the "country-made bread" from the one and the throwing-away of the flowers and the actual people concerned from the other. (315)

It remains only for "Freud" to provide the concluding touch.

> Yes. You projected the two phantasies on to one another and made a childhood memory of them. The element about the alpine flowers is as it were a stamp giving the date of manufacture. I can assure you that people often construct such things unconsciously—almost like works of fiction. (315)

Having argued successfully that memories imputed to childhood are compromise formations based on adult wishes and desires, Freud articulates the concept of "screen memory." Here, he pursues the idea that his subject's memory represents not only his fantasies of material success but also his libidinal impulses. At this point, moreover, the (fabricated) distinction between Freud and his subject virtually dissolves, as the one begins to complete the thought processes of the other.

When Freud suggests that "love" plays a less prominent role in the memory scene than he might have supposed, his subject immediately objects, offering his own bold interpretation. "No," he interposes, "You are mistaken. The essence of it is its representation of love. Now I understand for the first time. Think for a moment! Taking flowers away from a girl means to deflower her" (316). At this point, Freud's subject takes the lead, developing on his own the idea that such an explicit thought could not find its way into conscious memory. "In that case," he muses, "the phantasy that has transformed itself into these childhood memories would not be a conscious one that I can remember, but an unconscious one?" "Unconscious thoughts which are a prolongation of conscious ones," Freud prompts, to which his subject responds, "I can go on with it now myself. The most seductive part of the whole subject for a young scapegrace is the picture of the marriage night... But that picture cannot venture into the light of day: the dominating mood of diffidence and of respect towards the girl keeps it suppressed. So it remains unconscious" (316).

Freud describes the above process as one in which adult unconscious wishes "slip away" into childhood, where they find disguised expression in the form of memories experienced as genuine. Freud's subject summarizes this argument for himself, reiterating his doubts about the possibility of retrieving any valid childhood memories.

> If that is so, I have lost all faith in the genuineness of the dandelion scene. This is how I look at it: On the two occasions in question, and with the support of very comprehensible realistic motives, the thought occurred to me: "If you had married this or that girl, your life would have become much pleasanter." The seminal current in my mind took hold of the thought which is contained in the protasis and repeated it in images of a kind capable of giving that same sensual current satisfaction. This second version of the thought remained unconscious on account of its incompatibility with the dominant sexual disposition; but

this very fact of its remaining unconscious enabled it to persist in my mind long after changes in the real situation had quite got rid of the conscious version. In accordance, as you say, with a general law, the clause that had remained unconscious sought to transform itself into a childhood scene which, on account of its innocence, would be able to become conscious. With this end in view it had to undergo a fresh transformation, or rather two fresh transformations. One of these removed the objectionable element from the protasis by expressing it figuratively; the second forced the apodosis into a shape capable of visual representation—using for the purpose the intermediary ideas of "bread" and "bread-and-butter occupations." I see that by producing a phantasy like this I was providing, as it were, a fulfillment of the two suppressed wishes—for deflowering a girl and for material comfort. (317–18)

Freud's subject has internalized the concept of a "screen memory," to the point that his style of argument and language use, e.g. "protasis," and "apodosis," are indistinguishable from that of Freud. Yet a problem remains. Freud's argument is so convincing that it appears to leave no room for the possibility of untrammeled childhood memory. "But now that I have given such a complete account of the motives that led to my producing the dandelion phantasy," Freud's subject muses, "I cannot help concluding that what I am dealing with is something that never happened at all but has been unjustifiably smuggled in among my childhood memories" (318).

Here Freud pulls back, claiming that the adult fantasies find expression by attaching themselves to a "memory trace" from childhood, "the content of which offers the phantasy a point of contact" (318). At the same time, the process by which the composite memory is formed may distort its source to the point where the original memory is irretrievable. "It is very possible," Freud concludes, "that in the course of this process the childhood scene itself also undergoes changes; I regard it as certain that falsifications of memory may be brought about in this way too" (318). As a result, childhood memories may be regarded as "real," but we cannot be assured that they are true.

At this point, Freud's essay winds down. He offers an example drawn from V. and C. Henri to indicate the sexual content of a memory of a child breaking off a branch from a tree, then summarizes his findings. It is not the manifest content of a screen memory that matters but rather its deformed representation of unconscious wishes and conflicts. Despite Freud's assurances regarding the reality of memory traces from childhood, he emphasizes the element of "falsification" to an extent that renders them impossible to confirm, much less to access in uncontaminated form. Freud's final paragraph includes *all* childhood memories in this description. Memory, as a result, emerges as a process of construction. "It may indeed be questioned," he states, "whether we have any memories at all *from* our childhood: memories *relating to* our childhood may be all that we possess. Our childhood memories show us our earliest years not as they were but as they appeared at the later periods when the memories were aroused." Hence, "the childhood memories did not, as people are accustomed to say, *emerge*; they were *formed* at that time. And a number of motives, with no concern for historical accuracy, had a part in forming them, as well as in the selection of the memories themselves" (322). Memory, for Freud, is a kind of trickster, a canny yet unreliable narrator, a creator rather than a transcriber of reality.

To make matters even more complex, "Screen Memories" is a trickster narrative, offering itself as a faithful recreation of an encounter between Freud and his subject in the form of a Platonic dialogue, when in fact the essay presents Freud in dialogue with himself. In this respect, "Screen Memories" may be regarded as an aspect of Freud's self-analysis, his individual practice of life-writing, the point of which in this instance is to demonstrate the constructed nature of adult memories from childhood. Freud, in effect, writes a fictionalized account of his own inner musings in order to argue that memory itself is a writer of densely composed fictions. The unreliable narrator Freud represents memory as equally unreliable.

The self-reflexiveness of Freud's essay renders the very ground of his narrating selfhood unstable. Through an examination of his own "screen memory," Freud arrives at a conception of the fictional nature of all memory constructions. He cannot help, in this fashion, deconstructing his own memories, even as he articulates them. In choosing a personal reminiscence to demonstrate his point that memory itself is a mental artifact, Freud positions himself as a memoirist who is making himself up. Reading this essay is a bit like contemplating the M.C. Escher lithograph of two hands, each in the process of delineating the other.

Memory according to contemporary neuroscience

Despite the subjective manner of his theorizing, Freud's account of the formation of screen memories bears an interesting resemblance to the current neural network model of normal memory functioning. Based on new techniques (such as fMRI) of observing the brain on the level of neural activity, contemporary neuroscience conceives of memory encoding and retrieval as a process rather than a product. Memory does not exist in a specific location in the brain, nor does it consist of data that can be retrieved in fixed and immutable form. Rather, memory takes place in the present moment, as a result of the activation of neural pathways in the brain. It occurs as an interaction between a present stimulus and a previously activated neural network.[9] Summarizing this process, neuroscientist Daniel Schacter writes:

> Connectionist or neural network models are based on the principle that the brain stores engrams by increasing the strength of connections between different neurons that participate in encoding an experience. When we encode an experience, connections between active neurons become stronger, and this specific pattern of brain activity constitutes the engram. Later, as we try to remember the experience, a retrieval cue will induce another pattern of activity in the brain. If this pattern is similar enough to a previously encoded pattern, remembering will occur. (1996, 71)

Yet memory does not reside wholly or solely in the engram. Instead, it is a composite formation, entangling the previously encoded network of neural activity with the so-called retrieval cue, a separate and distinct pattern of neural connections that derive from the present stimulus. As Schacter explains:

> The "memory" in a neural network model is not simply an activated engram, however. It is a unique pattern that emerges from the pooled contributions of the cue and the engram. A neural network combines information in the present environment with patterns that have been stored in the past, and the resulting mixture of the two is what the network remembers. (71)

If this model is correct, it is impossible to retrieve a memory pure or intact. In Schacter's words, "When we remember, we complete a pattern with the best match available in memory; we do not shine a spotlight on a stored picture" (71). This idea, he admits, "is difficult to accept." Yet "we must leave behind our familiar conception if we are to understand how we convert the fragmentary remains of experience into the autobiographical narratives that endure over time and constitute the stories of our lives" (71).[10]

For both Freud and Schacter (who translates the neuroscience of memory into lay terms), our memory systems are comprised of past and present elements, which interact in complex and unpredictable ways. Schacter's engram corresponds to Freud's memory trace, while his retrieval cue offers a rough parallel to Freud's charged stimulus, which prompts the formation of a screen memory. Missing from Schacter's account is the meddling interference of the unconscious, which deforms childhood memory so as to forestall the expression of forbidden wishes or desires. Yet the two agree on a key point: one cannot access a childhood memory (or any memory for that matter) in its original form. Each conceives of memory as a work in progress, in effect a moving target.

Freud, the subjective theorizer of memory, represents memory as a writer of complex fictions. Schacter does not go quite so far, but he does demonstrate the inherently unstable and malleable nature of memory construction and retrieval. The only memory that we can experience is one that is inevitably enmeshed with the present moment. Because memory literally only "happens" in the present, it is subtly altered by each instance of recall. There is no more room in Schacter's theory for the concept of a pure or accurate memory than there is in Freud's.

Memoir as a postmodern literary genre

The popularity of the memoir genre in the late twentieth and early twenty-first centuries has drawn serious critical attention.[11] In *Reading Autobiography: A Guide for Interpreting Life Narratives* (2010), co-authors Sidonie Smith and Julia Watson provide a comprehensive overview of the various narrative practices that constitute "life-writing," of which memoir writing is a specific subset.

They consider, among other matters, the significance of memoir in the development of identity politics (addressing matters of sexual orientation, race, ethnicity, class, and gender), in the articulation of postcolonial subject positions, in human rights narratives and in the literature of trauma and witness. Memoir, through its emphasis on individual experience, participates in all of the above, while occupying a privileged position within the overall field of life-writing. For Smith and Watson, memoir "refers generally to life writing that takes a segment of a life, not its entirety, and focusing on interconnected experiences" (274). They observe that memoir has eclipsed its parent genre autobiography, which lays claim to greater inclusiveness and completeness. Because memoir supplies what is missing from the more august autobiographical form, they maintain, it might be viewed as a deconstructive practice, troubling ideas of selfhood in both public and private terms.

At least part of the appeal of memoir is due to its status as a nonfiction genre, purporting to describe what "actually happened," and hence to deliver an unmediated view of reality. Yet surely another aspect of memoir's popularity owes to its liberal use of the rhetorical strategies that characterize fiction writing. Memoir writers set scenes, develop characters, create dialogue, while also making use of conflict, crisis, and resolution to provide a satisfying narrative arc. The result often reads like fiction at the same time that it satisfies the reader's desire for a "true" story.[12] Most readers do not pause to consider how the use of the fiction writer's toolkit may compromise the supposedly factual nature of the memoir product. Only when the veracity of a specific memoir is called into question—as, for instance in the case of James Frey's best-selling addiction/recovery memoir *A Million Little Pieces* (2003)—does this vexed issue arise.[13] Even then the discussion may center not on the inherently fictionalizing nature of such devices but rather on the truth of fact. Frey was taken to task for exaggerating or inventing (hence "lying" about) certain aspects of his experience at Hazelden, the rehabilitation center he attended. Admitting to these transgressions, Frey added a disclaimer to subsequent editions of his book, indicating that he had taken certain liberties in composing his experience. Yet, in its very construction, the memoir Frey wrote represents "reality" in a mediated way, as does any memoir that relies on the storytelling strategies of the fiction writer. What happened can never be recalled verbatim, nor would such material (should such a feat be possible) make interesting reading. By inventing details of scene and dialogue, creating composite characters, and compressing and rearranging events, the memoir writer necessarily "fictionalizes" his or her experience.

A few, though not many, writers foreground the instability of their subject matter and narrative, explicitly calling attention to the constructed nature of their endeavor. Lauren Slater in *Lying* (2000), for instance, deliberately questions her own self-presentation as someone diagnosed variously as epileptic, manic-depressive, schizophrenic, or suffering from borderline personality disorder. Is any of these diagnoses accurate? How are we to judge, given Slater's self-professed tendency to stage dramas to draw attention to herself? At key moments, Slater suggests that one or more of her diagnoses is real, while at others she regards them as metaphors for the way that she views the world.[14] There is no way to resolve this issue in the light of Slater's title, which gives her permission to lie outright.

Mary Karr offers a more subtle instance of this kind of dilemma in her immensely popular memoir of a dirt-poor Texas childhood, *The Liar's Club* (1995). Karr's representation of her upbringing by a sophisticated and well-educated, but alcoholic, mother whose unpredictable behavior and outbursts of rage border on the deranged is riveting in its intensity. Karr, known chiefly as a poet before the publication of *The Liar's Club*, offers a highly dramatic tale of childhood trauma that reads as grippingly as fiction. Unlike Slater, she does not openly subvert the truthfulness of her narrative. At the same time, her title, which refers to the tall tales told by the members of her father's poker club, reminds the reader that she, too, may indulge in the habit of prevarication for effect.

Some degree of lying, whether intentional or rhetorical (due to the fictionalizing nature of narrative construction), seems an inevitable by-product of the memoir genre. Memoir's very imperative to provide shape and meaning to lived experience, as well as to convey a vivid sense of that reality, causes it to veer away from the nonfiction standard of truth of fact toward the more relaxed expectations of fiction.

Add to the above the inherently unreliable nature of memory and memoir ceases to merit the nonfiction label, if such a designation requires a strict, journalistic type of adherence to truth of fact. Memory, according to both Freud and Schacter, is a shape-shifter, constantly revising itself under the pressures of self-censorship (Freud) and/or the changing ground of life experience (Schacter). Under the best of circumstances, and with the best of intentions, we cannot give a completely accurate account of our past. To this extent, memoir may be regarded as a form of self-construction, a useful means of narrating selfhood, but by no means an unmediated one. There is no Eden of innocent self-awareness to be obtained by this most intimate and confessional of literary forms.

Psychoanalysis as a memory-based discipline

Psychoanalysis, in Freud's theory and practice, emerged from his profound self-interrogation at a moment of life-crisis and as such constitutes a unique form of autobiography, one that he represented as universal in its application. Occasionally, in his desire to put his ideas forward in a neutral, disinterested, or "scientific" way, he disguised the extent to which his illustrative material was drawn from his own experience: "Screen Memories" is a case in point. Yet the implications of this seemingly minor essay—appearing roughly in tandem with (and as a result mostly eclipsed by) Freud's monumental study of dreams—raises questions about the discipline of psychoanalysis as a whole. If, indeed, we have no memories that are accurately retrievable from childhood, as both Freud and contemporary neuroscientists claim, then how is analysis to be conducted and how might one validate its results?

In classical practice, the psychoanalyst listens to the patient's narrative and seeks to find its points of vulnerability: the places where false continuity is maintained, or where incoherence erupts. The analyst also attends to the ways in which the patient repeats with, or "transfers" onto her, patterns of interaction engendered by significant others, especially by powerful parental figures. In the light of intersubjective and countertransference theory, he also attends to his own reactions, taking note of emotional responses that the patient elicits, which might derive from or reflect (unresolved) personal issues in the analyst's own life.[15] Such a multiply charged task is clearly challenging. When you add to this equation the condition that no one's memory is absolutely reliable—neither that of the patient nor that of the analyst—one wonders what (in such an unstable environment) can be aimed for or accomplished.

If a patient's memories are always already mediated, either by the interference of unconscious wishes and desires or simply by the mutative process of memory formation, what exactly is the analyst to take as his "real" life history? If there is no way of ascertaining what actually happened in a patient's past, how can one assess the degree of his distortion of that past? In analyzing himself, Freud felt confident that he could unravel the subterfuges of his own unconscious mind to the point of being able to theorize its workings. Yet who can say that he was right? If the unconscious is sufficiently wily, may it not also elude the most conscientious of investigators?[16]

Traditionally, moreover, the form of evidence offered by psychoanalytic theorists takes the form of the analytic vignette or case history, which not only provides the testing ground of the analyst's theoretical activity, but also serves as its "proof." Yet the form of the case history is itself highly stylized, and even deliberately fictionalized, in order to protect the confidentiality of the analytic encounter and the patient's privacy. Names, occupations, aspects of life history, and even genders may be altered in the service of patient anonymity—the understanding being that the information offered in this guise is nonetheless "true" to the analyst's memory and to the patient's experience of reality. Whose word do we have for this? Generally speaking, only that of the analyst, whose persuasiveness depends on various factors: the degree to which the theory offered extends and/or transforms insights offered by established theoretical models; the match between the theory proposed and the (admittedly massaged) evidence provided; and the rhetorical expertise of the writer/analyst. In classical practice, there is really no "proof" at all—only the analyst's more or less persuasive presentation of his patient's dilemmas and how they might best be understood, if not resolved.[17]

The emergence of intersubjective theory, while acknowledging the two-person exchange aspect of psychoanalysis—one that involves two vulnerable people with individually conflicted life histories—by addressing these issues in a self-conscious way, does not eliminate them as problems to be confronted. Rather, it highlights the mutable, malleable, and unstable nature of the psychoanalytic enterprise as a whole. The trend, in more recent psychoanalytic writing, toward the analyst's inclusion of his/her own interior musings in the exposition of an individual patient's case history, calls explicit attention to the process that Freud, in "Screen Memories," wished to suppress, that is to say the degree to which the analyst is writing/inventing him or herself in the process of engaging with/analyzing a patient.[18]

Memory systems are inherently flawed and unreliable: this Freud understood as a result of examining his own, seemingly "real," childhood memories. We may have no memories, as he baldly stated, from our childhood, only ones that are elliptically related to it. Does this mean that we must abandon memory altogether as a guide to our wishfully constructed (and reconstructed) life narratives? If so, what accounts for the continuing popularity of the memoir genre, not to mention the vitality of psychoanalysis as a set of evolving theories and practices?

I suggest that the desire to understand oneself and one's history, as well as to project future goals and possibilities, is an aspect of human subjectivity that, if not inherent, is difficult to eradicate. The fact that memory, as fungible as it is, underpins this effort does not render the effort itself useless or invalid. Rather, it acts as a caution, a reminder that no self-construction, no matter how thoughtful, insightful, scrupulously or even scandalously honest, can ever be complete. Memory is wily and elusive, a charismatic, yet unreliable, narrator at heart. At the same time, no one in his right mind would wish for its absence—as represented, for instance, by traumatic brain injury, dementia, or Alzheimer's disease. That individual memory (the medium of psychoanalysis and of memoir) is flawed does not mean that it has no power or significance. Rather, it reminds us that we are engaged in a complex process of investigating, constructing, and revising the trajectories of our lives—until we die. Freud, as needful as he was to disguise the autobiographical ground of "Screen Memories," understood both the peril and the necessity of the memoirist's labor of self-invention.

Notes

1   Steven Marcus (1985) offers one of the most compelling arguments for a literary reading of Freud in his essay "Freud and Dora: Story, History, Case History," where he treats Freud's text as a form of modernist writing. Shoshana Felman (1987) makes a strong case for viewing psychoanalysis and literature as equally viable interpretive modes—where neither exercises ascendancy over the other.

2. Like his interpretation of *Oedipus Rex*, Freud's understanding of Hamlet's delay in avenging his father's murder in Shakespeare's play as evidence of repression of Hamlet's own wish to kill his father is less the key to the play's meaning than one among many possible interpretations. Contemporary psychoanalytic theory does not, in any case, focus on the incest/murder themes so central to Freud's thinking, but rather on the child's need to separate from the dyadic mother/infant bond and the role of the father (or the paternal function) in accomplishing that separation. The unsuitability of Freud's oedipal drama (dependent on the threat of castration) to girls has prompted much commentary from feminists and psychoanalytic theorists. For a comprehensive critique of the Oedipus complex as it pertains to female development, and an alternative literary and psychological model, see Nancy Kulish and Deanna Holtzman (2008).

3. The Nobel Prize–winning neurobiologist Eric Kandel comments on his dissatisfaction, as psychiatric resident, with the "lack of concern among psychoanalysts for conducting objective studies, or even for controlling investigator bias." As he observes,

> the data gathered in psychoanalytic sessions are almost always private. The patient's comments, associations, silences, postures, movements, and other behaviors are privileged. Of course, privacy is central to the trust that must be earned by the analyst—and therein lies the rub. In almost every case, the only record is the analyst's subjective accounts of what he or she believes happened. (2006, 366–67)

He lauds recent developments in psychoanalytic thought that emphasize evidence-based psychotherapy and the (rather more difficult) "attempt to align psychoanalysis with the emerging biology of mind" (368).

4. Freud, on more than one occasion, called attention to the imaginative (hence literary) aspect of his writing. See in particular his comment: "I have not always been a psychotherapist. Like other neuropathologists, I was trained to employ local diagnoses and electro-prognosis, and it still strikes me myself as strange that the case histories I write should read like short stories and that, as one might say, they lack the serious stamp of science" (1893–95, 160).

5. Peter Homans (1989) and Mark Edmundson (1990) both regard Freud's self-analysis and the invention of psychoanalysis as acts of self-creation. While Homans stresses the element of mourning (cultural as well as personal) in Freud's labor of introspection, Edmundson focuses on Freud as a literary writer, placing his achievement in the context of giants such as Milton, Wordsworth, and Emerson.

6   Peter Gay describes *The Interpretation of Dreams* as "an autobiography at once candid and canny, as tantalizing in what it omits as in what it discloses" (1988, 104). Later, he expands on this comment to characterize the bulk of Freud's writing.

> Most of Freud's writings bear the traces of his life. They are entangled, in important but often quite unobtrusive ways, with his private conflicts and his pedagogic strategies. *The Interpretation of Dreams* is an outpouring of self-revelations pressed into the service of science. The case of Dora is a public wrestling match between emotional needs and professional duties. "Little Hans" and "Rat Man" are more than just clinical documents, Freud drafted them to support the theories he had developed in his deeply subversive *Three Essays on the Theory of Sexuality*. (267)

7   James Strachey (1962/1986) points to the autobiographical ground of "Screen Memories," referring the reader not only to the Freud/Fliess correspondence edited by Ernst Freud (1975) but also to Freud's own writings, e.g., *The Interpretation of Dreams* (1900) and *The Psychopathology of Everyday Life* (1901), for corroborating evidence.

8   The publication of the correspondence between Freud and his friend Eduard Silberstein (Boehlich ed. 1990), where Freud confessed his teenage infatuation with Gisela Fluss, leaves no doubt about the autobiographical origin of this narrative.

9   Daniel Schacter's (1996) description of this process, though expressed in his own idiom, is representative of current thinking. See also Eric Kandel's (2006) detailed account of the neural bases of memory systems (short-term, long-term, implicit, and explicit). In this chapter, I am concerned only with the workings of long-term personal memory. Traumatic memory, as manifest for instance in post-traumatic stress syndrome and a subject of much scientific and psychological interest, is outside the bounds of this inquiry.

10 Current memory theory has begun to influence literary culture, as evidenced by Umberto Eco's novel *The Mysterious Flame of Queen Loana*, where a neurosurgeon explains to the protagonist who has (temporarily) lost his subjective memory:

> "You can't think of memory as a warehouse where you deposit past events and retrieve them later just as they were when you put them there," Gratarolo said. "I don't want to get too technical, but when you remember something, you're constructing a new profile of neuronal excitation. Let's suppose that in a certain place you had some unpleasant experience. When afterward you remember that place, you reactivate that initial pattern of neuronal excitation with a profile of excitation that's similar to but not the same as that which was originally simulated. Remembering will produce

a feeling of unease. In short, to remember is to reconstruct, in part on the basis of what we have learned or said since. That's normal, that's how we remember. I tell you this to encourage you to reactivate some of these profiles of excitation, instead of simply digging obsessively in an effort to find something that's already there, as shiny and new as you imagine it was when you first set it aside. The image of your parents in this photo is the one we've shown you and the one we see ourselves. You have to start from this image to rebuild something else, and only that will be yours. Remembering is a labor, not a luxury." (2004, 25)

11 The memoir boom, often said to have peaked, shows no signs of losing momentum. Rather, nonfiction writing (often of the memoir variety) has surpassed literary fiction in sales and popularity. Autobiographical modes of writing have also penetrated the halls of academia in the form of personalized literary criticism, though this genre does not enjoy the status of memoir per se. For a thoughtful analysis and consideration of this genre (as well as an example of its practice) see Nancy Miller's *Getting Personal* (1991).

12 Patricia Hampl freely admits that memoirists resort to invention, consciously blurring the boundary between fiction and nonfiction. In defense of her own practice, she writes:

> Memoir must be written because each of us must possess a created version of the past. Created: that is real in the sense of tangible, made of the stuff of a life lived in place and in history. And the downside of any created thing as well: we must live with a version that attaches us to our limitations, to the inevitable subjectivity of our points of view. We must acquiesce to our experience and our gift to transform experience into meaning. (1999, 12)

Many psychoanalysts, who are well acquainted with the painful and (potentially) healing aspects of a patient's unfolding and recreation of his life history, would agree with this statement, I believe. See in particular Donald Spence (1982) and Roy Schafer (1992).

13 The question of the degree to which memoir writers may deliberately alter details of their experience to make for a more satisfying read was raised in a prominent way by the publication of Judy Blunt's best-selling memoir *Breaking Clean* (2002), where she took far fewer liberties than Frey. Blunt portrayed her Montana rancher husband as literally breaking her typewriter in frustration with her unhousewifely behavior. Called to account over this single narrative detail, Blunt admitted that she had embellished the incident, pointing out that she had first written this chapter of her book as a short story for a fiction-writing class. Frey's transgressions were on a larger scale, though his confession was surprisingly similar. He had originally attempted to

publish his book as a novel. Failing that, he circulated it to agents as memoir without, however, changing the elements of the manuscript that he had knowingly fictionalized. More recently, Jon Krakauer (2011) sparked a furor over the nonfiction book *Three Cups of Tea* (2006) by Greg Mortenson, by claiming that key events in the book never happened. Mortenson, who spearheaded a movement to establish schools for girls in northern Pakistan and Afghanistan, has been subject to severe scrutiny as a result of this charge, as his book is not strictly speaking "personal," serving as it does as a fundraising vehicle for his philanthropic organization Central Asia Institute.

14 Slater offers many justifications for the slipperiness of her narrative practice. Indeed, the front cover of her book reads: "There is only one kind of memoir I can see to write and that's a slippery, playful, impish, exasperating text, shaped, if it could be, like a question mark." The following statement is also representative: "And anyway, just because something has the feel of truth doesn't mean it fits the facts. Sometimes, I don't even know why the facts should matter. I often disregard them, and even when I mean to get them right, I don't. I can't. Still, I like to write about me. Me! That's why I'm not a novelist" (2000, 145).

15 The fields of intersubjective and countertransference theory are too vast to explore in the confines of this essay. For an especially cogent overview see Theodore Jacobs (1999), himself a major contributor to this body of theory (1991). See also Adrienne Harris (2011).

16 The unconscious, by its very nature, cannot be fully known. I take this to be an axiom not only of Freud's writing but also of such influential successors as Jacques Lacan (1977a) and Wilfrid Bion (1962), both of whom stress the appeal and ultimate frustration of attempting to fix its meanings.

17 Fred Griffin offers an interesting example of the constructed nature of the psychoanalytic case history by literally making one up (based on his own experience). His aim is not to demonstrate the status of the case history as a variation of fiction writing but rather to illustrate how his engagement with the reading of fiction aided his self-analysis. His broader point concerns the role of imagination in the analytic encounter. As he concludes, "In many ways, the intersubjective constructions (fictions) we create in the analytic situation are the core of the analytic work. Each construction is a 'lie that tells the truth'" (2004, 710). Novelists, story-tellers, poets, and memoirists—all of whom seek to give expression to an emotional truth—would most likely agree with this last sentence.

18 Thomas Ogden's detailed explorations of his own (seemingly wool-gathering) musings in the course of his analytic sessions serves as a case in point. See, for instance, *Conversations at the Frontier of Dreaming* (2001).

6

Literature and Psychoanalysis

> *We know now that a text is not a line of words releasing a single "theological" meaning (the "message" of the Author-God) but a multi-dimensional space in which a variety of writings, none of them original, blend and clash. The text is a tissue of quotations drawn from the innumerable centres of culture.*
>
> ROLAND BARTHES, "THE DEATH OF THE AUTHOR"

Overview

What do psychoanalytic discourse and literary discourse have in common, and how do they diverge? There is no simple set of answers to these questions, as neither psychoanalysis nor literature can be apprehended as a single, definable entity. We speak of psychoanalysis and of literature as if they were nouns or objects, when they function more properly as verbs or forms of motion.

That Freud took inspiration from literature, most notably in his theorization of the Oedipus complex (Masson 1985, 272–73), and credited poets and fiction writers with intuitive knowledge about dreams and the working of the unconscious (Freud 1908) is widely recognized.[1] Teasing out the meanings in Freud's acknowledgment of his indebtedness to literary artists is a more troubled and troubling endeavor.

Adding to the complexity of this question, psychoanalysis as Freud conceived it does not come down to us as a fixed and internally consistent body of theory. Freud's texts interact with one another in myriad ways, repeating, revising, and commenting on one another as if to represent an ongoing internal conversation, rather than a logically ordered set of ideas.

Freud's speculative bent not only gave him the freedom to posit the Oedipus complex as a universal psychic structure but also to imagine Leonardo da Vinci's early life (1910b), to propose a myth of the primal horde to explain the development of human morality and civilization (1913b), and to invent an entirely new history for Moses as a non-Jew (1939). It also allowed him (when necessary or convenient) to change his mind. A case in point is Freud's shift from the so-called "topographical" model of psychic functioning based on the relationship of conscious to unconscious mental processes to the "structural" model of mind that posits interactions among the ego, superego, and id.

The mobility and flexibility of Freud's thinking proved an asset to him in the accretive, revisionary, and evolutionary nature of his theorizing. It also opened the door to further revisions and alterations of his ideas, authorizing his followers to exercise their own innovative and creative powers. Hence, it makes more sense to refer to psychoanalysis in the plural than in the singular form. When we talk about this highly complex and mobile body of theories and practices, we are engaging not with psychoanaly*sis* but rather with psychoanaly*ses*.

The same may be said of literature, which consists of many genres (poetry, fiction, drama, and creative nonfiction), which have diverse points of origin, evolutionary histories, and cultural manifestations. The history of literary criticism is equally complex, spanning many centuries, cultural traditions, and national boundaries.

How, then, is it possible to address the question of the relationship between two such powerfully influential, yet also challengingly mobile, modes of discourse, and representation? For the purpose of this chapter, I want to begin with the assumption that literature and psychoanalysis are plural entities in themselves, subject to mutation and change, yet mutually and fruitfully inter-involved over the course of the twentieth century and beyond. Each, you might say, is a moving target, yet their individual trajectories may be examined at significant moments of intersection.

Here, I assume that both psychoanalysis and literature, as diverse and distinctive as they are in their histories and concerns, participate in the broad sociocultural movements of their time. Neither exists in a vacuum, but rather as one strand among many of the material, intellectual, social, esthetic, and political forces that shape our time.[2] Yet there is also a significant difference between these two powerful modes of discourse. Psychoanalysis originated fairly recently—with the theoretical endeavors of Sigmund Freud, who took pains to establish himself as sole founder of a new discipline.[3] From this point of view, one might say that Freud, like other great thinkers before him, contested major tenets of the belief system he inherited—as a physician, neurological researcher, and bourgeois citizen of fin-de-siècle Vienna—and effectively transformed them. Over 150 years after his birth, one may also say that his ideas (admittedly in diluted form) have permeated Western culture. Who, for instance, is unfamiliar with the terms Oedipus complex, penis envy, castration anxiety, infantile sexuality, the unconscious, or the id? And, who, after Freud, would deny the wish-fulfilling properties of dreams or the hidden significance of everyday slips of the tongue?[4] Not only have Freudian neologisms entered our common vocabulary but Freud's focus on the irrational properties of the human mind has also contributed to modernism's subversion of the Enlightenment ideal of reason as a guide to politics and human behavior.

Beginning with the above assumptions—that neither literature nor psychoanalysis is unitary, that both discourses are embedded in the specifics of their time and place, and that they are complexly inter-involved over the course of the twentieth century—I nevertheless want to highlight some very general points of convergence between them.

Both forms of discourse assume that meaning is (in Freud's terms) latent rather than manifest. Hence, all forms of discourse, whether literary or individual, call for (and benefit from) interpretation. In addition, they both make use of and seek to elucidate strategies of displacement and concealment, most commonly symbol and metaphor. As such, they are equally overdetermined, hence irreducible to a single set of meanings.

These areas of resonance are significant, I believe, in terms of the broad shift from modernism to postmodernism over the course of the twentieth century. The relationship between psychoanalytic and literary (cum philosophic) discourse both reflects and contributes to this trend.

Finally, I want to suggest that the current tendency (among psychoanalytic as well as literary scholars and theorists) to read Freud's texts through a mobile set of interpretive strategies returns Freud to his own literary and autobiographical bases.[5] In this respect, his ideas remain interesting and useful insofar as they continue to open themselves to new insights and meanings, just as literary texts sustain their readership through ever-evolving processes of interpretation.

Broad developments and significant interactions

Much of the early history of psychoanalysis and literary interpretation, in the United States at least, reflects the emphasis on orthodoxy that Freud himself fostered among his followers and that flourished in post-war American culture through a generation of analysts who fled Nazi Germany. Many of these practitioners, trained by Freud or members of his inner circle, helped to found institutes that emphasized adherence to such key Freudian concepts as the Oedipus and castration complexes, with their concomitant formulations of masculinity and femininity. Such ideas not only resonated with the ideal of the nuclear family that evolved in the aftermath of the Second World War but also helped to sustain it.

Many literary critics, discontent with the strictures of the forty-year domination of the New Criticism, which banished all forms of "extra-literary" consideration (such as cultural, biographical, historical, or psychological issues) from the realm of textual interpretation, rebelled, in part, by embracing Freud's focus on the role of sexuality in human behavior, as well as his theory of "coded" meaning. Such critics happily discovered phallic symbols, as did Freud, in images of upright or elongated objects and female symbols in any kind of enclosed or inner space. For some writers as well as critics, such symbol hunting seemed not only obvious but also reductive. Yet it was hard to ignore this new approach to literature and literary criticism.

A writer like Vladimir Nabokov would publicly reject Freudian ideas while clearly flaunting them in his comic/satiric and profoundly transgressive novel *Lolita* (1955). A much younger (though now aging) writer such as Philip Roth would not only embrace Freud but also turn him on his head in his equally comic/satiric and profoundly transgressive novel *Portnoy's Complaint* (1969). Once writers themselves began to engage with Freud's ideas through adoption or contestation, the game changed. Freud was now a part of the culture at large and, as such, subject to deformation, alteration, and creative invention.

Social movements also had an impact. The 1950s' American ideal of the father-dominant, mother-submissive family in which dads worked to support families domestically managed by women raising children at home gave way to the social upheavals and challenges of the second wave of feminism initiated by Betty Friedan's *The Feminine Mystique* (1963), published in the midst of the Civil Rights movement of the 1960s. Combined with the anti–Vietnam War movement of the late 1960s and early 1970s, the feminist movement challenged Freud's ideas about female sexuality and feminine development, hence also helping to undermine Freud's focus on the foundational status of the Oedipus complex.

In the meantime, post-Freudian theorists (including his own daughter Anna Freud) had noticed something missing from the magisterial oedipal construct: the newly significant preoedipal period, which Freud acknowledged but chose not to theorize and which vitally involved those of his followers (many of them women) who undertook child analysis and/or observed mother–infant interactions.[6] The school of object relations (Bowlby 1969; Fairbairn 1952; Guntrip 1968; Klein 1975a; Mahler 1968; Winnicott 1971), which emphasized the role of the mother in early infant development, introduced many new paths in psychoanalytic theory and practice, which resonated with the feminist focus on women writers (past and present) and on themes that concern women in their roles as mothers and daughters. Feminist literary critics now turned their attention from a critique of stereotypical forms of "masculine" behavior in male-authored texts to women writers' explorations of female issues and concerns, including the various possibilities of feminine subjectivity and desire (Abel 1989; Gardiner 1985; Gilbert and Gubar 1979; Hirsch 1989; Lilienfeld 1980; Showalter 1977; Suleiman 1985).

The broad shift in psychoanalytic theory from oedipal to preoedipal matters of investigation corresponded with the social movement of second wave feminism in a way that supported not only the claims of women writers to "equal time" in the publishing world but also literary critics' focus on the ways that women authors have represented their experience(s) across the centuries. Some elements of idealization of women as mothers, present in Freud's own texts, persisted in this period, with the result that women's capacities for relatedness, empathy, and ethical concern for the welfare of others were celebrated over men's focus on abstract reasoning and principles of justice and morality (Chodorow 1978; Gilligan 1982; Ruddick 1989). The attempt to articulate a new and positive form of feminine identity—based in part on assumptions about mothers' capacities for and commitment to caregiving—has come under attack from many quarters and remains (to this day) a matter of debate. In a cultural sense at least, we remain unable to answer Freud's vexed and vexing question: "What does a woman want?" (quoted by Jones 1955, 421).

Part of the difficulty, both in theory and in literary production, may lie in the problem of infinite regress when it comes to matters of origin. Freud rather neatly sidestepped this issue by beginning his theoretical labor not with the moment or fact of birth, as his friend Otto Rank did in his articulation of "birth trauma" (Rank 1924, 1952), but with the advent of the Oedipus complex, a much later development focused on the male child's rivalry with his father for the love and possession of his mother. To the extent that Freud thought about the preoedipal period, he consigned it to shadows, like the Minoan–Mycenaean period of human prehistory (Freud 1931). What we cannot remember, we may not theorize, he appears to have maintained—failing to imagine the practices of his own daughter Anna Freud in observing the behavior of very young children, much less the theoretical activities of Melanie Klein, who also pioneered the field of child analysis (A. Freud 1922–1935; Klein 1921–1945).

Freud's avoidance of theoretical investigation of the preoedipal period (as I have previously argued) allowed him to preserve his personal idealization of maternal care, yet he also had a point about our collective lack of memory of the earliest stages of life. Mothers may remember, but babies do not. An entire body of speculative theory has arisen around this problematic awareness. How can we describe our own origins if we simply cannot recall, much less articulate, them?

Preoedipal theory, post-Freud, has taken several different paths. The British and American branches of the object relations school have focused on the figure of the mother and the significance of how she relates (in healthy or troubled ways) to her newborn and developing infant. Even at best, these schools, however sensitive to individual styles of parenting, tend to lay the burden of normal or optimal child development on the mother. The more recent school of attachment theory—based on close mother–infant observations and hence more "evidentiary" in its processes and formulations— is even more focused on the mother's responsibility for her child's early ego development and capacity for relationship (Bowlby 1969; Fonagy 2001; Seligman 2000; Schore 1994; Stern 1985). Neither of these schools emphasizes the mother's own history of mothering, much less the notion that no one is ideally "mothered" into the world.

Freud's own mother, as I have emphasized in previous chapters, was unable to offer her undivided attention to her first-born son, given that she was pregnant with his younger brother Julius, not long after his own birth, and suffered the loss of this child within a year. Although one may credit Freud's conviction that his mother was particularly devoted to him and believed in the special nature of his destiny, one can also understand how Freud as a child may have experienced her distraction with the cares of her household, including those of his six younger siblings.[7] That he was entrusted to the care of nannies in his earliest years suggests as much. Freud, at least, did not experience the kind of undivided attention from his mother that both object relations theory and attachment theory seem to prescribe for optimal infant development.

A counteridealizing, yet ultimately unrevolutionary trend, emerged in France through the influential writings of Jacques Lacan, who regarded himself as Freud's true heir, rescuing his radical insight into the irrationality of the unconscious from what he viewed as the reductive emphasis of American ego psychology. Lacan made use of French structuralism and Saussurian linguistics to transform Freud's ideas into his own idiom (Lévi-Strauss 1989; Saussure 1977).

For Lacan, who was also sensitive to the Dada and Surrealist movements in art, the realm of the preoedipal represented a field of speculation as well as potential subversion of the oedipal drama, which both instigates and sustains patriarchy. Given that the preoedipal period precedes the onset of declarative memory, along with verbal control, it represents a time when the ego is both fluid and disorganized. In this state of disorientation, it does not differentiate itself from the maternal matrix, nor does it conceive of individual identity as it may function in the social order.[8]

In Lacan's myth of origins, the authority and presence of the father (his *non* prohibiting incest, along with the power of his *nom*, his name and what it signifies in terms of his role in maintaining the structure of the family and society) instigate a rupture in the undifferentiated mother–infant relationship. The father, in this narrative, represents the necessary third term that signals not only the infant's access to language and signification but also its introduction into the social order.

Lacan's reformulation of Freud's Oedipus and castration complexes deemphasizes the role of drive or desire (i.e., the wish to murder one's father in order to have sex with one's mother) in favor of a more abstract conceptualization of how and why infants separate from their mothers. Each narrative has its tragic aspect, as neither permits the infant (presumably male) to achieve satisfaction in terms of having the mother all to itself. Renunciation (as in Freud's key concept of sublimation as the effort to redirect prohibited wishes and desires into socially acceptable activities) marks both stories. Yet there is a significant difference, which stimulated Lacan's feminist follower/critics to introduce new psychoanalytic and writerly options.

Lacan appears to valorize the position prior to paternal intervention as represented by the father's *non*, while also insisting on its necessity to participation in society and culture. His writings, as a result, have the paradoxical effect of both undermining and affirming the patriarchal status quo. The preoedipal period (renamed the Imaginary in his unique terminology) represents the actual or primary state of confusion, disorientation, and fragmentation of the ego, over which a socially acceptable form of integration (imposed by the father's function) is overlaid. Civilization, thus linguistically and psychically organized, is something of a sham. Exposing the nature of this sham allows Lacan to dance on the border, as it were, between the preoedipal and oedipal periods, seeming to endorse the revolutionary prospect of ego dissolution while also affirming the necessity of the father's role and function in maintaining the patriarchal organization of human society.

It is perhaps no wonder that the writings of Lacan's feminist followers (most notably Hélène Cixous and Catherine Clément [1986], Luce Irigaray [1985], and Julia Kristeva [1986] seem both liberated and constrained by his theoretical formulations. Each has sought, through theoretical formulations and writerly practices, to investigate the potential for creative disruption embedded in the preoedipal period. For these women, the lack of firm ego boundaries that characterizes the infant's relationship to its mother permits a freedom of internal organization, which may find adult expression in certain forms of writerly representation, loosely described as *l'écriture féminine*. Such so-called "feminine writing," in contrast to rationally ordered or logically sequential forms of expression, allows for the eruption of unconscious images, fantasies, and desires.

In some instances, these women associate the capacity for producing this kind of writing with the biological condition of being female and celebrate women's special proclivity for and access to *l'écriture féminine*. At other times, they maintain that such kinds of writing are not only open to men but have also been successfully practiced by them, as works by Marcel Proust, James Joyce, Jean Genet, and others demonstrate.[9]

French feminism, as represented by these women's collective writings, had a significant impact on advancing awareness of and appreciation for avant-garde forms of literature, as experimental kinds of writing seemed more closely to approximate preoedipal experience(s) than did male-centered, oedipally organized texts. In this sense, French feminist theory and writing endorsed the literature of modernism over that of nineteenth-century realism. At the same time, French feminists' adherence to Lacan's model of the acquisition of language and access to the Symbolic order (Lacan's substitution for Freud's term civilization) prevented them from finding an alternative to patriarchy. To some degree also, their idealization of the mother/infant bond and the preoedipal period as one of freedom from patriarchal constraint led to criticisms of their work for reinstating stereotypes of women as creatures ruled by nature and emotion, as opposed to culture and reason.

As a result of conflicting currents, the differences within feminist literary criticism seem not to have come to resolution so much as they have shifted ground. Social concerns, instead, have taken center stage in recent decades, focusing on such issues as race, class, and gender identity, including issues of sexual orientation and transsexuality. In this arena, the work of Lacan has been less significant than that of his French philosophical contemporary, Michel Foucault.

Foucault's work critiques psychoanalysis as a discipline enmeshed in the culture of its time (especially in terms of its understanding of the diverse forms of human sexual expression), hence, one that is subordinate to historical/materialist analysis (Foucault 1978). Foucault, in this sense, takes aim at Freud's somewhat easy assent to the assumptions about masculinity and femininity embedded in the social order of his day.

Foucault's work inspired and intersects with trends in contemporary GLBT (gay/lesbian/bisexual/transgender) studies, which flourish in the United States and elsewhere. If gender identity, as Judith Butler claimed in *Gender Trouble* (1990), is not a matter of anatomical or biological destiny, but rather one of social construction, then we may all be freed from gender stereotypes based on how we look or are perceived by others.

Butler's early work owes much to Foucault's efforts to expose and to deconstruct the cultural assumptions about sexual behavior that Freud inherited and partially transformed but also transmitted in his formulation of the Oedipus complex. Despite Freud's affirmation of the bisexual disposition of both sexes, his Oedipus construct assumes that boys are normally heterosexual, as are girls—regardless of the fact that this construct does not explain female development as comfortably as it does the evolution of heterosexuality in boys and men. In her emphasis on the social construction of masculinity and femininity, Butler strove to liberate both men and women from the constraints of heteronormativity.

Toward postmodernism

Movements in psychoanalytic theory and in literature and literary studies, as I have suggested earlier, do not move together in lockstep fashion, but rather speak to one another across disciplinary developments, as across national, historical, and cultural boundaries. As a result, I have chosen to focus on moments where these two powerful modes of representation have impacted and challenged each other, with the effect of stimulating new forms of psychoanalytic and literary discourse.

The opening of psychoanalytic investigation and theory to the preoedipal period neglected by Freud proved both productive and problematic in terms of literary/cultural study. On the one hand, it alerted women writers, readers, and critics to a field that had been obscured and prompted vital response—not only in terms of the publishing world (which began to recognize the quality of women's writing as well as the possibility of reaching new markets) but also in terms of the exploration of new subjects, e.g., women as daughters and as mothers, in addition to their forms of sexuality and expressions of subjectivity. On the other hand, it revived discussion about women's roles as mothers and caregivers, which has led (in some instances) to an intensification of pressure on mothers to provide "ideal" care to their newborns and preschool-age children. The contemporary (admittedly middle-class) "liberated" woman seems to be able to "have it all," but cannot embrace this role without internal conflict, and in some instances, intense anxiety, and/or guilt.[10]

While the debate about women in the workplace continues as a matter of social concern, the writerly and literary critical exploration of women in their roles as mothers and daughters seems to have subsided, due perhaps to the theoretical impasse reached in the conflict between the object relations view of women and that of French feminism, neither of which found a way of undermining or overturning the Oedipus complex as the engine of civilization and (patriarchal) culture. Instead, historical pressures and considerations, combined with Foucault's social constructivist turn toward cultural-political analysis, introduced new subjects of interest. I would describe the nature of this turn as postmodern.

From a psychoanalytic perspective, this shift may be attributed to two important developments: the recognition of the subjective involvement of the analyst in the process of treatment (under the general rubric of countertransference and intersubjective theories), and the emergence of trauma theory. These two strands of psychoanalytic thought, developing along somewhat parallel lines, have not only affected each other but also have connected with a significant trend in literary/cultural studies toward the investigation of the history of the twentieth century as traumatic—hence disruptive of previously understood notions of stability in human nature and behavior.

There is an additional point of intersection here between Freud's (and his successor Lacan's) emphasis on the driving and determining forces of human behavior as beyond our rational control (represented in dream formation, the unconscious, eros, the death instinct, and the id), but postmodern psychoanalytic literary and theoretical practices take these assumptions further.

Early in his practice as an analyst, Freud observed the phenomenon of transference: the patient's tendency to replay and relive emotional dramas from the past, as evident in his feelings of love/hate toward the therapist (Freud 1905, 1912b, 1915). Much later, he recognized the ways that the (insufficiently self-aware) analyst might do the same in reverse, reacting to her patient on the basis of personal issues and conflicts (Freud 1912b, 1937). While Freud readily acknowledged that the process of self-analysis continues throughout life and may never be complete, he did not actively theorize the concept of countertransference as it is understood today.

Over the course of the latter half of the twentieth century, the representation of the analyst as securely in possession of the kind of knowledge that enables her to apprehend and articulate the unconscious conflicts of her patient has diminished to the point of near vanishing. In place of the image of an all-knowing and largely silent analyst, whose mind serves as a blank screen for projection of the emotions of the patient, a radically different conception and set of practices has emerged. Instead of being a one-way street of disclosure, the psychoanalytic process is now generally understood as a two-person form of engagement, in which both partners are subjectively involved. The difference between analyst and patient is less one of emotional distance or disinterested observation on the analyst's part than one of specific training, including years of personal analysis, leading to the capacity for insight.[11]

Although this crucial development in psychoanalytic theory might seem, to many of us today, a matter of common sense, it has had significant consequences. Freud's conception of the superior, self-contained, and scrupulously objective analyst (as best represented perhaps by himself) can no longer be sustained. Even Lacan, one of Freud's most staunch defenders, challenged the role of the analyst as the one ideally "supposed to know." In his emphasis on the turbulent and disruptive tensions of the preoedipal (Imaginary) period, Lacan sided with artists and revolutionaries, hence contributing to the undermining of all forms of authority, including his own as well as that of Freud.

Countertransference theory does not seek to undermine key psychoanalytic formulations, such as the Oedipus and castration complexes, but rather to focus on the mobile and contingent process of interaction established in the consulting room (Gabbard 1995; Jacobs 1999). It introduces its own kind of "relativity theory" into psychoanalysis as a collection of ideas and practices. At the same time, it cannot exclude from consideration the kinds of social, political, material, and cultural concerns highlighted by Foucault. In this respect, the evolution of psychoanalysis over the course of the twentieth century (continuing into the twenty-first) corresponds with dominant movements in literature and literary criticism. Each has moved away from the kinds of grand narrative that characterized the nineteenth century along with their emphases on human order, reason, and (the potential for) progress.

Intersubjective theory takes the ideas embedded in countertransference theory to new levels of speculation and uncertainty (Mitchell 1993). If, as seems the case, the analyst is involved in a profoundly emotional and culturally inflected subjective encounter, what kind of communication occurs and how might one describe it?

Following Lacan and other theorists' leads into the realm of the nonverbal as represented by the preoedipal period, some analysts, e.g., Wilfred Bion (1962) and Thomas Ogden (1994a, 1997), have posited a form of nonverbal interaction between analyst and patient that "happens" on the level of the unconscious in each partner. This unconscious and inarticulate type of communication may, via the special sensitivity of the analyst, find its way into words—and thence into conscious processing.

Melanie Klein's (1921–45) notion of projective identification, which theorized some of the ways in which patients might induce their analysts to feel what they were feeling, spoke to this kind of unconscious communication, although her near contemporary Wilfred Bion immersed himself more intimately in this realm of speculation. The contemporary American psychoanalyst Thomas Ogden has made this idea more accessible in his articulation of the "intersubjective analytic third," by which he attempts to delineate the space in which the unconscious of both the analyst and the patient may communicate. For Ogden, access to this realm of communication involves the analyst's activity of reverie, which Ogden does not view as an expression of the analyst's distraction, boredom, or lack of connection with his patient, but rather as a sign of his deep, unconscious communication.

The turn in psychoanalytic theory and practice to an emphasis on the nonverbal realm of the preoedipal period not only parallels but also supports the turn toward recognition of the analyst's subjectivity in the process of treatment and the unconscious (unverbalized) elements of his or her response to patients and the interaction between them.

Rather than pursuing Freud's emphasis on the significance of renunciation and sublimation in the evolution of human culture and civilization, his followers (intentionally and to some degree inadvertently) stress the unpredictable, unruly, inarticulate, and sometimes destructive urges that reside in and emanate from the realm of the unconscious. The development of trauma theory in the latter half of the twentieth century not only coincides with this overall trend, but also furthers it in significant respects.

In the aftermath of the Great War, Freud commented on the effects of trauma as a physical and/or psychic shock to the system so profound as to unhinge a previously "healthy" personality, but he did not pursue this subject at length—other than to posit the existence of an ominous "death instinct" in human nature that accompanies the desire to live and sustain life, and to observe the tendency to repeat past experiences of pain and suffering rather than act to resolve them (Freud 1920).

While clearly indebted to Freud's formulations, trauma theory was slow to develop, achieving significant momentum in the post–Vietnam War era in the United States as a result of two forms of activism: Vietnam War veterans who spoke out about their enduring psychic and physiologic wounds; and women who called attention to the long-term bodily and emotional effects of rape, battery, incest, and other forms of sexual abuse (van der Kolk, McFarlane, and Weisaeth, eds. 1996). Once again, social experience intersected with and helped to stimulate new areas of research and development in literary and psychoanalytic production. Not only is this field in a state of fluid and rapid development but there is also an interesting new partner in the game—neuroscience, with its technology of real-time brain imaging (fMRI) and related research into the functions and dysfunctions of memory.

A consensus has emerged among psychoanalysts and neuroscientists regarding a specific aspect of trauma: its inaccessibility to verbal processing and (hence) narrative construction. For members of the psychoanalytic community, this means that trauma victims have no effective form of speech or language through which to integrate their disruptive experience(s) into the ongoing narrative of their lives (van der Kolk and van der Hart 1991). The field of Holocaust studies, especially as it relates to the testimonies of its survivors, has a particular interest in this concept, as it correlates with an understanding of the Holocaust as essentially unspeakable, hence outside the realm of ordinary narrative representation. For many in this field (as for others who research the effects of other historical traumas), there is no way to give expression to the full horror of such events (Lanzmann 1991).

Neuroscientists approach this issue from a different, yet corroborating, perspective. In their view, the sudden (or repeated) shock of trauma releases the stress hormone cortisol in such a way as to interfere with the normal, memory-forming, function of the hippocampus (Schacter 1996). Not being able to compose a proper memory of the event, the trauma victim relives it as if it were still happening, in the form of flashbacks, fight or flight responses, and recurring nightmares (Schacter 1996). In this view, the past is never past, but rather a daily, unbidden, and violent presence.

Although Freud did observe some of these phenomena, he did not investigate them in depth, due in part to his commitment to the process of bringing previously unconscious and nonverbalized aspects of human experience into the light of psychoanalytic treatment and dialogue. Trauma theory poses a challenge to this perspective. The increasing emphasis within psychoanalysis as a developing body of theory and practice on the preoedipal period (inaccessible to individual consciousness and articulation) leads, however, to precisely this kind of impasse.

What we cannot remember, we cannot put into words, which in turn we cannot make meaningful sense of. In a curious way, the trajectories of psychoanalytic theory and practice, of literature and literary analysis—and more recently the neuroscience of trauma—articulate similar problems over the course of the twentieth century. If key aspects of human experience are truly "beyond words," how are we to speak or write?

I do not want to suggest that psychoanalysts, and here I mean to include psychologists and clinical social workers, despair of treating their patients because they are no longer certain of what they know, or how to deal with the murky realms of nonverbal experience and communication. On the contrary, psychoanalysis as a set of theories and treatment modalities appears to be thriving, as it attempts to come to grips with some of the more extreme forms of human suffering that characterize our time. That definitive answers are not forthcoming does not invalidate the energy engaged, but rather speaks to the density and complexity of the problems at issue.

Nor do I wish to indicate that the modernist experiment in literature and literary study has reached a dead end with the advent of postmodern theories and practices. While it is clear that many writers (poets, fiction writers, and memoirists) have adopted a set of postmodern ideas and forms of writing that strive to embody the problem(s) inherent in the process of representation, it would be difficult to find any who argue against writing, authorship, or publication per se. Even those who assent to Roland Barthes' (1968) notion of textual production as an effect of social and material culture (the so-called "death of the author") claim individual responsibility and ownership when it comes to matters of royalty or copyright.

To state this case as simply as possible: we keep trying to give expression to what seems to be, by its very nature, elusive and ultimately (perhaps) inexpressible.

Postmodernism

Psychoanalysis, like literature and other forms of meaning-making, strives to illuminate the most urgent questions of our time. In the current shift between modernist and postmodern worldviews, it reflects our deep concern, as well as our anxiety and uncertainty, about the future. Psychoanalysis as a discipline is not unitary (as Freud had hoped) but rather highly heterogeneous, containing within its broad embrace many conflicting theories and treatment modalities.

The same might be said of the world of literary production and reception where there is no longer an agreed-upon canon of great authors, much less a hierarchy of literary value, but rather a plethora of genres, styles, voices, and critical views, all competing for attention in a rapidly changing media environment and equally evolving set of social networks connecting writers, audiences, and critics.

Most people most of the time, I believe, would find such developments more hopeful and salutary than otherwise. The downside, of course, is that we do not quite know where we are going. "There's no map," as Tom Stoppard's character Alexander Herzen says toward the end of the second play in his trilogy *The Coast of Utopia* (2003), which portrays the ferment of revolutionary Europe in the middle of the nineteenth century.

Modernism contained within itself the seeds of postmodernism, the consequences of which we have yet to comprehend, much less to theorize, in terms of the world we live in today—as dominated as it is by international conflict, local genocidal actions and violations of human rights, extremist movements and ideologies, financial markets and practices that only the most elite among us can manipulate or understand, as well as nuclear and environmental threats to global survival.

The current focus on trauma theory may represent a very real engagement not only with the extremely painful history of the twentieth century but also with our own (terrified if not terrorized) concern about what may lie ahead. Many contemporary writers seek to engage these kinds of issues on the level of subject matter as well as narrative form, e.g., Don DeLillo (1985), Louise Erdrich (1988), Colum McCann (2009), Toni Morrison (1987), Zadie Smith (2012), and David Foster Wallace (1996), to name only a handful of fiction writers. At the same time, popular literature hardly seems to change, relying as it does on clearly defined characters and conventional structures of conflict and resolution.

The upside to this confusion of tongues in the state of contemporary culture is the freedom (in plural political societies) to choose the narrative or treatment modality that is not only most resonant with one's history, cultural background, and system of belief but also most individually useful and productive. The downside is that there is no universal psychic paradigm to which everyone can turn for insight and understanding.

Freud himself, though a participant in this series of developments, hardly imagined such a cacophonous state of affairs. Rather, he pictured a seamless line of descendants who would promulgate his ideas for the benefit of future generations. Early in his career, he conceived of an ideal successor, a "crown prince," who would ensure the continuity, as well as the purity of the ideas he articulated.[12] One after another, however, these younger (primarily male) followers fell away. Even his own daughter Anna Freud, who professed her loyalty in personal and ideological ways, helped to inaugurate the field of child analysis and preoedipal studies, which have called many of his most cherished concepts into question.

Freud, in spite of his particular genius, seems not so much to have provided a means of relieving the neurotic dilemmas he observed in himself and his late Victorian and early-twentieth-century compatriots as to have opened a Pandora's box of problems and issues for our own and future generations to address.

Reading between the lines

If, in our current state of global (multi-sexual, multi-cultural, multi-historical, multi-national, and multi-financial) awareness, we no longer feel comfortable with the idea of mastery—in terms of philosophy, religion, social theory, literature, or psychoanalysis—how might we move forward?

I'd like to propose a rather humble thesis, beginning with the assumption that each of us, born into our own family system, time, and place, attempts to find personal meaning in our lives—even when these attempts appear to be thwarted by conditions (most often material/historical) beyond our control.

Freud was a major thinker in striving to make sense of the world he inherited and vigorously participated in, which also exceeded his ability to theorize in a universal way for all time. In this sense, he reflects many assumptions that most of us no longer take for granted: that he was the inheritor of a tradition of master theorist/philosophers, who could guide and lead mankind into a less suffering, if not also more "enlightened," future. At the same time, we continue to read him and to be inspired by his work. Why?

The reason, I believe, is that Freud wrote like a writer—that is to say in a manner that allows readers to engage with his ideas in multi-textual ways.[13] Because of his somewhat meandering, hypothetical, anecdotal, metaphoric, and often self-questioning style, he offers opportunities for us as readers to engage in a silent (perhaps subconscious or even unconscious) conversation with him, allowing us to ponder our own thoughts, feelings, and experiences in relation to his.

Freud, on the page, is the least coercive of theorists, allowing for doubt, conjecture, and even creative disagreement with him, which, in turn, invites new ideas and formulations. While Freud himself may have deplored the defection of individual disciples, the enduring legacy of his writing (not unlike that of literary authors over time) has been to enable creative response and adaptation.

Like children who become the unwitting legacies of their parents' psychic histories, psychoanalytic, as well as literary, writers inherit the tangle of history, theory, and (partially processed) experience that precedes them. In the best of circumstances, they do not blindly adhere to or repeat these histories.[14] Rather they transform them in the light of their own life trajectories and sources of inspiration.

Ironically, for Freud, the aspects of his writing that exercise the most appeal for contemporary writers and theorists draw from ideas he hinted at, instead of fully developing. It is as if late-twentieth and twenty-first-century readers explore the regions that Freud himself could glimpse but not directly address. These include the preoedipal period (which Freud considered too shadowy to investigate), the phenomenon of mourning (which he regarded as too ordinary to theorize), and trauma, a subject that prompted him to hypothesize repetition compulsion and the death instinct (Freud 1917, 1920).

While opening these areas of interest, Freud himself did not pursue their implications, leaving them for others to mine more deeply. It is for this reason, I believe, that contemporary psychoanalytic theorists routinely pay tribute to him, citing those (mostly fragmentary) statements in his texts that authorize their own views and speculations. Not only do they seek in this way to honor Freud's achievement but also to establish a line of continuity between his work and theirs. At the same time, contemporary psychoanalytic theories and theorists diverge widely from their source, so much so that Freud himself would regard many (if not most) as defectors and/or apostates.

The current emphasis on the two (or three) person nature of psychoanalytic treatment, along with the fascination with pre- or nonverbal aspects of early life, and their adult corollaries in the unrepresented nature of traumatic experience(s), has moved psychoanalysis in the direction of avant-garde literature, which also seeks to explore such elusive states of mind and being. Both discourses seem to be asking the same kinds of questions. What forces beyond our conscious awareness drive or control our actions? Who or what is speaking through us as we struggle to shape our own poetic or narrative structures of meaning? Are some aspects of human experience genuinely inaccessible to representation? If so, what can we hope to comprehend, much less articulate? Finally, what kinds of social/political relations can be formed in the light of these issues and awarenesses?

Although I do not have answers to these questions, I want to suggest that Freud not only contributed to the dominant historical movement of his time toward the shaping of modernity but also helped—through the polysemous and unstable nature of his own writing practices—to enable postmodernism, which calls into question every aspect of authority (who "authors" our beginnings and what can be said about them?), including the authority of Freud himself.

That Freud wrote like a writer, that is to say, recognizing that all forms of writing are tentative forays into the unknown, not only establishes his body of work among the classics of twentieth-century literature but also affirms his role in the development of contemporary postmodern reality.

Notes

1 We know, as I have noted earlier, that Freud was well-acquainted with Sophocles's drama, having studied it extensively as a student and having fantasized that he might one day receive a bust with an inscription from it as a tribute to him in later life (Rudnytsky, 1987). One might argue, on these grounds, that Freud was predisposed to interpret his own instinctual life in terms of Sophocles's drama. If this is the case, then one might also maintain that the trajectory of psychoanalysis has been intertwined with that of literature from its inception.

2 Freud's insistence on the universality of his theories had a dampening effect on studies of his work in sociopolitical terms. Among those who have sought to locate Freud's achievement in terms of the science and culture of his times, Peter Gay (1988), Peter Homans (1989), Carl Schorske (1981), Frank Sulloway (1979), and Eli Zaretsky (2004) are especially cogent.

3 Freud insisted that he not only invented psychoanalysis but also that he had no precursors. His need to establish his status as founder of a new discipline also fueled many of his quarrels with his early disciples. Those who diverged from his thinking—such as Alfred Adler, Sándor Ferenczi, Wilhelm Stekel, and (perhaps most painfully) Carl Jung—were banished from his inner circle, their

works considered anathema. Ironically, Freud's greatest and most loyal supporter, his daughter Anna Fraud, also diverged from the fold through her development of child analysis and the investigation of the preoedipal period that derives from her work. Ernest Jones, Freud's first major biographer, may have been his best supporter, as he strove to represent Freud in the way that he most wished to be remembered. In his three-volume biography (Jones 1953–57), he set a precedent that no one, including the extraordinarily learned Peter Gay (1988), has superseded or overturned.

4 Jonathan Lear (2005) makes this point most succinctly. He says simply that in today's culture we "speak Freud."

5 I have argued in Chapter 1 that Freud's theoretical endeavor, especially in its earliest stages, constitutes a unique form of autobiography, as his major insights, e.g., dream interpretation, the Oedipus and castration complexes, derived from his self-analysis. The resonance of Freud's ideas with other social developments of his time have not only ensured his place in the history of modernism, but have also provided the inspiration for contemporary theories and practices, many of which alter his conceptions to the point that he would hardly recognize them. What Freud invented, in my view, is not an objective science of mind but rather a new form of subjective self-inquiry. The power of his discovery is in no way diminished by its lack of "scientific" status. To make such a claim would be like saying that James Joyce's *Ulysses* (1922) or Marcel Ptoust's *In Search of Lost Time* (1922–31) have nothing to teach us about the workings of the human mind.

6 In *The Spectral Mother* (1990), I examine in detail Freud's approach/avoidance response to the figure of the mother and his corresponding inability (or unwillingness) to theorize the preoedipal period.

7 I discuss the possible disappointments and losses of Freud's early life and the ways they may have impacted his theoretical activity more extensively in Chapters 1 and 3 of this book. Other significant treatments of Freud's relationship with his mother include: Hardin (1987; 1988a,b), Holt (1992), Slipp (1988), and Swan (1974).

8 Lacan famously posited a "mirror stage" of development (1977b), at which point the infant catches sight of itself in a mirror, which reflects back an image of physical and psychic cohesion. This image provides an illusion of internal coherence, which, in turn, fosters the infant's developing ego. Such an ego, based on the alluring, yet inaccessible image in the mirror, is as frustrating as it is unreal. In Lacan's mode of thinking, we never coincide with the image of ourselves that we perceive as integrated and whole, at the same time that we rely on just such an image to function within the social order. The "mirror stage" in this way constitutes a "heads you lose, tails you lose"

deal, which the drama of human development requires. To accept this bargain involves living with a necessary split: the simultaneous embrace and alienation from a selfhood that is a fictional construct at best. To reject it is not only to refuse participation in the human social exchange that Lacan terms the Symbolic order, but it is also to consign oneself to the realm of failed interaction and communication that constitutes psychosis.

9 I have discussed this issue at greater length in *The Spectral Mother* (1990). Among the feminist psychoanalytic theorists I refer to here, Julia Kristeva (1986) seems the clearest in her assertion that *l'écriture féminine* may be practiced by men as well as women. As the issue of feminism in the academy has lessened in significance and intensity, so too have many of the debates among feminists about the possibility and/or nature of *l'écriture féminine*.

10 In many ways, the "choice" of wife-and-motherhood over career is a false one, as the majority of women in the United States must work either to support their single-parent families or to supplement the family income. The "choice" not to earn a salary is open only to those women and families whose (single-earner) incomes make it possible for one partner to stay at home. Few contemporary writers address the painful conflicts that women who do not have such a choice deal with in their day-to-day lives. A notable exception to this "silence" is Barbara Almond's *The Monster Within: The Hidden Side of Motherhood* (2010), which explores women's feelings of guilt, shame, and (sometimes) rage about their demanding, and often conflicting, social roles as wives, mothers, and wage-earners.

11 There is an interesting parallel between the development of countertransference theory in psychoanalysis and reader-response criticism in literary studies, which deposed the literary text as the primary source of meaning in order to relocate it in the minds of individual readers (Bleich 1975; Fish 1967; Holland 1968; Iser 1974). Whereas the New Criticism had assumed the text itself as the arbiter of its meaning(s), which the assiduous reader could decode or discover through close textual analysis, subsequent modes of interpretation (feminist, Marxist, queer, and postcolonial) have assumed the primacy of the reader, including her cultural background and individual life history.

12 Freud, as both of his major biographers point out (Jones 1953–57; Gay 1988), was concerned about his succession. At the same time, he had a tendency (which he himself admitted) to quarrel with some of his most intimate male friends. This propensity characterized his relationship with Josef Breuer and with Wilhelm Fliess, long before the defections of Alfred Adler and Wilhelm Stekel. Freud

was particularly pained by Carl Jung's unwillingness to affirm the centrality of the libido in human consciousness and behavior, as he had relied on him as an honorary son, to ensure that his message would transcend the narrow Jewish circle of his earliest supporters.

13 Steven Marcus, in his seminal essay "Freud and Dora: Story, History, Case History" (1985), considers the radical hypothesis that Freud, in his Dora case history, was writing a unique kind of modernist fiction. Not many critics have followed his lead in regarding Freud primarily as a writer of fiction, or perhaps, even more appropriately, as a writer of memoir. Implicitly, however, philosopher/psychoanalytic/critics such as Jacques Derrida (1978) read Freud's texts not for their overt content but for their subtextual resonances and even subversive implications. A deconstructionist (or postmodern) reading of Freud will, by its very nature, read on the margins of Freud's texts, seeking for the moments of rupture, disruption, contradiction, and/or reversal of conscious meaning. We read Freud today as he taught us to read dreams, that is to say, with an eye to disguise, displacement, and cryptic expression. In this sense, Freud's texts are literary, open to endless conjecture, and interpretation.

14 Harold Bloom's enormously influential *The Anxiety of Influence* (1973) may be said to have opened (and expanded) the subject of how literary writers regard their predecessors. Heavily influenced by Freud's conception of the psychological weight that fathers impose on sons, Bloom nevertheless created a paradigm of his own, which emphasizes the burden on "strong" poets of the achievement of their forbears. In order to withstand such a burden, poets must "misread" their predecessors in order to establish their own originality. A more contemporary version of this kind of psychological burden and influence has been proposed by Hans Loewald (1960), who suggests that the drama of "influence" may take another turn, in the direction of introjection, which allows for the ghosts of the past to assume the supporting role of ancestors. I doubt that Bloom would approve of Loewald's view of psychological health as based on a friendly as opposed to an antagonistic relationship to one's immediate past, but Loewald's idea has merit in terms of how twenty-first-century theorists might confront the history of traumatic loss that our twentieth-century forebears have bequeathed us.

PART THREE

Ghosts and Ancestors

7

Reflections on Melancholia and Mourning

Ghosts and ancestors

> *Scientific examination of the spiritual or "occultist" experience demonstrates that haunting can emerge from the forgotten depths of our own past, and assume physical and externalized form, now independent of the memories that spawned it, as Athena sprang from the head of Zeus, of him but at once free of him. Memories and ghosts are not so easily distinguished as previous generations have assumed.*
>
> ARTHUR PHILLIPS, *ANGELICA*

At the outset of his career, Freud described the unconscious as indestructible, comparing the power of unconscious wishes to specters, which "are only capable of annihilation in the same sense as the ghosts in the underworld of the *Odyssey*—ghosts which awoke to new life as soon as they tasted blood" (1900, 553. n.1). Freud's early-twentieth-century audience would easily have identified his allusion to Book XI of Homer's epic poem, which describes Odysseus's descent into the underworld to seek the guidance of the blind prophet Teiresias.

In order to attract the spirits of the dead, Odysseus pours libations of milk, honey, and wine before sacrificing a lamb and a ewe; their response is instantaneous.

> Now the souls gathered, stirring out of Erebos,
> Brides and young men, and men grown old in pain,
> And tender girls whose hearts were new to grief;
> Many were there, too, torn by brazen lanceheads,
> Battle-slain, bearing still their bloody gear.
> From every side they came and sought the pit
> With rustling cries; and I grew sick with fear. (XI, 40–46)

Like creatures out of a modern-day horror movie, such as the classic *Night of the Living Dead* (1968), these ghosts are drawn by the smell of blood. It is no wonder that Odysseus shrinks back in fear. Summoning his courage, he bars passage to the sacrificial pit until he has spoken with Teiresias, who not only offers him a preview of the trials he must undergo but also explains the secret of communing with the dead. Those "who enter where the blood is/Will speak to you, and speak the truth," he says, "but those/Deprived will grow remote again and fade." Armed with this knowledge, Odysseus calls out to his mother (whose death succeeded his departure from Troy) and whom he questions about the fates of his father, wife, and son. She satisfies his desire for knowledge of their lives, but flees his embrace, being "impalpable/As shadows are, and wavering like a dream" (231–32). Nor can Odysseus remain indefinitely in the underworld without losing his own flesh and blood vitality. Yet he entertains the stories of many more ghosts—some historical, some mythological—before he begins to feel anxious that the "shades in thousands, rustling/In a pandemonium of whispers, blown together" intend to hold him captive in the realm of death.

I begin with this episode of Homer's *Odyssey* because it speaks to a level of Freud's own half-spoken (hence partly unconscious?) thought; he relegates it to a footnote, after all, which he does not trouble to explain. Assuming that his readers share his familiarity with classical literature, he may take our understanding for granted. Ghosts are frightening, they crave blood, yet they also possess knowledge that is occult (hidden that is to say from ourselves and perhaps even forbidden); hence we seek their company. At the same time, too close an intimacy with the dead may cause us to linger in the shades, neglecting the richness, movement, and promise of our own lives.

Although Freud refers here to the immaterial (or spectral) realm of the unconscious, which finds expression through the language of dreams, his ghost metaphor resonates on many other levels. Hans Loewald, for instance, extended Freud's allusion into a rich description of the therapeutic process, whereby unconscious (often preoedipal) object relationships are reenacted in the transference, awakening "to new life" through the therapeutic interaction and what Loewald terms "the blood of recognition." As he states: "The transference neurosis, in the technical sense of the establishment and resolution of it in the analytic process, is due to the blood of recognition, which the patient's unconscious is given to taste so that the old ghosts may reawaken to life" (1960, 29). Loewald, whose subject is how psychoanalysis works (when it does) to bring about psychic change, describes this process by extending and transforming Freud's elliptical reference to the *Odyssey*.[1]

> Those who know ghosts tell us that they long to be released from their ghost life and laid to rest as ancestors. As ancestors they live forth in the present generation, while as ghosts they are compelled to haunt the present generation with their shadow life. Transference is pathological insofar as the unconscious is a crowd of ghosts, and this is the beginning of the transference neurosis in analysis: ghosts of the unconscious, imprisoned by defenses but haunting the patient in the dark of his defenses and symptoms, are allowed to taste blood, are let loose. In the daylight of analysis the ghosts of the unconscious are laid and led to rest as ancestors whose power is taken over and transformed into the newer intensity of present life, of the secondary process and contemporary objects. (Loewald 1960, 29)

Loewald's contribution to Freud's fragmentary allusion—through his elaboration of the transformation of ghosts into ancestors—forms the basis of my own speculations on the relationship between melancholia and mourning and by extension on contemporary theorizations of selfhood and representation.

Where Freud sees ghosts awakened "to new life" in the process of dream formation, which provides the unconscious with an elusive means of representation, Loewald perceives the process of the transference as one where ghosts of former loves and losses appear in the consulting room, to be analyzed, acknowledged, and befriended in treatment. For Freud, the ghosts of the unconscious make a brief (and largely enigmatic) appearance before fading again from view. For Loewald, they change in character as a result of making their presence felt, and (finally) known. Both Freud and Loewald were well-acquainted with ghosts, and each was a sensitive reader of Homer's poem, but I want to suggest that Loewald had a more dynamic understanding not only of the meaning of Odysseus's descent into the underworld but also of the way that patients may transform the fearful, threatening, and even deadly aspects of their histories into sources of wisdom.

While the *Odyssey*, in its emphasis on triumph over adversity, provides the template for Western narratives of adventure, it also offers a surprising level of psychological depth, due in part to Book XI. What Homer says, in effect, is that in order to move forward in such a way as to achieve his goal of returning home to Ithaca, Odysseus must revisit the past. Only in the realm of the dead can he find the wisdom he seeks (from Teiresias) about the dangers that lie ahead and how best to engage them. Loewald reads Odysseus's encounter in a hopeful way. We may, he imagines, by recognizing our private ghosts initiate a meaningful dialogue with them, one that may free us from sterile patterns of repetition (or endless wandering) while opening new avenues of development.

My argument adopts Loewald's process-oriented perspective. While melancholia (like our modern-day understanding of depression) generally refers to a condition of stasis, mourning (even as a part of speech) suggests motion. To adopt another, more literary, kind of language, I associate melancholia with the condition of being haunted by fearful apparitions from the past, which threaten our own liveliness or capacity to be-in-the-world, while I see mourning as a process of actively conversing with the dead.

Living with the dead

In loss and at the upper limit in old age (which will be different for every person), we may not want to "free" ourselves from the emotional bonds which have secured us to others we have loved so that we may "invest" our energy elsewhere. We do not detach ourselves from our losses. Instead we live with them. And then we die with them ... It may be not that we are detaching ourselves from others but that we have refused to untie the bonds which have attached us to those we have lost. We may begin to live with the dead.

KATHLEEN WOODWARD, "BETWEEN MOURNING AND MELANCHOLIA"

Any serious discussion of the psychological processes of mourning must begin (but not end) with Freud. In his classic essay "Mourning and Melancholia" (1917), composed before the Great War had revealed the extent of its devastation on European culture, Freud began to speculate on one of the more intransigent aspects of human suffering—melancholia—which for the sake of elucidation he contrasted with the more ordinary (and self-resolving) process of mourning.[2] While mourning and melancholia share "exciting causes due to environmental influences," e.g. "the loss of a loved person," or "of some abstraction which has taken the place of one, such as one's country, liberty, an ideal, and so on" (243), they follow different trajectories. Whereas mourning gradually dissipates and comes to an end, melancholia circles around itself, exhausting its victim, sometimes to the point of self-annihilation. Because Freud views mourning as routine and unproblematic, he does not have much to say about it apart from the following, rather chilly, conjecture:

> Each single one of the memories and situations of expectancy which demonstrate the libido's attachment to the lost object is met by the verdict of reality that the object no longer exists; and the ego, confronted as it were with the question whether it shall share this fate, is persuaded by the sum of the narcissistic satisfactions it derives from being alive to sever its attachment to the object that has been abolished. (255)

We simply detach, in time, from the dead.

Freud's description of melancholia, in contrast, involves a rich panoply of symptoms and behaviors, due in part to its entrenched (hence pathological) nature and its corresponding resistance to treatment. Mourning he regards as a "no brainer"; it is the enigma of melancholia that challenges and engages his intellectual powers, precisely because it is so difficult to alleviate.

Melancholia has a long history of association with creativity, achievement, and even genius, which may account in part for the appeal of Freud's exploration of this subject.[3] Think, for instance, of the exceptional nature—and self-torment—of Shakespeare's Hamlet. Contemporary studies of melancholia (under the guise of its prosaic cousin depression) abound, in part because of its endurance over time despite its changing nomenclature, but also because of its continuing power to elude relief, not to mention cure. We remain interested in melancholia, not only because it seems to pervade Western culture but also because we still do not quite know what to make of it.

Freud's contributions to this effort, while groundbreaking, are far from definitive. In "Mourning and Melancholia" he initiated a conversation—specifically about the role of early object relations and ambivalence toward the loved/lost object—that is ongoing. Increasingly, however, the line of demarcation that Freud drew between mourning and melancholia (as normal vs. pathological responses to loss) has blurred, to the point of altering the terms of contemporary discourse. We speak now—in the aftermath of the twentieth century (generally regarded as traumatic in its global conflicts and smaller-scale genocidal wars)—of psychological disorders so complex as to confound not only the possibility of amelioration, but also that of representation itself.[4] For Freud, melancholia was puzzling in its intransigence; for us, it is a "normal" (and intransigent) response to the tragedies of history.

The question I want to pose is how we have gotten from the place that Freud inhabited (theoretically at least) to where we are now, and where we might go from here. An exploration of this question will help to position my argument about the significance of Odysseus's descent into the underworld to converse with the dead, and hence also clarify my view of the relationship between ghosts and ancestors. This reading, in turn, informs my understanding of Freud's place in the world of psychoanalysis today.

Freud offers a succinct and compelling portrait of melancholia, the distinguishing features of which are "a profoundly painful dejection, cessation of interest in the outside world, loss of the capacity to love, inhibition of all activity, and a lowering of the self-regarding feelings to a degree that finds utterance in self-reproaches and self-revilings, and culminates in a delusional expectation of punishment." In every respect but one, he claims, "the same traits are met with in mourning. The disturbance of self-regard is absent in mourning; but otherwise the features are the same" (244). The remainder of Freud's essay is taken up with this critical difference. Mourning, he states, dissipates in time because it involves a gradual withdrawal from a loved object considered separate from the self, hence one that can eventually be surrendered. Melancholia, in contrast, feeds on ambivalence. The lost object is loved and hated in equal measure. The element of hatred, instead of being vented on the object, is directed toward the self. In addition, the lost object, instead of being recognized as integral to itself, has been incorporated or swallowed up, as it were, into the melancholic's own being. There it survives as a kind of undead presence, attacking its host from within.

The melancholic manages in this way to preserve the lost object but at an enormous cost. Feelings of anger or hatred that might have found expression (and relief) when directed outward consume the melancholic instead.

Freud's analysis of melancholia is arresting and powerful, in part because he paints a portrait that we can recognize of the person who is simply unable to "get better," "move on," or "snap out of it." It is also a portrait of what we might describe as clinical depression. Just as important, however, is Freud's theoretical foray into the role of ambivalence in early childhood development and the construction of the ego, both of which have inspired subsequent theorists and remain lively matters of question and debate.

The melancholic, according to Freud, denigrates him or herself to an exceptional degree, a situation that has nothing to do with reality but rather with hostile feelings due to disappointment in the loved/lost object that have been turned back against the self. Freud's description of this process, while complex, is also innovative in terms of his understanding of the internal structure of the ego.

> An object choice, an attachment of the libido to a particular person, had at one time existed; then, owing to a real slight or disappointment coming from this loved person, the object-relationship was shattered. The result was not the normal one of a withdrawal of the libido from this object and a displacement

of it on to a new one, but something different, for whose coming-about various conditions seem to be necessary. The object cathexis proved to have little power of resistance and was brought to an end. But the free libido was not displaced on to another object; it was withdrawn into the ego. There, however, it was not employed in any specified way, but served to establish an identification of the ego with the abandoned object. (249)

In other words, the abandoned object loses its independent existence, its otherness, and becomes instead an aspect of the self, where it cannot (it would seem) be given up without severe internal damage. "Thus the shadow of the object," Freud resonantly concludes, "fell upon the ego" (249).

In what follows, Freud offers an extremely condensed and highly speculative account of the early stages of ego development. The melancholic, Freud assumes, must once have formed an attachment to a real person. Something about this attachment, however, was not robust, having been "effected on a narcissistic basis, so that the object-cathexis, when obstacles come in its way, can regress to narcissism" (249). Because the melancholic only partly understands the love object as separate from himself, he succumbs easily to the process of internalization that Freud describes. More than this, Freud posits that all human relationships begin with identification—in effect, with a form of self-love or narcissism.

How does this work?

Identification, Freud explains,

> is a preliminary stage of object-choice ... it is the first way—and one that is expressed in an ambivalent fashion—in which the ego picks out an object. The ego wants to incorporate this object into itself, and, in accordance with the oral or cannibalistic phase of libidinal development in which it is, it wants to do so by devouring it.

Freud does not really pursue the implications of this line of argument, except to note that those who succumb to melancholia are more susceptible than others to "regression from narcissistic object-choice to narcissism" (250). Having incorporated the lost love object into the self, the melancholic suffers inwardly from the ambivalence (primarily feelings of hatred) that characterized the lost relationship.

As a result, "the self-tormenting in melancholia, which is without doubt enjoyable, signifies, just like the corresponding phenomenon in obsessional neurosis, a satisfaction of trends of sadism and hate which relate to an object, and which have been turned round upon the subject's own self in the ways we have been discussing" (251). Here, Freud seems to reach a limit in his theorization of melancholia. Granted, the lost loved object has been incorporated into the melancholic's ego (where it need not be relinquished), but the lost hated object resides there as well. As long as the melancholic persists in denigrating himself instead of expressing rage against the lost object, he will be unable to escape the prison of his illness. "We see," he observes, "that the ego debases itself and rages against itself, and we understand as little as the patient what this can lead to and how it can change" (257). Melancholia, for Freud, represents a form of mourning interminable.

Freud would seem at this point to have exhausted his own argument but he goes on. How to account for the sudden shift on the part of some patients from melancholia to its affective opposite mania? Here Freud introduces a resonant metaphor, one that will insinuate itself (in transformative ways) into the psychoanalytic literature that follows.

Some instances of melancholia, it seems, do run their course, though Freud is unsure how. So "cathected" is the melancholic to her internal object that it is hard to understand how such an attachment might be dissolved. At this point, Freud introduces the metaphor of the "open wound," which I have highlighted in Chapters 2 and 3. This wound, Freud states, draws "to itself cathectic energies," a process that empties the ego "until it is entirely impoverished" (253).

The wound metaphor, suggestive (in Freud's vocabulary) of female castration, rarely appears in his writing—hence its significance here. An "open wound" is problematic precisely because it does not close, much less offer closure. Freud returns to this image in the last paragraph of his essay, still puzzling around its possible meanings in relation to the melancholia/mania nexis. It must be so hard to "detach" from the loved/hated object, he speculates, that the effort involved erupts (into mania) once it is freed. Here is Freud's full description of this process:

> The accumulation of cathexis which is at first bound and then, after the work of melancholia is finished, becomes free and makes

mania possible must be linked with regression of the libido to narcissism. The conflict within the ego, which melancholia substitutes for the struggle over the object, must act like a painful wound which calls for an extraordinarily high anti-cathexis. (258)

This image does not so much suggest calm detachment as forced withdrawal, like a willed turning away from a terrifying prospect, such as the edge of a precipice, the depths of a whirlpool, or the petrifying face of Medusa.

However one might wish to interpret this passage, it causes Freud himself abruptly to break off. "But here," he says, "once again, it will be well to call a halt and to postpone any further explanation of mania until we have gained some insight into the economic nature, first, of physical pain, and then of the mental pain which is analogous to it" (258).

Freud's introduction of the subject of early ego development into his discussion of melancholia, though fragmentary, offered a productive line of theory for his followers. Karl Abraham, from whom Freud borrowed the idea of the internalization of the lost object as an oral, or "cannibalistic" act, describes melancholia as a "regression of the libido to the oral stage and the mechanism of introjection" (1927, 419), processes that he views as intimately connected. "As I hope to be able to make quite clear," he states, the introjection of the love-object is an incorporation of it, in keeping with the regression of the libido to the cannibalistic level" (420). For Abraham, the ambivalence that characterizes the melancholic's response to the lost (internalized) object derives from the oral sadistic phase of libido development.

In the original phase of object incorporation, he states, "the child is not yet able to distinguish between its own self and the external object... There is as yet no differentiation made between the sucking child and the suckling breast." Hence, "the child has as yet neither feelings of hatred nor of love." This pre-ambivalent phase is succeeded by one in which "the child exchanges its sucking activity for a biting one" (450). In the biting stage, "the individual incorporates the object in himself and in so doing destroys it... As soon as the child is attracted to an object, it is liable, even bound, to attempt its destruction." As a result, "the ambivalent attitude of the ego to its object begins to grow up" (451). In order to achieve full object love—one in which the object is regarded neither as an aspect of the self nor as the target of destructive impulses—the child must proceed through at least two more phases. Abraham summarizes the child's progress from oral to anal to genital stages of development as follows:

> Within the first—the oral—period, the child exchanges its preambivalent libidinal attitude, which is free from conflict, for one which is ambivalent and preponderantly hostile towards its object. Within the second—the anal-sadistic period, the transition from the earlier to the later stage means that the individual has begun to spare his object from destruction. Finally, within the third—the genital—period, he overcomes his ambivalent attitude and his libido attains to its full capacity both from a sexual and a social point of view. (453)

The significance of Abraham's mapping of melancholia onto this developmental scheme is greater than it might appear. Far from being static, in this view, melancholia manifests a surprising degree of motility. If, as Abraham argues, melancholia represents a regression (to a primitive level of ego organization), it surely must be amenable to progression (to a mature form of object love) as well. By linking Freud's notion of the melancholic's incorporation of the lost object to a stepwise process of libido development, Abraham opens the seemingly intractable condition of melancholia to change. Indeed, Abraham associates the treatment possibilities for melancholic patients with their capacity to form a transference relationship with the analyst, hence their (prior) achievement of the genital phase, or capacity for mature object love.

In addition to mapping melancholia onto the process of ego development, Abraham suggests that mourning differs from melancholia in degree rather than in kind. Mourning, like melancholia, for instance, involves the internalization of the lost object, a view that Abraham takes care to distinguish from that of Freud:

> True, Freud has made the very significant observation that the serious conflict of ambivalent feelings from which the melancholiac suffers is absent in the normal person. But how exactly the process of mourning is effected in the normal mind we do not at present know. Quite recently, however, I have had a case of this sort which has at last enabled me to gain some

knowledge of this till now obscure subject, and which shows that in the normal process of mourning, too, the person reacts to a real object-loss by effecting a temporary introjection of the loved person. (435)

In mourning, this internalized object can serve not only as a source of torment but also as one of solace. To demonstrate this point, Abraham offers an example from his clinical practice. A recently widowed patient, who suffers from a dislike of eating, a symptom resembling "the refusal to take nourishment met with in melancholiacs," suddenly improves, to the point of enjoying a "good meal in the evening" (436). That night he dreams that his wife (who had died as the result of an operation for cesarean section) comes back to life, her severed parts rejoined. The dreamer embraces her "with feelings of the liveliest joy." In another part of the same dream, he finds himself in a dissecting room, which reminds him "of slaughtered animals in a butcher's shop" (476). Abraham interprets the second part of the dream as a cannibalistic fantasy in which the dreamer ingests the body of his deceased wife. Connecting the two parts of the dream, he concludes that "consuming the flesh of the dead wife is made equivalent to restoring her to life" (436).

In the immediate aftermath of his loss, the widower "abandoned himself to his grief ... as though there were no possible escape from it." In this state of mind, he flirts with the idea of his own death. Later, however, he begins "to work off the traumatic effect of his loss by means of an unconscious process of introjection of the loved object" (436). This process of introjection, in turn, leads to the comforting thought: "My loved object is not gone, for now I carry it within myself and can never lose it" (437). In this instance of "normal" mourning, introjection allows the bereaved person to retain the lost object as a consoling presence within.

Abraham's theorization of introjection as a critical element in mourning as well as melancholia collapses one of the major distinctions between them. These two processes, in Abraham's formulation, are more similar than not. Indeed, he states that "this psychological process is, we see, identical with what occurs in melancholia. I shall try to make it clear later on that melancholia is an archaic form of mourning." Conversely, "the work of mourning in the healthy individual also assumes an archaic form in the lower strata of his mind" (437).

Melanie Klein, Abraham's pupil and analysand, extends his scheme of development while offering her own theorization of the infant's inner world, which she sees as vitally engaged (and reworked) in the process of mourning.[5]

For Klein, the essential features of mourning and melancholia are the same. Both mourning and melancholia for her (as for Abraham) involve a process of introjection rooted in ambivalence, ultimately derived from and modeled on infantile stages of development. Where Abraham offers a sequential model of pre-ambivalence (the oral phase) followed by intense ambivalence (the anal sadistic phase), eventuating in mature object love (the genital phase), Klein focuses on the problematics of ambivalence as expressed in what she terms the "paranoid-schizoid position," succeeded by the "depressive position" in the organization of the infant's inner world. Both theorists offer a progressive scheme (which impacts their understanding of the processes of mourning and melancholia), but Klein offers a richer and more dramatic picture of the infant's struggles with its painfully divided feelings than does Abraham.

For Klein, the inner (unverbalized and unverbalizable) life of the infant is a field of conflict. "In the very first months of the baby's existence," she claims, "it has sadistic impulses directed not only against its mother's breast, but also against the inside of her body: scooping it out, devouring the contents, destroying it by every means which sadism can suggest" (1935, 116). While these allegedly aggressive impulses derive from within, the infant (unable to tolerate its own destructive wishes) projects them outward onto the loved/hated object, its mother. For the infant, whose desire for satisfaction is insatiable, the mother who offers her breast is "good," whereas the mother who withholds it is "bad." Hence the infant's internal world is dominated by fantasies of the "good" and "bad" breast, the latter of which is perceived as an agent of persecution. While the infant is, in effect, experiencing its own ambivalence, it attributes both "good" and "bad" states of being to outside forces, projected onto its primary (presumably maternal) caregiver. In Klein's words, "the ego tries to defend itself against internalized persecutors by the processes of expulsion and projection." Such a process, she observes, also characterizes "the most severe psychoses" (117).

The infant, in Klein's view, is more than a little "crazy." Yet, normally (or perhaps optimally), it progresses to a more organized stage, where it can tolerate its warring impulses by containing feelings of frustration and hatred directed toward the unsatisfying breast, while also acknowledging love and gratitude toward the nurturing breast. Klein describes this achievement as the "depressive position," a difficult, yet necessary victory in the complex trajectory of human development.

In the depressive position, the infant is able to withstand its inner conflict precisely because it conceives of the loved/hated object as enjoying an independent existence, which also entails an awareness of loss. "Not until the object is lived as a whole," Klein states, "can its loss be felt as a whole" (118). The ability to tolerate mixed feelings advances the infant's development toward full object love, but at the cost of acknowledging its painful condition of separation. Nor is this achievement entirely stable. "[B]ased on the paranoid state and genetically derived from it," the depressive position, once attained, is subject to regression (130). The real loss (through death for instance) of a loved object threatens to undo this fragile state of internal balance. Klein describes this process in some detail in her (partly autobiographical) essay "Mourning and Its Relation to Manic-Depressive States" (1940), where she virtually collapses Freud's distinction between mourning and melancholia.

Klein begins with a key statement likening the process of early development to that of mourning. "In my view," she states, "there is a close connection between the testing of reality in normal mourning and early processes of the mind. My contention is that the child goes through states of mind comparable to the mourning of the adult, or rather, that this early mourning is revived whenever grief is experienced in later life" (1940, 147). She elaborates on this statement as follows:

> In normal mourning early psychotic anxieties are reactivated; the mourner is in fact ill, but, because this state of mind is so common and seems so natural to us, we do not call mourning an illness. (For similar reasons, until recent years, the infantile neurosis of the normal child was not recognized as such.) To put my conclusions more precisely: I should say that in mourning the subject goes through a modified and transitory manic-depressive state and overcomes it, thus repeating, though in different circumstances and with different manifestations, the processes which the child normally goes through in his early development. (157)

Klein, as we know, was testing her theory along her own pulse as she was no stranger to mourning—neither as a child nor as an adult.[6] Two of her siblings had died when she was young; her son Hans perished in a mountain-climbing accident in the mid-1930s; and her daughter Melitta (also a psychoanalyst) quarreled with her and later broke with her. As a result, Klein's description of the unraveling of the mourner's inner world reads with special urgency.

The adult mourner, according to Klein, is projected backwards in time, where she undergoes the process of intense ambivalence that the baby once experienced. The outcome of infant mourning, so critical to its growth and development, is never a sure thing. Rather, it must be relived with each significant loss. The adult mourner descends into the underworld, as it were, of its archaic responses to its first love, a world as full of persecuting as gratifying elements. In such a state, the mourner's very being seems in danger of breakdown, into the externalized battle between good and evil forces that had once threatened to tear it apart. While Klein acknowledges the mourner's need to reestablish the "lost loved object in the ego," she also understands the magnitude of this task, involving as it does the struggle to reinstate the mourner's "internalized good objects (ultimately his loved parents), who became part of his inner world from the earliest stages of his development onwards" (156).

Klein's summary of this process is compelling:

> The pain experienced in the slow process of testing reality in the work of mourning thus seems to be partly due to the necessity, not only to renew the links to the external world and thus continuously to re-experience the loss, but at the same time and by means of this to rebuild with anguish the inner world, which is felt to be in danger of deteriorating and collapsing. Just as the young child passing through the depressive position is struggling, in his unconscious mind, with the task of establishing and integrating his inner world, so the mourner goes through the pain of re-establishing and re-integrating it. (156)

The process of mourning plunges the adult back into the psychosis of early development, in which "fears of being robbed and punished by both dreaded parents—that is to say, feelings of persecution are revived" (156). The way out of such a painful condition lies in the reconstitution of the depressive position, culminating in the rebuilding of the mourner's inner world, which in turn "characterizes the successful work of mourning" (167).

Following Abraham's lead, Klein distinguishes mourning from melancholia on the basis of the mourner's ability to reestablish "the lost loved person in his ego," a task the melancholic fails to perform. The afflicted individual, she explains, "is reinstating his actually lost loved object; but he is also at the same time reestablishing inside himself his first loved objects—ultimately the 'good' parents—whom, when the actual loss occurred, he felt in danger of losing as well." While the melancholic succumbs to its state of inner chaos, the successful mourner succeeds in "rebuilding his inner world, which was disintegrated and in danger," hence surmounting grief and attaining "true harmony and peace" (174).

Klein's highly original contributions to the growing body of theory focused on the preoedipal period have had a major impact on the conceptualization of mourning and melancholia. By locating both along the spectrum of infant development—one that at its most primitive level mimics psychotic processes of mentalization—she prepares the ground for the kinds of questions posed by Lacan and his followers concerning language and representation.

Lacan (1977b) focuses on the languageless aspect of the preoedipal period, which renders it inaccessible to conscious awareness. Like Klein, he conceives of an infant whose initial state of being is disorganized, its body uncoordinated, its inner world dispersed. A key step in development, as described in Chapter 6 of this book, occurs during the "mirror stage," at which point the infant (presumably viewing itself in a mirror) forms an image of a coherent, though illusory, selfhood. This (false) image of integration propels further development. Another key moment occurs when the infant encounters the so-called "Law of the Father," a refinement of Freud's concept of the paternal threat of castration. Here, Lacan introduces a transformative idea—that the father's possession of the physical penis is separate from and not synonymous with his possession of the immaterial phallus, which (through its power of prohibition) represents the functions of language and signification. Hence, it is the function of the father, rather than his individual embodiment, that matters as the agent that interrupts the mother/infant dyad and precipitates the child's entry into the social circuits of language and culture.

For Lacan, the threat of castration is less physical than symbolic, yet its impact is no less powerful, as it instigates a dramatic change in the infant's nonverbal connection (if not fusion) with its mother, while compensating for this loss with access to the social worlds of language and representation. For Klein, the moment at which the infant becomes fully "human" is when it begins to acknowledge and to integrate its radically divided feeling states. Lacan's view is significantly different, as he locates the crisis of infant development in its recognition of the father's name/phallus/prohibition/law as representative of the requirement of its development into a full member of society. For Klein, the function of the father is not especially relevant to the infant's transition from the paranoid/schizoid to the depressive position, though she does not seek to revise Freud's oedipal construct. For Lacan, Oedipus reigns over the most crucial phase of human development, though in a strangely nonmaterial form, not as a person but as "the law," against which one may, of course, rebel.

Julia Kristeva, one of a group of French theorists who have drawn on the work of Lacan while critiquing it from a feminist standpoint, addresses the issue of melancholia in a way that combines Kleininian and Lacanian ideas in a new synthesis.

Kristeva's discussion of melancholia in *Black Sun* (1989) begins with a description of how it feels to be depressed. Speaking in the first person, she says "I am trying to address an abyss of sorrow, a noncommunicable grief that at times, and often on a long-term basis, lays claims upon us to the extent of having us lose all interest in words, actions, and even life itself" (3). Such a condition, far from being conducive to creativity, leads "to silence, to renunciation" (3). True melancholy constitutes a timeless state of nonmeaning, precisely because it is inaccessible to symbolic representation.

Kristeva links melancholia, in this respect, to the infant's initial languageless condition. Hence, "the melancholy person appears to stop cognizing as well as uttering, sinking into the blankness of asymbolia or the excess of an unorderable cognitive chaos" (33). Like Klein, Kristeva views the adult experience of melancholia as a regression to and reenactment of an earlier, more primitive state of being. Like Lacan, she views the infant's first experience as literally *infans,* that is to say without speech. For her, as for Lacan, the access to language instituted by the "Law of the Father" is a crucial step in development, at the same time that it alienates the infant from its true desire, which is full possession of the mother.

In the state of fusion with its mother, the infant is not aware of anything missing. In such a blissful union, the infant has no need, no lack, hence no desire. The possibility of coming into being for the infant depends on a radical separation from the maternal matrix, which it cannot perceive in terms of separate individuality or personhood but only as the inexpressible, primordial "Thing." Kristeva describes this process as follows:

> From the analyst's point of view, the possibility of concatenating signifiers (words or actions) appears to depend upon going through mourning for an archaic and indispensable object—and on the related emotions as well. Mourning for the Thing—such a possibility comes out of transposing, beyond loss and on an imaginary or symbolic level, the imprints of an interchange with the other articulated according to a certain order. (40)

The infant's first sense of loss inevitably involves the loss of mother, conceived by the child as the utterly gratifying, hence irreplaceable, "Thing." The only compensation for such a breach is the (admittedly displaced) recovery of the irredeemable object through language. As Kristeva states, "if I did not agree to lose mother, I could neither imagine nor name her" (41).

The drama of human development is thus inherently tragic. In order to live and to grow, we must lose the only "Thing" we ever really want(ed). What we get in return is the privilege of giving expression (through words and other symbolic means) to the obscure objects of our desire. "Verbal sequences only turn up," Kristeva affirms, "if a trans-position is substituted for a more or less symbiotic primal object, this trans-position being a true reconstitution that retroactively gives form and meaning to the mirage of the primal Thing." In order to imagine what we have lost, we must first give it up, a process that Kristeva describes as a form of mourning. "That critical task of transposition," she states, "consists of two facets: the mourning gone through for the object (and its shadow the mourning for the archaic Thing), and the subject's acceptance of a set of signs (signifying precisely because of the absence of object) only thus open to serial organization" (41).

The "Law of the Father" requires separation from the mother as the price of entry into culture, a necessarily patriarchal mandate for Kristeva as for Lacan. In order to accomplish this painful task, the infant must practice "negation," a forced turning away from the seduction of possession of the mother, compensated for by the ability to possess one's loss, so to speak, through the power of naming. If this notion seems paradoxical, it is. An actual loss is the prerequisite for the so-called "negation" of loss in language. Here is Kristeva's explanation of her use of the word negation:

> Signs are arbitrary because language starts with a negation (*Verneinung*) of loss, along with the depression occasioned by mourning. "I have lost an essential object that happens to be, in the final analysis, my mother," is what the speaking being seems to be saying. "But no, I have found her again in signs, or rather since I consent to lose her I have not lost her (that is the negation), I can recover her in language. (43)

The individual who refuses to subscribe to this Faustian bargain practices "denial" as opposed to negation. "Depressed persons," Kristeva maintains, "*disavow the negation*: [italics in the original] they cancel it out, suspend it, and nostalgically fall back on the real object (The Thing) of their loss, which is just what they do not manage to lose, to which they remain painfully riveted" (43–44). By denying "negation," the depressed individual seeks to cling to the lost object of desire, which remains unnamed due to the absence of signification.

Attempting to clarify this difficult set of distinctions, Kristeva restates them as follows: "I shall call *denial* the rejection of the signifier as well as semiotic representatives of drives and affects. *Negation* will be understood as the intellectual process that leads the repressed to representation on the condition of denying it and, on that account, shares in the signifier's advent" (44). Another way of conceptualizing her position (though not necessarily one that Kristeva would approve) is that the melancholic seeks to reinstate a relationship with an object that she cannot properly name because she rejects the notion that such a relationship ever had to be relinquished. In seeking nostalgically to recover a lost union with "The Thing" (ultimately the primordial mother), the melancholic also forecloses the "Law of the Father," as Kristeva makes clear. "The denial of the signifier is shored up by a denial of the father's function, which is precisely to guarantee the establishment of the signifier" (45).

In Kristeva's tragic universe, we cannot win for losing. Separating from the maternal matrix requires a catastrophic loss, one that is only partially compensated for by access to the signifier, hence the capacity to give voice to one's devastation. Melancholics, in this view, are inherent rebels, refusing to accede to the "Law of the Father," which is synonymous with the human condition, but they pay an enormous price. "Denial of negation," as Kristeva observes, "deprives the language signifiers of their role of making sense for the subject" (52). As a result, "denial annihilates even the introjections of depressive persons and leaves them with the feeling of being worthless, empty." Here, Kristeva invokes Freud's view that the melancholic relentlessly denigrates himself. She advances Freud's argument, however, by maintaining that melancholics use their depression like "a drug that allows them to insure a narcissistic homeostasis by means of a nonverbal, unnameable. (hence untouchable and omnipotent) hold over a nonobjectal Thing" (48). Is it any wonder that the melancholic, in Kristeva's view, is in some sense "locked in," unable to act, to communicate, much less to hope for change?

Kristeva provides not only a powerful depiction of the melancholic's existential state of being but also a theoretical construct to explain it. While building on the work of her predecessors (Freud, Abraham, Klein, and Lacan), she also anticipates current lines of theory and investigation. Her emphasis on the "stasis" of melancholia as inaccessible to language and representation is particularly relevant—not only to contemporary (neurobiologically based) theories of trauma but also to the psychoanalytic concept of "the crypt," which gives expression to the idea of a deadness within that describes the pain of the feeling of melancholia, as well as its resistance to speech and action. Kristeva describes such a condition as follows:

> The spectacular collapse of meaning with depressive persons—and, at the limit, the meaning of life—allows us to assume that they experience difficulty integrating the universal signifying sequence, that is, language ... The dead language they speak, which foreshadows their suicide, conceals a Thing buried alive. The latter, however, will not be translated in order that it not be betrayed; it shall remain walled up within the crypt of the inexpressible affect, anally harnessed, with no way out. (51)

Kristeva's description of the melancholic's walled-in state of suffering, which she imagines as a kind of inner tomb, seems to offer no possible exit. Yet she does offer a glimmer of hope. "It will be the task of analytic interpretation," she affirms, "to search for depressive meaning in the vault where sadness has locked it up with the mother, and tie it to the signification of objects and desires" (63). If, as Kristeva maintains, one falls ill of melancholy as a result of an inability properly to mourn mother, that is to say to give up one's attachment to the primordial "Thing," then the path to recovery involves precisely such a task of mourning, which in turn requires an engagement with *Verneinung* or the "Law of the Father." "Such melancholy persons," she declares, "triumph over the sadness at being separated from the loved object through an unbelievable effort to master signs in order to have them correspond to primal, unnamable, traumatic experiences" (67).

As evident in the work of Julia Kristeva, Lacan's introduction of the question of signification and the "Law of the Father" into considerations of the child's transition from a preverbal state to the acquisition of language has had a major impact on discussions of mourning in relation to melancholia. Where Abraham and Klein tend to collapse the distinction between these two processes, Kristeva (and by implication Lacan) implies that melancholia in its reversion to a preverbal (fantasized) union with the "Thing" is intractable and untreatable to the extent that the melancholic subject refuses *Verneinumg*, that is to say its existential condition of separation. In this sense, Kristeva collapses the distinction between so-called ordinary mourning and melancholia while also raising the stakes. In responding to current loss by regressing to an earlier stage of development, the mourner/melancholic must once again accomplish the herculean task of losing mother. Because melancholia involves a loss of the language-making function per se, this task may appear (to some) to be insuperable. Contemporary theories of melancholia—now linked to the study of trauma—suggest at times that the overwhelming nature of traumatic loss, which bypasses or disallows the possibility of symbolic articulation, prevents the melancholic from finding an exit from his or her misery. In *Black Sun*, Kristeva presents a realistic but somewhat more hopeful view.[7]

Kristeva's understanding of melancholy owes much to the work of Nicolas Abraham and Maria Torok, who describe melancholia as a kind of inner tomb or crpyt in which the lost object is secretly interred and preserved (hence not lost) within the self. Abraham and

Torok distinguish between mourning and melancholia along lines that resemble Loewald's distinction between ghosts and ancestors, portraying the former as the result of "introjection" (a process) and the latter as the outcome of "incorporation" (a fantasy).

Citing Sándor Ferenczi, who coined the term "introjection," Abraham and Torok redefine it as the means by which the infant ego begins to form itself around the awareness of its own emptiness (of the mother's breast), accompanied by its ability to fill itself with words as substitutes.[8] "The transition from a mouth filled with the breast to a mouth filled with words," they state, "occurs by virtue of the intervening experiences of the empty mouth. Learning to fill the mouth with words is the initial model of introjection" (128). Introjection, in this view, constitutes a form of mourning, a recognition of loss that elicits attempts at substitution, which eventuate in communion with others. Hence "the passage from food to language in the mouth presupposes the successful replacement of the object's presence with the self's cognizance of its absence. Since language acts and makes up for absence by representing, by giving figurative shape to presence, it can only be comprehended or shared in a 'community of empty mouths'" (128). Introjection is a more or less continuous process across the life span, which functions as a means of "broadening the ego" (127) through an ongoing process of object loss, succeeded by acts of verbal symbolization.

Abraham and Torok regard such a mourning process as involving not the introjection of the lost object itself but rather the subject's libidinal investments in it, that is to say "the sum total of the drives, and their vicissitudes as occasioned and mediated by the object" (1994, 113). This distinction is crucial, as it contrasts sharply with the process of incorporation, which seeks to swallow the loss whole, hence obviating the need to acknowledge its reality, including the task of inner reorganization.

Incorporation constitutes a rejection of mourning, "the refusal to claim as our own the part of ourselves that we placed in what we lost; incorporation is the refusal to acknowledge the full import of the loss, a loss that if recognized as such, would effectively transform us" (127). Abraham and Torok's description of the resulting "intrapsychic tomb" that the process of incorporation erects within is highly dramatic:

> Inexpressible mourning erects a secret tomb inside the subject. Reconstituted from the memories of words, scenes, and affects,

the objectal correlative of the loss is buried alive in the crypt as a full-fledged person, complete with its own topography. The crypt includes the actual or supposed traumas that made introjection impracticable ... Sometimes in the dead of night, when libidinal fulfillments have their way, the ghost of the crypt comes back to haunt the cemetery guard, giving him strange and incomprehensible signals, making him perform bizarre acts, or subjecting him to unexpected sensations. (130)

For Abraham and Torok, melancholia as represented by the inner crypt amounts to a form of haunting. They liberally employ the rhetoric of ghosts, tombs, and phantoms to emphasize this point. At the same time, the melancholic so haunted is unaware of his or her loss. Rather, the loss is immured, due in part to its secrecy but also to its unspeakability. A loss that is not recognized is inaccessible to self-consciousness, and by extension to representation. For Abraham and Torok (as for Kristeva), the absence of speech and communicability renders melancholia a static condition. The loss, made "dead" within the self, leads to the death-in-life of melancholia.

Whereas mourning implies the existence of a social world through the subject's attempts at signification—an implicit address to the Other—melancholia (locked in silence) is individual and solitary. Like Kristeva, Abraham and Torok regard melancholia as an extreme condition, languageless and virtually inaccessible. Like Kristeva, however, they offer an escape hatch, through the laborious process of breaching the tomb and liberating the ghosts that reside therein primarily through the process of psychoanalysis as based in the transference, the coded means by which analysands relive the past in the present through their attachment to the person of the analyst. Dreams, physical symptoms, puns, slips of the tongue, and other encrypted forms of speech such as anagrams, may also provide clues to the seemingly unnamable secret within. While aware of the difficulty of undertaking such an analytic task, Abraham and Torok remain guardedly optimistic about the possibility of converting melancholia into ordinary mourning. Just as importantly, they stress the social dimension of mourning, as a process that connects the mourner to her community through the medium of speech. This aspect of their thinking opens the question of the relationship between mourning and melancholia to the fields of culture and politics.

Abraham and Torok's concept of the phantom, elaborated from that of the crypt, moves these issues into the broader social world through the subject's incorporation of other people's secrets, unnamable losses, hence also their ghosts. The phantom is not the result of the individual subject's trauma or loss, but rather the effect of an intergenerational transmission of silence around an unnamable secret, a secondary form of haunting or legacy as it were. A ghost of this kind feels doubly alien, as its origin is twice removed from the subject, encrypted by a parent or elder of the previous generation yet passed on in powerful, though muted, form. "What comes back to haunt," as Abraham states, "are the tombs of others" (172). "The phantom," as he explains, "is a formation of the unconscious that has never been conscious—for good reason. It passes—in a way yet to be determined—from the parent's unconscious into the child's" (171).

In her essay "Between Mourning and Melancholia: Roland Barthes' *Camera Lucida*" (1991) Kathleen Woodward contrasts Freud's view of mourning as detachment from the dead with Barthes' seeming refusal of mourning (not quite synonymous with melancholia) as a condition somewhere in-between the poles of unbearable and incommunicable pain and the renunciation and abandonment of the lost object. This is, needless to say, a delicate task, yet one that seeks to bridge the divide introduced by Freud between these two powerful psychic experiences—a division that subsequent theorists have partly collapsed (Abraham and Klein) but also partly reconstituted (Kristeva and Abraham and Torok).

Woodward seeks, as she states, "a discourse about mourning more expressive than that provided by psychoanalysis, a discourse that would combine the affective dimension of the experience of mourning with theoretical descriptions of mourning as a process" (112). She explores ways of talking and writing about grief and mourning that include an awareness that "some people come to terms with their grief by learning to live with their pain and in such a way that they are still in mourning, but no longer exclusively devoted to mourning" (116). She finds this kind of discourse in Barthes' meditation on a photograph of his mother as a child that he discovered only after her death.

Barthes, in Woodward's view, does not want to "get over" his loss, at the same time that he does not wish merely to sink into it, to immure himself in a timeless and irreparable state of grief. On the one hand, he does not seek to transform his grief but rather to sustain it, as if to construct an interior memorial, such as the kind of crypt described by Abraham and Torok. On the other hand, Barthes clearly desires to communicate his distress. As Woodward observes, "cryptic incorporation ... is hidden from oneself. But Barthes wishes to keep his pain no secret." Hence, he "seeks to remain in mourning, to retain his psychic pain," while also sustaining his connection to the larger social world. "We may conclude here," Woodward affirms, that Barthes' grieving process "occupies a middle position *in between* mourning and melancholia" (119), one that seeks neither to negate the loss, nor to succumb to it, but rather (somehow) to live with it. In this sense, Barthes chooses to "live with the dead."

The theorists whose work on mourning and melancholia I have surveyed point (albeit individually and idiosyncratically) to a position not unlike that of Woodward in her meditation on Barthes' process of mourning/melancholia. They distinguish between the ordinary (and normally self-healing) process of mourning and the more entrenched and intractable problems posed by melancholia, while emphasizing the relationship of mourning and melancholia to early developmental stages and the role of language (and other processes of symbolization) in the creation and maintenance of social bonds. Abraham and Torok, in particular, raise the question of how the individual relates to her invisible pre-history as well as to the immediate present. Their concept of the phantom anticipates contemporary dialogues concerning the relevance of psychoanalytic theories of melancholia and mourning to our experience of social life, including the forms of collective violence— and collective responses thereto—that affect nearly everyone in a global environment. I suggest that Loewald's distinction between "ghosts and ancestors," accompanied by Woodward's concept of "living with the dead," may help to guide us into (if not through) this difficult terrain.

Haunting

The ghost makes itself known to us through haunting and pulls us affectively into the structure of feeling of

> *a reality we come to experience as a recognition. Haunting recognition is a special way of knowing what has happened or is happening.*
>
> AVERY GORDON, *GHOSTLY MATTERS*

The question I wish to pose, if not to resolve, is how one may be haunted by one's personal or social past without succumbing to the psychological threats so acutely described by Freud and his followers. Here, I want to suggest that the psychic entities Loewald refers to as ghosts correspond in a metaphoric sense to the persecuting agents described by Klein as active in the paranoid/schizoid position, which dissolve the organization of the ego and lead in extreme cases to the kind of death-in-life depicted by Kristeva, Abraham, and Klein as an inner tomb or crypt. In addition, I want to propose that Loewald's notion of converting ghosts into ancestors through the labor of psychoanalysis corresponds to the action of mourning on melancholia proposed by Woodward—a process that seeks not to forget or abandon the dead but rather to acknowledge their ongoing existence within. Such a mourning is neither static nor terminable but rather a lifelong engagement with the challenges posed by love and loss, that is to say by living itself.

Haunting, in this sense, is hardly a condition to be avoided. Rather, it is a sign of attention to the conscious and unconscious dimensions of suffering that form the crucible of our selfhood, hence shaping the choices we make and ultimately our paths in life. I propose a sketch here (rather than a theory) of what this kind of haunting entails, making use of somewhat scattered yet related sources that address the question of how we might begin to talk in a psychoanalytically informed way about the question of communal or social loss. I will focus on a few key texts, which offer significant insights and avenues for further exploration.

Judith Butler's essay "Melancholy Gender: Refused Identification" (1997) reads Freud's essay on melancholia in relation to his later thoughts on the construction of the ego to produce an original argument concerning the formation of the heterosexual subject, a process that extends well beyond the individual melancholic to society at large. As she observes, "in *The Ego and the Id* (1923), Freud himself acknowledges that melancholy, the unfinished process of grieving, is central to the formation of the identifications that form the ego" (134). Because the ego, according to Freud, "is a precipitate of abandoned object-cathexes" (135), it transcribes and memorializes our history of early loss. One such loss for the heterosexually organized subject is love for the parent of the same sex. Such love, repudiated and repressed, preserves its existence in the form of (disavowed) melancholy—a grief that can hardly be named, much less mourned. As a result, we are faced with "the question of ungrieved and ungrievable loss in the formation of what we might call the gendered character of the ego" (136).

A subject so constituted, according to Butler, is by virtue of its coming-into-being melancholic. While the girl, in this system of logic, must renounce her love/desire for her mother (perhaps originary in Kristeva's sense), the boy is required to disavow his love/desire for his father. Butler describes the boy's dilemma as follows:

> Becoming a "man" within this logic requires repudiating femininity as a precondition for the heterosexualization of sexual desire and its fundamental ambivalence ... Indeed, the desire for the feminine is marked by that repudiation: he wants the woman he would never be ... His wanting will be haunted by a dread of being what he wants, so that his wanting will always be a kind of dread. (137)

For Butler, haunting is not a positive term. Rather, it refers us to the commonplace understanding of ghosts as agents who wish us harm and who require an enormous effort to repel, if not to vanquish. Haunting in this view involves a more or less continuous battle with the undead, or return of the repressed.

The widespread (if not universal) repudiation of same sex love/ desire, Butler argues, leads not only to the social pathology of homophobia but also to prohibitions on mourning large-scale social loss—as represented, for instance, in the obstacles to grieving the massive death toll of the early AIDS epidemic. Such prohibitions, she observes, ultimately engender rage.

The question naturally arises of how to counter such collective haunting, how to give expression to the underlying structure of ambivalence that gives it life and hence to relieve the pressures of gendered melancholia that Butler so cogently articulates.

Although the dilemma Butler describes seems irremediable, her position is not without hope; she does offer something resembling an alternative or remedy. While acknowledging the problematic of "speaking the unspeakable," she discusses the possibility of communal political action as an antidote to accumulated rage that feeds on itself, assuming (in some instances) "suicidal proportions" (148). "The emergence of collective institutions for grieving," she states, "are thus crucial to survival, to reassembling community, to rearticulating kinship, to reweaving sustaining relations. Insofar as they involve the publicization and dramatization of death ... they call for being read as life-affirming rejoinders to the dire psychic consequences of a grieving process culturally thwarted and proscribed" (148).

Butler's use of Freud's conception of the "melancholy" construction of the ego (as foreshadowed in his essay "Mourning and Melancholia" and more fully articulated in *The Ego and the Id*) to address the social pathology of homophobia provides a bridge between the realm of the individual psyche and the world of sociopolitical relations. The German psychoanalysts and social theorists Alexander and Margarete Mitscherlich offer an even more ambitious approach to connecting these two spheres. In *The Inability to Mourn* (1967/1975) they propose that the postwar German response to the collapse of the Nazi regime amounted to a collective form of denial or "forgetting" of the immediate past in the service of economic reconstruction and national self-reinvention. Such an avoidance of awareness of the devastations inflicted on others and suffered by themselves on the part of the German people blocked the possibility of the kind of mourning process the Mitscherlichs regard as necessary to the maintenance of a healthy body politic. Although I cannot do justice here to the complexity of the Mitscherlichs's argument, I want to point to some of their key observations—as they touch on all of the issues under discussion.

In invoking the "self-protective forces of forgetting, denying, projecting, and other similar defense mechanisms" in their analysis of the postwar attempt to obliterate knowledge of the past, the Mitscherlichs describe a process that bypasses both mourning and melancholia. Mobilized on a national scale, such "manic" defenses functioned, in their view, as a means of avoiding "mass melancholia," a condition (unconsciously) perceived as a threat to economic recovery (25). "The gain," they conclude, "from the ability to forget, this alienation from one's own past, this erection of a collective taboo, is very substantial. If Germans had to live with the unvarnished memory of their Nazi past ... their ego could not easily integrate it with their present way of life" (20). The German public, the Mitscherlichs maintain, neither "introjected" their guilt, rage, humiliation, and loss (as in the mourning process) nor did they "incorporate" it (as in melancholia). "The Federal Republic," they state, "did not succumb to melancholia: instead, as a group, those who had lost their 'ideal leader,' the representative of a commonly shared ego ideal, managed to avoid self-devaluation by breaking off all affective bridges to the immediate past" (28).

Such an extreme strategy resembles, in part, Abraham and Torok's formulation of the crypt: the relegation of unacceptable states of mind to a sealed container within. Yet even the construction of a crypt represents an acknowledgment (however estranged) of the pain of loss. If, as I am suggesting, both mourning and melancholia may be viewed as responses to the condition of being "haunted," then the psychic mechanism described by the Mitscherlichs may be understood as a refusal of haunting. If there is no past, there can be no ghosts. Collective, as well as individual, history requires an underworld, a place where the dead may continue to live.

First published in the 1960s, *The Inability to Mourn* focuses less on the dynamics of mourning and melancholia than on their failure to emerge. The Mitscherlichs stress instead the absence of a national German response to the horrors imposed by the Hitler regime on its enemies internal and external, vividly describing the cascading consequences of such a collective loss of affect.

> Close examination shows three kinds of reaction by which insight into the overwhelming burden of guilt was kept at bay. In the first place, a striking emotional rigidity was evidenced in response to the piles of corpses in the concentration camps, to the disappearance into captivity of entire German armies, to the news of the slaughter of millions of Jews, Poles, and Russians, and to the murder of political opponents in one's own ranks. Such rigidity is the sign of emotional repudiation: the past is derealized, all pleasurable and unpleasurable involvement is withdrawn from it, it fades like a dream. This quasi-stoical attitude...also made it possible, in the second step, for Germans to identify themselves with the victors easily and without any sign of wounded pride. This shift of identification also helped ward off the sense of being implicated, and prepared the way for the third phase: the manic undoing of the past, the huge collective effort of reconstruction. (28)

The Mitscherlichs's analysis of such ruthless detachment—resembling in some respects the attitude attributed by Freud to the successful mourner in his essay "Mourning and Melancholia"—is not itself without empathy, although I do not expect every reader to agree with me in this assessment.

In order for the German people to come to terms with their Second World War past, the Mitscherlichs imply, they must descend into the underworld of their own conflicted emotions first by succumbing to the very melancholia they sought to avoid through "derealization" of what had occurred, and then by actively struggling with the persecutory agents of guilt, shame, loss of self-worth, depression, and despair. Is such a recognition of national melancholia and the subsequent labor of mourning even possible? If so, how?

The Mitscherlichs do not propose easy solutions. However, they do distinguish between the stasis of "melancholy self-reproach" and the more productive work of mourning (63). Melancholy may be the first step, but it is not necessarily the last. When we lose a person or an ideal we have loved, there is an understandable desire to turn away from reality, "clinging to the medium of hallucinatory wishful psychosis" instead (62). Yet in a successful mourning process "the loss is eventually introjected" through a painful process of acceptance that "must be struggled for, learned, and accomplished" (62). No one truly relinquishes an important love object without such a struggle, as the ending of such an attachment also "involves a partial loss of the self, as if by amputation" (63). For the Mitscherlichs, we both lose and (and in some sense) regain ourselves through mourning.

By descending into the underworld of melancholia, however, we incur the risk of being so assaulted by the ghosts of our own accusatory memories and emotions that we permanently lose our way. Haunting, in this sense, is double-edged. It may serve as a prompt to those feelings and reminiscences that we have excluded or occluded from consciousness and sought to banish from personal, cultural or historical awareness, or it may instigate a process of engagement with painful kinds of ambivalence, which may lead, in turn, to personal growth, if not transformation.

Repudiating the past, in the Mitscherlichs' view, incurs a kind of psychic numbing that further impedes the descent into melancholia, hence also the possibility of active mourning. In this respect, their work anticipates the development and elaboration of trauma theory—an interdisciplinary area of research that includes psychoanalysis, social theory, history, neurobiology, cultural studies, the literature of testimony, and even fiction. The current popularity of this field is a complex phenomenon with no simple point of origin, though the emergence of Holocaust studies in the latter half of the twentieth century serves to some extent as its most compelling instance and continuing point of reference.

Though hardly the first to call attention to the soul-destroying effects of extreme physical or psychological abuse, Freud was nevertheless one of the first to attempt to theorize it. Early in his career, he believed that childhood sexual "seduction" (a polite term for incest) might help to explain some of his female patients' puzzling symptoms. Later abandoning this hypothesis, he developed a theoretical stance and clinical method that emphasized internal (as opposed to external) sources of pain and conflict. In *Beyond the Pleasure Principle* (1920), however, he returned to the issues raised by externally imposed suffering, as evident, for instance, in the psychological distress of combat veterans of the First World War commonly referred to as "shell shock." Though relatively normal before their service, such veterans seemed unable to "forget" their war experiences or to resume their previous lives. Instead they became stuck, fixated on their terrible memories, which returned to them (as if in instant replay) in response to random stimuli from the environment, or in the form of recurring nightmares.

While sensitive to these conditions, Freud does not focus on them directly, except to comment on the element of "repetition compulsion" in the veterans' insistent nightmares—as in the behavior of others (including children) confronted by the painful reality of loss. His example of the "fort-da" game played by his favorite grandson Ernst, which consisted of the child's throwing a spool out of his cot, then reeling it back by a string, prompts Freud's extended meditation on the so-called "death instinct." This idea, so charmingly presented by way of personal anecdote, effectively displaces the subject of "shell shock," as well as that of trauma generally, for at least another generation.

The development of trauma theory over the course of the twentieth century has been so well reviewed by Bessel van der Kolk, Lars Weisaeth, and Onno van der Hart in their essay "History of Trauma in Psychiatry" (1996) that I will not rehearse it here.

Suffice it to say that the trajectory that has brought psychoanalysts, historians, sociologists, and neuroscientists into meaningful dialogue has emerged through a lengthy process of gestation. I want to call attention here to a significant aspect of trauma theory that bears on the question of melancholia, mourning, and what I choose to call haunting. This matter concerns the disruption of normal memory formation, leading to problems in mental representation, which in turn pose obstacles to treatment. On this point, there is a convergence of thinking between psychoanalytic and neuroscientific research.[9]

This area of (ongoing) investigation intersects, moreover, with the questions of language and signification posed by Lacan and his followers in regard not only to early developmental stages but also to those affective conditions—like melancholia—that recall and reenact such primitive states of being. At stake in this body of theoretical and observational research is a critical question: to what extent are extreme mental states, such as the ones induced by trauma, susceptible to speech and other forms of social communication? Are some human experiences simply "unspeakable," or unrepresentable, hence relegated to historical amnesia or the perpetual silence of an unbreachable tomb?

Freud was not the first, it seems, to comment on the psychic difficulties associated with trauma. The nineteenth-century French psychologist Pierre Janet not only observed patients who suffered the kinds of reactions described by Freud in *Beyond the Pleasure Principle* but he also speculated about the ways such individuals deal with their painful experiences through a process of memory dislocation. Such persons, according to Janet, are unable to integrate their shocking realities into ordinary narrative memory. Rather, they store such memories separately in sealed compartments of the brain. Such memories exist in fragmentary form, are not susceptible to integration into the kinds of autobiographical narratives we construct over the course of our lives and hence remain static or impervious to change. Summarizing Janet's position, van der Kolk and van der Hart conclude:

> Under extreme conditions, existing meaning schemes may be entirely unable to accommodate frightening experiences, which causes the "memory" of these experiences to be stored differently, and not to be available for retrieval under ordinary conditions:

it becomes dissociated from conscious awareness and voluntary control ... When that occurs, fragments of these unintegrated experiences may later manifest recollections or behavioral reenactments. (427)

For Janet, traumatic memory differs in important respects from ordinary narrative memory. Freud echoes this idea in his observations about the phenomenon of "repetition compulsion." Kristeva validates it in her description of the kind of melancholia that refuses signification, finding expression (when it does) only through the form of sporadic symptoms. Van der Kolk and van der Hart summarize Janet's position as follows: "in contrast to narrative memory, which is a social act, traumatic memory is inflexible and invariable. Traumatic memory has no social component; it is not addressed to anybody, the patient does not respond to anybody: it is a solitary activity" (431). The failure to make sense of an overwhelming experience leads not only to dysfunctions of memory but also to dysfunctions of symbolization, which in turn erect barriers to social interaction. "The crucial factor that determines the repetition of trauma," van der Kolk and van der Hart conclude, "is the presence of mute, unsymbolized, and unintegrated experiences" (436).

Evidence from the field of cognitive neuroscience confirms Janet's observations. The release of stress hormones triggered by traumatic experiences most likely affects how they are encoded and preserved in the brain. Hyperarousal of the amygdala, the seat of emotional response, for instance, may override the normal functioning of the hippocampus, which plays a significant role in the formation of narrative memory. In consequence, "severe or prolonged stress can suppress hippocampal functioning, creating context-free fearful associations which are hard to locate in space and time" (442). The result is not simply a failure to organize traumatic experience "in words and symbols," but a different kind of organization altogether, which manifests itself "on a somatosensory or iconic level as in somatic sensations, behavioral reenactments, nightmares, and flashbacks" (443).

The question posed by Janet's (and subsequent theorists') exploration of traumatic memory is not unlike that raised by Kristeva in regard to the insular condition of melancholia, as well as that of Abraham and Torok concerning the fortress-like nature of the crypt. For Janet, the answer lies in the recovery of ordinary memory functioning, residing primarily in its story telling capacity, which permits the split-off experience to be "integrated into existing meaning schemes" (440). Janet, however, was not confronted with patients suffering from the kind of massive emotional trauma borne by survivors of the Holocaust. Such experiences seem to transcend ordinary categories of response not only because they involve the survivors' excruciating personal losses but also because they refer to (and implicate survivors in) a collective experience of loss that is difficult if not impossible to imagine, much less to integrate into an existing meaning scheme. Events that expose a fault line in our understanding of history or human nature challenge such a possibility.

To their credit, van der Kolk and van der Hart do not shy away from these issues. Many concentration camp survivors, they observe, simply cannot connect their war experiences with the lives they have led since. Rather, they exist in two time frames simultaneously, "not exactly a split or doubling but a parallel existence" (448). Here van der Kolk and van der Hart raise an important (and unanswered) question:

> Can the Auschwitz experience and the loss of innumerable family members during the Holocaust really be integrated, be made part of one's autobiography?... How can one bring the traumatic experience to an end, when one feels completely unable and unwilling to resign oneself to the fact that one has been subjected to this horrendous event or series of events. How can one resign oneself to the unacceptable? (450)

Posing this question in terms that extend beyond the individual experiences of survivors to include us as readers, van der Kolk and van der Hart ask, "whether it is not a sacrilege of the traumatic experience to play with the reality of the past?" (450).

Perhaps the Holocaust (like some modern-day genocidal equivalents) constitutes the kind of human reality that is not only "unspeakable" for those who suffered and survived it but also in its essence "unrepresentable," that is to say fundamentally at odds with the goal of integration in the form of narrative memory. One may not wish to mourn such a reality, as in the psychoanalytic sense of introjection, but rather to do what? To suffer it as the interminable malady of melancholia or to pay it endless tribute in the form of an inner mausoleum? Historical events of the magnitude of the Holocaust raise precisely these kinds of agonizing questions.

Cathy Caruth, in her introduction to the second volume of a special issue of *American Imago* titled "Psychoanalysis, Culture and Trauma," restates some of these issues in especially urgent language. "The phenomenon of trauma," she observes, "demands historical awareness and yet denies our usual modes of access to it. How is it possible ... to gain access to a traumatic memory?" (1991, 417). As a result of its elusive manner of encoding, the trauma "seems to evoke the difficult truth of a history that is constituted by the very incomprehensibility of its occurrence" (419). In the face of such obstacles, she refers her readers to the position taken by Claude Lanzmann, the director of the documentary film *Shoah*, who rejects "understanding" as a possible or desirable goal, and who claims further that "there is an absolute obscenity in the very project of 'understanding'" (421). What Lanzmann offers in the place of "understanding" is the "creative act of listening," which "creates new ways of gaining access to a historical catastrophe for those who attempt to witness it from afar" (422). Such listening, in turn, allows for the transmission of an experience that conveys its own incomprehensibility. It exists, as such, as "the transmission of a gap" (422).

It is important to note here that Caruth does not attempt to resolve the question of how the victim of trauma might, could, or should relate to his experience. Rather, she refers to the potential for social engagement between traumatized subjects and those who choose to attend to them through whatever means they are able to communicate their distress. She concludes that "the attempt to gain access to a traumatic history, then, is also the project of listening beyond the pathology of individual suffering, to the reality of a history that in its crises can only be perceived in unassimilable forms" (423).

The question remains: if some kinds of psychic experience are "unassimilable," whether in individual or collective terms, how does one acknowledge or attend to them? Not to make such an attempt (as the Mittscherlichs cogently argue) seems even more "obscene" than trying to impose an artificial and inappropriate scheme of "understanding."

Here, I would like to propose the conceptual usefulness of the idea of haunting—as a means of both recognizing the genuinely inarticulate aspects of human consciousness and historical experience and of crediting the special kinds of knowledge or information they convey.

The work of Avery Gordon (1997), who perceives inadequacies in the formal disciplines of both psychoanalysis and sociology, is relevant in this regard. Where psychoanalysis lacks attention to the social, political, and historical dimensions of human experience, she maintains, sociology fails to register the emotional resonance of the past and hence its impact on the unfolding of the present and future. Gordon offers a socially based theory of haunting to address these issues. Stating the central thesis of her book, she writes:

> *Ghostly Matters* is about haunting, a paradigmatic way in which life is more complicated than those of us who study it have usually granted. Haunting is a constituent element of modern social life. It is neither premodern superstition nor individual psychosis; it is a generalizable social phenomenon of great import. To study social life one must confront the ghostly aspects of it. (7)

Gordon presents three case studies or instances of what she calls haunting: a reading of the absence of a historical woman (Sabina Spielrein) from the photograph of a psychoanalytic congress that she attended and two extended analyses of works of fiction, one by the Latin American novelist Luisa Valenzuela, the other by the African-American writer Toni Morrison.

The specter of Sabina Spielrein, she argues, calls attention to her unacknowledged role in the elaborately spun theories of the two men whose lives she connected: Carl Jung and Sigmund Freud. Valenzuela's novel depicts the progressive derangement of a Spanish psychoanalyst who attempts and fails to treat an Argentinian woman who is suffering from her country's political repression and terrorist practice of "disappearing" its own citizens. The sudden disappearance of this woman from the analyst's treatment room leads him on a journey to her country of origin to uncover the mystery of her vanishing, a journey that not only challenges his sanity but also reveals to him the publicly disavowed aspect of Argentina's brutal politics.

Morrison's novel, by reviving and retelling the story of Margaret Garner, an actual African-American woman who tried to murder her children when she was threatened by a return to slavery after her arduous journey to freedom, portrays the protagonist Sethe's haunting by the ghost of her slaughtered daughter, who (as a revenant) gives expression to the history of slavery as an institution in the United States.

It is impossible for me to do justice to the complexity of Gordon's analyses of these three instances—one a quasi-literary interpretation of a suppressed historical record, the other two investigations of the sociopolitical roots of literary fictions. Instead, I want to call attention to some of the assumptions underlying her argument.

Not only does the past inform the present in readily observable ways (as in the impact of economic chaos in Weimar Germany on Hitler's rise to power), but it also "haunts" it in less easily discernible, hence "ghostly" ways. These ghostly elements, precisely because they subsist below (or beyond) the level of conscious thought, are especially difficult to name, much less to exorcise. The inexpressible nature of what is not seen, not known, not even imagined, poisons public discourse and public life. It is not only individuals who suffer, in consequence, but entire societies and institutions of government.

Gordon proposes a theory to describe the ongoing effects of historical trauma (such as slavery or "disappearance") on societies at large, an issue that borders on the Mitscherlichs's questions about how to deal with "mass melancholia" avoided or suppressed. The especially difficult nature of this set of issues returns us, once again, to the conundrum of how to gain access to and to represent the so-called "unrepresentable."

Gordon's solution is not perfect but it is certainly appealing. The forms of fiction, she suggests, are particularly suitable to the indirect means of expression employed by ghosts. Specters, as emanations of an individual or collective psyche, are not strictly speaking real. As such, they can only make their presence felt obliquely through irrational (or nonrational) means. They appear and disappear sometimes in the guise of dreams or nightmares. They speak through whispers and suggestion and sometimes (it seems) even in tongues. They don't seek to make any kind of sense. Yet they tell us exactly what we need to know but do not want to hear.

Gordon describes the effect of the ghost of Sethe's murdered child as an embodiment not only of Sethe's maternal conscience but also of that of the silent history that led to Sethe's agonized moment of decision. "What gestures the unspeakable?" she writes. "In this other sociology, which is willy-nilly another politics, the ghost gesticulates, signals, and sometimes mimics the unspeakable as it shines for both the remembered and the forgotten" (150). The ghost, according to Gordon, does not need to make sense; she needs only to make her presence felt.

It is a given for Gordon that societies as well as individuals are haunted by their experiences of violence and suffering.[10] The question is not whether ghosts exist, but how to engage them. In her view, both Valenzuela and Morrison, through the strategies of fiction, offer a means of articulating the shape of what is missing from personal and institutional structures of meaning. Morrison, in particular, "provides a stunning example of how to hospitably and delicately talk to ghosts and through hauntings, which," Gordon asserts, "we must do" (182).

Here, I would like to return to Loewald's distinction between ghosts and ancestors. Whereas a ghost threatens to undermine or collapse the structures of meaning we rely on to make sense of our lives, an ancestor acts as a source of difficult knowledge that supports our efforts to live mindfully in the present. We fear ghosts as we fear ghouls or zombies who inhabit an underworld of torment. We revere ancestors as figures of wisdom who offer to guide us through the shades of the past. Deprived of ancestors, we are unmoored from our own histories, collective as well as individual. The difference between ghosts and ancestors might also be conceived as the difference between the undead and the merely dead. Whereas the undead paralyze us with fear, the merely dead stimulate our memories in ways that expand the possibilities of our present lives.

Mourning interminable

We are something other than autonomous ... but that does not mean that we are merged or without boundaries. It does mean, however, that when we think who we "are" and seek to represent ourselves we cannot represent ourselves as merely bounded beings, for the primary others who are past for me not only live on in the fiber of the boundary that contains me (one meaning of "incorporation"), but they

also haunt the way I am, as it were periodically undone and open to becoming unbounded.
JUDITH BUTLER, "VIOLENCE, MOURNING, POLITICS"

Insofar as we possess the gift of memory, we are also "haunted" by our individual and collective histories. Such haunting may take the form of dissociation, psychic numbing, or persecution—as in trauma or melancholia—or it may assume the shape of what Morrison calls "rememory," an active process of engagement with the dead. Lanzmann's conception of "listening" to the testimonies of Holocaust survivors, while also gathering and attending to available documentary records, constitutes such a process of engagement as do the "ghostly" fictions of writers like Morrison or Valenzuela.

But what about ordinary people? What is the magic process by which ghosts turn into ancestors, evil wizards into fairy godparents, or melancholia into so-called normal mourning?

Abraham, Klein, and even Kristeva might say that we already know the path having once tread it in infancy and early childhood. If, as they maintain, we experience some version of melancholia (in the form of ambivalence and inner persecution) in the process of moving from passionate attachment to our first caregiver(s) to a painful acceptance of separation, then we are already familiar with this path. Later losses—if indeed they return us to our first (though inarticulate) experiences of loss—offer the hope at least that we can make our way (like Hansel and Gretel retracing their trail of crumbs) through this dark wood again. Kristeva, by way of Lacan, poses an additional challenge. What if there is an insuperable barrier or gap between our adult speaking selfhood and our languageless condition as infants? Pursuing the Hansel and Gretel metaphor, what if the birds have eaten the crumbs? As each of us knows, some clinically depressed people do not make it out of the woods.

Here, I would like to juxtapose Freud's (barely theorized) notion of the ego as a "precipitate of abandoned object cathexes" with Judith Butler's concept of social subjectivity as one that is perpetually open to mourning.

In her essay "Violence, Mourning, Politics" (2004) Judith Butler returns to the issue of the "melancholy" construction of the ego, broadening her argument from the subject of gendered sexual identity and the forms of homophobia it incurs to the field of social relations and to social violence at large. She begins quietly yet also ambitiously: "I propose to consider a dimension of political life that has to do with vulnerability to loss and the task of mourning that follows, and with finding a basis for community in these conditions" (19). Given the helplessness of the newborn and its corresponding dependence on its primary caregivers, no human being can lay claim to absolute ego integrity or autonomy. Vulnerability to others (good, bad, or indifferent) not only describes our first physical experiences of life but also the manner by which we develop into individual subjects. Out of successive experiences of frustration, we come to understand that our caregivers are separate from us and we from them. Such experiences may be viewed as (relatively benign) steps in a process of mourning. At each stage, what we give up in terms of immediate satisfaction pushes us toward an exploration of our own powers, leading ideally to the capacity to take care of ourselves and to live on our own. Those who raised us will leave us, in time.

If one takes seriously (as Butler and theorists of object relations do) Freud's fragmentary utterance about the ego as taking shape through such a stepwise accommodation to loss, then one arrives at a position like that of Woodward, who views mourning as a process that does not aim to sever one's ties with the dead but rather to include them into the ever growing list of *dramatis personae* who populate our inner lives. In this way, we must consent to lose, but also continually to rediscover ourselves through loss.

Butler describes her own view of mourning as follows:

> I do not think that successful grieving implies that one has forgotten another person or that something else has come along to take its place ... Perhaps rather one mourns when one accepts that by the loss one undergoes one will be changed, possibly for ever. Perhaps mourning has to do with agreeing to undergo a transformation (perhaps one should say submitting to a transformation) the full result of which one cannot know in advance. (21)

In other words, mourning requires a return to the condition of helplessness (and potential undoing) that we felt as infants, which Abraham, Klein, and Kristeva so vividly describe. Butler articulates this dilemma in her own terms. "What grief displays," she states, "is the thrall in which our relations to others hold us, in ways that we cannot recount or explain, in ways that often interrupt the self-conscious account of ourselves we might try to provide, in ways that challenge the very notion of ourselves as autonomous and in control." As with desire, she observes, "one does not always stay intact" (23). Speaking again in the first person, Butler writes:

> I might try to tell a story here about what I am feeling, but it would have to be a story in which the very "I" who seeks to tell the story is stopped in the midst of the telling; the very "I" is called into question by its relation to the Other, a relation that does not precisely reduce me to speechlessness, but does nevertheless clutter my speech with signs of its undoing. I tell a story about the relations I choose, only to expose, somewhere along the way, the way I am gripped and undone by these very relations. My narrative falters, as it must. (23)

Mourning, Butler implies, renders us (at least temporarily) speechless. How can it not? The result of a successful mourning, however, might lead to an opening or expanded awareness of oneself, not only in terms of one's individual personal life but also in terms of one's relations to the larger social world. "To grieve," she states,

> and to make grief itself into a resource for politics, is not to be resigned to inaction, but it may be understood as the slow process by which we develop a point of identification with suffering itself. The disorientation of grief—"Who have I become?" or indeed, "What is left of me?" "What is it in the Other that I have lost?"—posits the "I" in the mode of unknowingness. (30)

For Butler, it is the shadow memory of our physical helplessness and vulnerability as infants that not only teaches us how to mourn but also opens us to the possibility of grieving the harms of others, including the losses of those whom we do not personally "know." She writes:

> I find that my very formation implicates the other in me, that my own foreignness to myself is, paradoxically, the source of my ethical connection with others. I am not fully known to myself because part of what I am is the enigmatic traces of others. In this sense, I cannot know myself perfectly or know my "difference" from others in an irreducible way. (46)

In other words, the parts of the self that are constituted by the "enigmatic traces of others" not only haunt us (benignly) through their foreignness or difference but also remind us of how vulnerable we are to the Other per se. "This unknowingness," Butler acknowledges, "may seem from a given perspective, a problem for ethics and politics. Don't I need to know myself in order to act responsibly in social relations?" Pursuing this question, Butler writes: "I am wounded, and I find that the wound itself testifies to the fact that I am impressionable, given over to the Other in ways that I cannot fully predict or control." As a result, "I cannot think the question of responsibility alone, in isolation from the Other; if I do, I have taken myself out of the relational bind that frames the problem of responsibility from the start" (46).

If, indeed, the ego is painfully constituted through loss, then it is also an open rather than a fixed structure—a loose scaffolding or fluid set of strategies by which we filter new experience and attempt to fit it into existing meaning schemes, as well as the means by which we admit and absorb that which is genuinely unfamiliar to us into our own being. Such an ego is continually under construction, made and remade through loss.

Freud's view of what I have elsewhere termed "the elegiac construction of the ego" (1990) is somewhat more conflicted than Butler's, although it clearly subtends the line of thought she develops from his texts. In *The Ego and the Id* (1923), Freud returned to the subject of melancholia, generalizing from the dynamic he had earlier theorized in "Mourning and Melancholia" (1917) to the manner by which we first come into being. "When it happens that a person has to give up a sexual object," he writes, "there quite often ensues an alteration of his ego which can only be described as a setting up of the object inside the ego, as it occurs in melancholia" (29). Such a process in adult life may be modeled, he observes, on the infantile experience of giving up a loved object.

> It may be that this identification is the sole condition under which the id can give up its objects. At any rate, the process, especially in the early phases of development, is a very frequent one, and it makes it possible to suppose that the character of the ego is a precipitate of abandoned object-cathexes and that it contains the history of those object choices. (29)

What exactly, in Freud's understanding, is introjected? Not the love object per se but rather the prohibition that disallows the ego's gratification of its desires. Nor is the loss of the original love object mourned as such; rather it undergoes a punishing kind of transmutation into the superego.

Let us assume for a moment that an infant's first loss involves its awareness of separation from its mother. The residue of this loss, in Freud's view, is not a maternal imago (as in the case of Barthes for instance), but rather a paternal one.

> The broad general outcome of the sexual phase dominated by the Oedipus complex may, therefore, be taken to be the forming of a precipitate in the ego, consisting of these two identifications in some way united with each other. This modification of the ego retains its special position; it confronts the other contents of the ego as an ego ideal or super-ego. (34)

In the above sense, the ego introjects a threatening (rather than a loving) parental ideal, which may explain why Freud invokes his earlier essay on melancholia. To introject this kind of loss into the early formation of the ego leads to a tormenting, rather than a consoling, presence within. To be so haunted is to be in pain.

Toward the end of *The Ego and the Id* Freud makes this association explicit by connecting the formation of the superego with the fear of death. Here also he invokes melancholia as a means of describing the sadistic functions of the superego: "The fear of death in melancholia only admits of one explanation: that the ego gives itself up because it feels itself hated and persecuted by the super-ego, instead of loved—being loved by the super-ego, which here appears as the representative of the id" (58). What the ego wants, in contrast, is to be loved. "To the ego, therefore," Freud affirms, "living means the same as being loved" (58), a function he attributes only to the super ego, which the super ego cannot provide.

Whereas for Butler (as for Abraham, Klein, and Kristeva) the task of ego construction involves "mourning mother," for Freud it means something rather more somber, the installation of a permanent Darth Vader–like figure into one's inner life. For this reason also his notion of the "wound" inflicted by melancholia does not suggest openness to the losses of others but rather an evacuation or emptying out of one's own inner resources, and hence also a call to the siren temptation of death.

For Freud, as I have maintained elsewhere, the condition of being wounded touched too closely on that of castration—to the loss of phallic mastery, independence, and power that he associated with feminine helplessness and vulnerability. Men, in his eyes, were not lacking, due to their possession of a penis. Women, being deprived of this privileged condition, could only hope to achieve acceptance of their physically deprived and socially inferior status in life. Being wounded (through loss or even the ordinary process of mourning), was not, as a result, a state of being that Freud was able to theorize in positive terms.

There is a significant (but also productive) irony here. If, as Freud and others have conjectured, the very process by which the ego comes into being is a "melancholy" one, that is to say haunted by its objects of first love and loss, then we are always and everywhere in mourning. At the same time, such a fundamentally "wounded" selfhood need not be construed as one that is merely helpless or deficient, much less deformed, as Freud's view of female castration suggests. Rather, the fluid organization of the ego may also be its greatest strength, if not also the means by which it develops the capacity to establish meaningful social relations.

Following Kristeva's line of thought, if the infant never "missed" mother, if its desires were immediately and completely satisfied, there would be no necessity for it to develop a means of articulating its needs through cries, gestures, and ultimately the full play of language. The process of signification arises out of a necessary mismatch between the self and the world. Language, as such, is an address to the Other, which in turn requires a recognition of the Other as separate from oneself. Language, however imperfectly, attempts to bridge this gap.

From this point of view, we should not expect experience to be fully "representable," as in completely present in words or through other means of symbolization. Words, as Lacan reminds us, are not things; they derive their meanings not from their inherent connection to the world of objects but rather from their differential relations with one another. We cannot, through language, capture the world as it is. Instead, we can only create an alternate universe, as it were, of ghostly forms.

This is a bad news/good news situation. On the one hand, we cannot own or possess the objects of our desire in a state of oneness or timeless gratification. We must take satisfaction, instead, in the fleeting, though real, pleasures of reaching toward them. If we experience the temporary illusion of plenitude, by which I mean the loss of our feeling of existential solitude, so much the better. But it can't last. On the other hand, our development of the capacity for language (and by extension symbolization) opens to us the possibility of participating in the community of others who constitute our social and cultural world(s). To refuse the process of signification (which Kristeva terms *Verneinung*) is to embrace isolation, if not entombment.

The point I am making here is familiar to theorists of postmodernism. It bears repeating, however, in the context of statements about forms of experience so extreme as to be "unspeakable" or "unrepresentable." Without minimizing the horrific nature of the events experienced by victims and survivors of the Holocaust (and other such manifestations of human inhumanity), I want to underscore the fact that no human experience can be fully captured in language. At the same time, because we are always in the position of seeking to communicate to ourselves and others what we see, how we feel, what we have undergone and what we think we "know," we are also capable of establishing the kinds of communities in which we can thrive. Because we cannot wrap our minds around historical events such as the Holocaust does not mean that they are condemned to silence or collective amnesia. The very attempt to speak the unspeakable establishes a dialogue, or multi-logue, that reaches (potentially at least) across ethnic, racial, and political divides as well as across generations. The fact that historical traumas such as the Holocaust cannot be explained by means of simple cause and effect or fit into existing meaning schemes does not mean that they cannot be spoken of at all. To argue such a position implies that some forms of melancholy are by their very nature mute and inaccessible to social intervention.

If, on the contrary, as I am suggesting, melancholy (communal as well as individual) constitutes a particular form of mourning that has gotten stuck, so to speak, in a powerfully felt and hence painfully real state of isolation and immobility, then there is at least a glimmer of hope.

Some experiences in life take us to the limits not only of our endurance, but also of our understanding. It is precisely because these experiences challenge our existing meaning schemes that we feel blocked, stymied, at a loss. At the same time, being faced with the limits of our understanding is not, in and of itself, the end of hope or possibility.

As Shoshana Felman, in her introduction to Claude Lanzmann points out, the conviction that we understand too well or too much can do harm. She connects the film work of *Shoah* with the work of psychoanalysis in the following way: "both work through gaps in understanding and at the limit of understanding, and even though the film incorporates a refusal of psychological understanding, and in a vaster sense a refusal of understanding as such" (1991, 477). By this, I do not take her to mean that it is futile to make any attempt at representation. Rather, I take her to mean that we cannot "know" even the content of our own experience fully. Rather than focusing on the (impossible) task of comprehending the reality of past, traumatic events, she calls attention, as does Lanzmann, to the process of transmission. That is to say to the address to the Other that depends, in turn, on our specifically human need and capacity for signification. As Lanzmann repeatedly insists, "the act of transmission is the only thing that matters" (478).

Effected by love

> *You are probably aware that our cures are brought about through the fixation of the libido prevailing in the unconscious (transference), and that this transference is most readily obtained in hysteria. Transference provides the impulse necessary for understanding and translating the language of the ucs; where it is lacking, the patient does not make the effort or does not listen when we submit our translation to him. Essentially, one might say, the cure is effected by love.*
> SIGMUND FREUD, LETTER TO CARL JUNG, DECEMBER 6, 1906

I have made a case here, for the similarities over the differences between melancholia and mourning—despite the clearly more problematic nature of melancholia. My argument is largely theoretical, that is to say, based in psychoanalytic theory as represented by classic authors and texts. Within this admittedly restricted field, there are many crosscurrents, though also a high degree of consensus regarding the evolution of the ego as constituted by a process that we might usefully describe as mourning. Just how this process takes place remains something of a mystery. Yet there seems a general truth in Freud's perception about the formation of subjectivity as "the precipitate of abandoned object cathexes." In this sense, we contain the ghost traces of those whom we love, lose, and mourn. In their first forms, these traces may be so buried within us that we are not only barred from direct access to them but are also unaware that they even exist. Later in life, they may take the form of conscious awareness or memory. In any case, the question remains: how do we communicate with ghosts in such a way as to transform them into ancestors?

For Odysseus, this was evidently not a problem. He gathered his courage and descended into the underworld to initiate a face-to-face conversation. Subsequent heroes of epic poetry and fiction have followed his example—from Virgil's Aeneas to Joyce's Stephen Dedalus—with similar results. More contemporary authors, such as Luisa Valenzuela and Toni Morrison, depict equally epic journeys and encounters with the disappeared and the dead. But these are fictions, imaginative constructions that function like extended metaphors, are they not?

I would like to conclude with a suggestion (not unlike an extended metaphor) for further thought.

When Odysseus engages with ghosts from the underworld, he learns things he did not already know, some of which, at least, help to guide him through the perils that lie ahead. There may be more wisdom in this encounter than is readily apparent, as Loewald so thoughtfully conjectured. Perhaps the point lies not so much in the specific knowledge conveyed as in the process of transmission itself?

For Freud, Loewald, and many contemporary theorists, the meaning and effectiveness of psychoanalysis emerges not so much through specific interpretations as through the slow revelation of the transference, including of course the analyst's reflections on her countertransference reactions. The process of transference—by which the patient reenacts his prior experiences of love and loss through the medium of the analytic relationship—brings old ghosts back to life. In this sense, the analytic session acts like a séance, calling spirits of the dead into the consulting room, not as disembodied presences but as aspects of the patient's current emotional responses. We are possessed by our ghost histories, so to speak, until we begin to engage them in a live form of conversation. If the transference works, the patient cares enough about his analyst to express the full range of emotion once felt but suppressed, ignored, or simply unthought. If the patient does not attach to the figure of the analyst, however, there is no possibility of communication. The ghosts choose either not to appear or not to speak.

Ghosts control us through their alienation from us, which amounts to a form of withholding. Once we allow them to share the same space with us, however, they gather near. When psychoanalysis works, as Freud and Loewald suggest, it works through the painful labor—and recognition—of repetition. It is not as though we share the same language with our internal specters, but rather that they speak through us to the point that we are compelled to acknowledge their presence. When this process occurs in a setting addressed to an Other who can properly attend to what we/they have to say, there is hope for change. Under these conditions, we may begin a conversation with the dead.

I do not mean to imply, by the above, that the only means of engaging the dead is through the means of formal psychoanalysis. Rather, I want to point to the element of communication at the heart of the psychoanalytic process, which may take many different forms, such as the documentary film project of Lanzmann's *Shoah*. Those who take the time to view and attend to this film sequence will be changed by the experience. Through the medium of artistic expression, the ghosts of others can become our own.

Representation does not need to be perfect. It just needs to happen. The process of representation, in itself, gives evidence of the desire to communicate across the gap of each person's awareness of his or her individual solitude. The desire to communicate, in turn, is motivated (for want of a better term) by love.[11]

If there is no one we ever love, then there is also no loss to grieve, hence no need to form other kinds of attachment in life. No need also for signification or an address to an Other. I see this as Butler's point in her meditation on social subjectivity, as I see it in Loewald's restatement of Freud's offhand allusion to ghosts in *The Interpretation of Dreams*.

That ghosts do not speak logically, consistently, or even consciously does not mean that we should ignore them. They remind us of our primary attachments in life, including our deepest wishes, dreams, and desires. They transcribe our personal histories of love and loss, which connect us, in turn, to the world at large.

Notes

1. This chapter grew out of a keynote address for a conference on "The Paradox of Melancholia: Paralysis and Agency," sponsored by the University of Flinders, Adelaide, Australia, in 2012. The challenge proposed by the organizers was to consider whether the paralysis typically associated with the condition of melancholia could also be viewed as a source of creativity or agency. In reviewing the literature on melancholia and mourning, I found a means of both distinguishing between them and demonstrating how they are similar. Hans Loewald's concept of turning ghosts into ancestors provided me with a framework for my discussion. At the conference, I discovered that Professor Prager also made use of this concept in his presentation "Mourning Becomes Eclectic: Racial Melancholia in an Age of Reconciliation." Loewald's formulation, which did not make a major impact at the time of its articulation in 1960, has since been embraced by many. Most recently, I encountered it in Norman Doidge's *The Brain That Changes Itself*, a book that explores the neuroplasticity of the brain, in the chapter titled "Turning Our Ghosts into Ancestors" (2007).
2. The literature on mourning is too vast to cite here. A collection of essays titled *On Freud's "Mourning and Melancholia"* (eds. Fiorini, Bokanowski, and Lewkowicz 2009) provides an excellent selection of contemporary responses to Freud's classic text, in addition to a comprehensive bibliography.
3. Juliana Schiesari documents this history in *Gendering Melancholia: Feminism, Psychoanalysis, and the Symbolics of Loss in Renaissance Literature* (1992), pointing out that only men were thought to suffer from this ailment. She conceives of her book as a "feminist reconceptualization of Klibansky, Panofsky, and Saxl's classic *Saturn and Melancholy* [1964], the thesis of which, about sadness and artistic triumph in the Renaissance, only tangentially speaks to women" (4). Among the many books on the subject of melancholy, *The Nature of Melancholy: From Aristotle to Kristeva* (ed. Radden 2000) provides a particularly useful collection of essays.
4. Many recent cultural critics make use of the term "melancholy" to describe the appropriate response to particularly virulent kinds of social pathology. Among these, I find the following especially compelling: Anne Cheng's *The Melancholy of Race* (2001), Paul

Gilroy's *postcolonial melancholia* (2004), and Wolf Lepenies' *Melancholy and Society* (1992). The collection of essays simply titled *Loss* (eds. Eng and Kazanjian 2003) offers a compendium of the many uses of melancholia in contemporary cultural studies.

5 Melanie Klein undertook analysis with Sándor Ferenczi after the death of her mother. Klein later credited him with fostering her interest in child analysis, stating in her *Autobiography* that "he very much encouraged my idea of devoting myself to analysis, particularly child-analysis" (Grosskurth 1986, 74). Later, she engaged in analysis with Karl Abraham for at least fifteen months in 1924–25. In her *Autobiography*, she comments on the significance of his thinking in the development of her own work:

> Abraham, who had discovered the first anal phase and linked it up with some work by Ophuijsen, came near to the conception of the internal objects. His work on the oral impulses and phantasies goes beyond F's work. It did not by any means go as far as my own, but it is on the same line ... I should say that A. represents the link between my own work and F's. (quoted in Grosskurth, 109)

6 For a full treatment of Klein's losses in life and how she may have transmuted some of her personal experiences in her theories, see Grosskurth (1986).

7 Issues of unrepresented states of being and how they enter into the treatment process are moving to the forefront of psychoanalytic thinking. See, in particular, the essays in *Unrepresented States and the Construction of Meaning: Clinical and Theoretical Contributions* (eds. Levine, Reed, and Scarfone 2013).

8 Ferenczi introduced the term "introjection" in his essay "The Meaning of Introjection" (1909). This term has been refined by Abraham and Torok (1994). Maria Torok takes issue with Ferenczi in her essay "The Illness of Mourning and the Fantasy of the Exquisite Corpse" (1994). "Incorporation," she writes, "is invariably distinct from introjection (a gradual process) because it is instantaneous and magical." "Introjection," in contrast, "seeks to introduce into it the unconscious, nameless, or repressed libido. Thus it is not at all a matter of 'introjecting' the object, as is all too commonly stated, but of introjecting the sum total of the drives, and their vicissitudes as occasioned and mediated by the object" (113).

9 See, for instance, the essay by van der Kolk and van der Hart titled "The Intrusive Past: The Flexibility of Memory and the Engraving of Trauma" (1991). The fixed nature of traumatic memory and its resistance to narrative integration has become something of a truism in both psychoanalytic and neuroscientific thinking.

10 Ricardo Ainslee, who does not use the term "haunting," analyzes the effects of communal trauma in his book *The Fight to Save Juarez: Life in the Heart of Mexico's Drug War* (2013). Stephen Frosh develops Gordon's thesis concerning social haunting in terms of historical traumas such as the institution of slavery and the Holocaust in *Hauntings: Psychoanalysis and Ghostly Transmissions* (2013).
11 The tone of Freud's letter to Jung, composed many years before the rupture of their relationship, is both formal and intimate. He precedes his seemingly offhand remark about a cure being "effected by love" by the humble observation:

> I have been reluctant for the same reason to say any more in public than that "this method [therapy] is more fruitful than any other." I should not even claim that every case of hysteria can be cured by it, let alone all the states that go by that name ... It is not possible to explain anything to a hostile public; accordingly I have kept certain things that might be said concerning the limits of the therapy and its mechanism to myself, or spoken of them in a way that is intelligible only to the initiate. (*The Freud/Jung Letters* 1974, 12)

This lengthy preface introduces one of Freud's most resonant statements—about the role of love in the therapeutic setting. It is as if he had to begin with doubts and disclaimers in order to speak from the heart.

Conclusion

This book addresses Freud's failures of mourning and their impact on his construction of theory. It also deals with the cultural task of mourning Freud, by which I mean adopting a stance toward the man and his work that acknowledges his power and influence while avoiding the hazards of idealization or denigration.[1] Too often in recent years, Freud skeptics have warred with his defenders in a way that leaves no room for moderation, much less revisionary thinking.[2] An either/or mentality has characterized the debate on Freud's relevance leading, on the one hand, to a total denial of the validity of his work, and on the other to an almost religious adherence to his texts and precepts.

I propose another path, one that Freud himself not only hinted at but also (inadvertently) fostered in his tentative formulations of the preoedipal period, which in turn involves the labor of mourning entailed in the struggle to attain a sense of independent selfhood. Psychoanalytic theories, post-Freud, focus heavily on the questions and problems generated by the earliest stages of development: attachment and individuation; unrepresented states of being; the processes of symbolization and acculturation; and trauma and mourning. That Freud himself did not develop these lines of thinking is no discredit to him. Rather, the very incompleteness of Freud's speculations opened avenues for future theorization.

Mourning Freud does not mean disparaging, ignoring, or forgetting him. Nor does it mean elevating him to a position that demands discipleship or submission to unquestioned authority. Rather, it means digesting his body of thought in a way that resembles the process of assimilating the memory of a departed loved one as an internal source of support and inspiration. Hans Loewald's concept of transforming "ghosts into ancestors" eloquently articulates this process. Whereas ghosts haunt us in ways that terrify and transfix us, preventing us from moving forward in our lives, ancestors act as internal guides and sources of wisdom.

In the first three chapters of this book, I maintain that Freud's life does not fit the major theory he derived from it: the Oedipus complex. Rather, the Oedipus complex serves to obscure a deeper, more private, and conflicted drama of mourning that Freud was unable to articulate. This drama took place, I believe, in the first four years of his life, as he lost first his young mother's primary care and attention, then a younger sibling, his nanny, and finally his beloved Freiburg home. All of these losses took place during the phase of life Freud later termed "preoedipal," meaning that it preceded the onset of hostility directed at the figure of the father as an agent of prohibition.

Freud's oedipal structure, which obscures the dynamics of the mother–infant relationship and the rich drama of development it entails, rests on the quicksand of mourning, a subject that Freud could glimpse but not directly address. Given his culturally normative assumptions about masculinity as active and femininity as passive, it is perhaps no surprise that the condition of loss made him uneasy. Repeatedly, Freud describes melancholia (pathological mourning) as a bleeding wound, evoking the imagery of castration. To mourn, he implies, renders one helpless, at a loss, wounded, and hence feminine.

The Oedipus complex, in contrast, offers a paradigm of masculine development centered on paternal threat and filial aggression. In this scenario, the boy's love for his mother is not thwarted by his immaturity, much less her rejection of him as weak and inferior. Rather, the powerful father prevents the fulfillment of his desire. As a result, the child's impulses remain aggressive in character and only temporarily diverted from their aim. Such a narrative sustains not only the family structure and patriarchal order Freud consciously upheld but also the masculine self-representation that he held dear.

It is ironic, and perhaps even inevitable, that the very areas Freud slighted or neglected in his theory have moved center-stage in the latter half of the twentieth century and beyond. I chart this trajectory in the middle part of this book, which focuses on the imbrication of psychoanalysis in the social, cultural, and political narratives of our time. In these chapters, I demonstrate the ways that psychoanalysis has altered our notions of personal subjectivity as well as the ways that our narratives of subjectivity (per feminism, cultural materialism, and critical theory) have altered the course of psychoanalysis.

In the concluding chapter of this book, I offer a reflection on the concept of mourning, beginning with Freud's groundbreaking essay "Mourning and Melancholia." I trace the complex trajectory of his line of thought through that of his followers Karl Abraham and Melanie Klein, to those of more contemporary theorists, such as Jacques Lacan, and Julia Kristeva. I relate this development to the increasing emphasis in psychoanalytic theory on the preoedipal period and the transition from preverbal states of awareness to the acquisition of language. I see trauma theory as related to these areas of inquiry through its emphasis on the failure of narrative and hence nonrepresented states of being.

This shift from the oedipal to the preoedipal period is consonant with new readings of Freud's fragmentary pronouncements about the development of the ego as the "precipitate of abandoned object cathexes." If, as Freud suggested, and as subsequent theorists have maintained, we come into life always already at a loss, then our lifelong task is to come to terms with this painful reality. Mourning implies not only a primary rupture but also a return (with each new loss) to our early childhood experience, until we die. This is not an especially cheerful message, but I think that Freud would consider it realistic.

How does this perception relate to current social realities?

We live our lives in the context of our times—including the complexly interwoven and internally inconsistent set of narratives (gendered, historical, material, and cultural) that we inherit from our forebears. At present and for our moment, Freud's oedipal theory (rooted in his drive theory) has less relevance than his episodic, cryptic, and incompletely formulated speculations about mourning. We are interested today in questions that Freud anticipated but did not fully articulate, such as the devastating capacity for human destructiveness as evidenced in our expressions of religious intolerance, violation of human rights, genocidal actions, and ever-present threat of nuclear holocaust. Freud in his later years developed the concept of the "death instinct" to give a name to such propensities but he did not offer anything like a program of action (nor perhaps did he imagine the need for one) to avert their worst forms of expression.

In today's unstable combination of cyber connectedness (and surveillance), global economics, and extreme political/religious conflict, we need something more than the fatalism of Freud's "death instinct" to guide us into the future. At the same time, his thinking about the problem of human malevolence (rooted in the necessary ambivalences of our earliest experiences) may offer some clues. The difficult process of mourning, which necessarily involves ambivalence (according to Melanie Klein and others), may be able to teach us not only to live with our painful internal conflicts but also to tolerate the social and political divisions we face on a daily basis. We are always renegotiating the terms of love and hate, not only in our personal relationships but also in the world at large. To the extent that we can come to terms with mourning—that is to say with our internally divided selves—we may also hope to become better citizens of the world.

Notes

1 Anton Kris (2013) addresses this issue in his eloquent essay "Unlearning and Learning Psychoanalysis," where he describes the process of "unlearning in psychoanalysis" as involving not only "cognitive retraining," but also *"revision of identifications and processes of mourning"* (341; italics in the original).
2 The "Freud Wars" of the 1990s seem to have abated but without coming to resolution. The issues raised by Frederick Crews (2006, 2017) and others about the lack of empirical evidence for Freud's primary tenets and interpretations (as expressed in his published case histories) have created a split in the intellectual community that has not produced a consensus—at least not from my point of view.

Freud is not "dead," yet his status has been challenged and hence remains vulnerable in terms of his influence over future generations. Psychoanalysis as an evolving discipline, and even more importantly as a praxis, retains its viability in Western culture, despite the many assaults on it in regard to its evidentiary base. Crews is a powerful voice in the ongoing conversation about the meanings and possible uses of psychoanalysis and psychoanalytic thinking in today's world. I find myself in agreement with him on many points of his argument, but I do not embrace his wholesale rejection of Freud and his relevance to the world we live in today.

In my own view, Freud's approach to the world he was born into and the political upheavals he experienced over the course of his lifetime was profoundly subjective as well as literary. Looking back on the history of the twentieth century, we turn as much to the literary masterpieces of this period as we do to professional historians to comprehend what happened and what it might have meant. It is sad to me that the movement to discredit Freud's contributions to the history of modernity contributes to the widening gulf between so-called scientific or evidence-based thinking and the more individual and intuitive expressions of the arts, including the literary arts, of which Freud was a master.

WORKS CITED

Abel, Elizabeth (1989), *Virginia Woolf and the Fictions of Psychoanalysis*, Chicago: Chicago University Press.
Abraham, Karl (1927), "A Short Study of the Development of the Libido, Viewed in the Light of Mental Disorders, Part I, Manic-Depressive States and the Pre-Genital Levels of the Libido," in *Selected Works of Karl Abraham*, ed. Ernest Jones, trans. Douglas Bryan and Alix Strachey, 418–51, London: Hogarth.
Abraham, Nicolas and Maria Torok (1994), *The Shell and the Kernel, Vol 1*, ed. and trans. Nicholas T. Rand, Chicago: University of Chicago Press.
Adelman, Janet (1992), *Suffocating Mothers: Fantasies of Maternal Origin in Shakespeare's Plays: Hamlet to the Tempest*, New York: Routledge.
Ainslie, Ricardo (2013), *The Fight to Save Juarez: Life in the Heart of Mexico's Drug War*, Austin: University of Texas Press.
Almond, Barbara (2010), *The Monster Within: The Hidden Side of Motherhood*, Berkeley: University of California Press.
Anspaugh, Kelly (1995), "Repression or Suppression? Freud's Interpretation of the Dream of Irma's Injection," *Psychoanalytic Review* 82: 427–42.
Anzieu, Didier (1986), *Freud's Self-Analysis*, trans. P. Graham, London: Hogarth.
Appignanesi, Lisa and John Forrester (1992), *Freud's Women*, New York: Basic/HarperCollins.
Bachofen, J.J. (1861; 1967), *Myth, Religion and Mother-Right*, trans. Ralph Manheim, Princeton, NJ: Princeton University Press.
Balmary, Marie (1982), *Psychoanalyzing Psychoanalysis: Freud and the Hidden Fault of the Father*, trans. Ned Lukacher, Baltimore, MD: Johns Hopkins University Press.
Barthes, Roland (1989), "The Death of the Author," in *Modern Literary Theory: A Reader*, eds. Philip Rice and Patricia Waugh, 114–18, London: Edward Arnold/Hodder and Stoughton.
Belleforest, F. de (1992), "The Historie of Hamblet, Prince of Denmark," in *William Shakespeare, Hamlet*, ed. C. Hoy, 134–43, New York: Norton.

Benjamin, Jessica (1988), *The Bonds of Love: Psychoanalysis, Feminism and the Problem of Domination*, New York: Pantheon.
Bernheimer, Charles and Claire Kahane, eds. (1985), *In Dora's Case: Freud-Hysteria- Feminism*, New York: Columbia University Press.
Bion, Wilfred (1962), *Learning from Experience*, New York: Basic Books.
Bleich, David (1975), "The Subjective Character of Clinical Interpretation," *College English* 36: 739–55.
Bloom, Harold (1973), *The Anxiety of Influence*, New York: Oxford University Press.
Blum, Harold P. (2016), "A Psychoanalytic Odyssey," *American Imago* 13: 417–34.
Blunt, Judy (2002), *Breaking Clean*, New York: Knopf.
Boehlich, Walter, ed. (1990), *The Letters of Sigmund Freud to Eduard Silberstein 1871–1881*, trans. Arnold J. Pomerans, Cambridge: Belknap/Harvard University Press.
Boose, Lynda and Betty S. Flowers, eds. (1989a), *Daughters and Fathers*, Baltimore, MD: Johns Hopkins University Press.
Boose, Lynda and Betty S. Flowers, eds. (1989b), "The Father's House and the Daughter in It: The Structures of Western Culture's Daughter-Father Relationship," in *Daughters and Fathers*, 19–74, Baltimore, MD: Johns Hopkins University Press.
Bowlby, John (1969), *Attachment and Loss*, London: Hogarth Press.
Breger, Louis (2000), *Freud: Darkness in the Midst of Vision*, New York: John Wiley & Sons.
Brome, Vincent (1983), *Ernest Jones: A Biography*, New York: Norton.
Burlingham, Michael (1989), *The Last Tiffany: A Biography of Dorothy Tiffany Burlingham*, New York: Atheneum.
Butler, Judith (1990), *Gender Trouble: Feminism and the Subversion of Identity*, New York and London: Routledge.
Butler, Judith (1993), *Bodies That Matter*, New York: Routledge.
Butler, Judith (1997), "Melancholy Gender/Refused Identification," in *The Psychic Life of Power*, 132–90, Stanford, CA: Stanford University Press.
Butler, Judith (2004), "Violence, Mourning, Politics," in *Precarious Life: The Powers of Mourning*, 19–49, London: Verso.
Byck, Robert, ed. (1975), *Cocaine Papers*, New York: NAL.
Campbell, Bebe Moore (1989), *Sweet Summer: Growing Up With and Without My Dad*, New York: Putnam.
Carotenuto, Aldo (1982), *A Secret Symmetry: Sabina Spielrein Between Freud and Jung*, trans. Arno Pomerans, John Shipley, and Krishna Winston, New York: Pantheon.
Caruth, Cathy, ed. (1991), *Psychoanalysis, Culture and Trauma II*, *American Imago* 48.
Caruth, Cathy, ed. (1996), *Unclaimed Experience: Trauma, Narrative, History*, Baltimore, MD: Johns Hopkins University Press.

Cheng, Anne (2001), *The Melancholy of Race: Psychoanalysis, Assimilation, and Hidden Grief*, Oxford: Oxford University Press.
Chodorow, Nancy (1978), *The Reproduction of Mothering: Psychoanalysis and the Sociology of Gender*, Berkeley: University of California Press.
Cixous, Hélène and Catherine Clément (1986), *The Newly Born Woman*, trans. Betsy Wing, Minneapolis: University of Minnesota Press.
Clark, Ronald W. (1982), *Freud: The Man and the Cause*, London: Paladin/Grenada.
Cooper, Arnold M. (1991), "On Metapsychology and Termination," in *On Freud's Analysis Terminable and Interminable*, ed. Joseph Sandler, 106–23, New Haven: Yale University Press.
Crews, Frederick (2006), *Follies of the Wise: Dissenting Essays*. Emeryville, CA: Shoemaker and Hoard.
Crews, Frederick (2017), *Freud: the Making of an Illusion*, New York: Henry Holt & Company.
Delillo, Don (1985), *White Noise*, New York: Viking.
Derrida, Jacques (1975), "The Purveyor of Truth," *Yale French Studies* 52: 31–113.
Derrida, Jacques (1976), *Of Grammatology*, trans. Gayatri Chakravorty Spivak, Baltimore, MD: Johns Hopkins University Press.
Derrida, Jacques (1978a), "Freud and the Scene of Writing," in *Writing and Difference*, trans. Alan Bass, 196–231, Chicago: Chicago University Press.
Derrida, Jacques (1978b), "Coming into One's Own," in *Psychoanalysis and the Question of the Text*, ed. Geoffrey Hartman, trans. J. Hulbert, 114–48, Baltimore, MD: Johns Hopkins University Press.
Dinnerstein, Dorothy (1976), *The Mermaid and the Minotaur: Sexual Arrangements and Human Malaise*, New York: Harper and Row.
Doidge, Norman (2007), *The Brain That Changes Itself: Stories of Personal Triumph from the Frontiers of Brain Science*, New York: Penguin Books.
Eagleton, Terry (1983), *Literary Theory: An Introduction*, Minneapolis: University of Minnesota Press.
Eco, Umberto (2004), *The Mysterious Flame of Queen Loana*, trans. Geoffrey Brock, New York: Harcourt.
Edmundson, Mark (1990), *Towards Reading Freud: Self-Creation in Milton, Wordsworth, Emerson, and Sigmund Freud*, Princeton, NJ: Princeton University Press.
Ellenberger, Henri (1970), *The Discovery of the Unconscious: The History and Evolution of Dynamic Psychiatry*, New York: Basic Books.
Elliott, Patricia (1991), *From Mastery to Analysis: Theories of Gender in Psychoanalytic Feminism*, Ithaca: Cornell University Press.
Eng, David L. and David Kazanjian, eds. (2003), *Loss*, Berkeley: University of California Press.

Epstein, William H. (1991a), *Contesting the Subject: Essays in the Postmodern Theory and Practice of Biography and Biographical Criticism*, West Lafayette: Purdue University Press.

Epstein, William H. (1991b), "(Post)Modern Lives: Abducting the Biographical Subject," in *Contesting the Subject: Essays in the Postmodern Theory and Practice of Biography and Biographical Criticism*, ed. William H. Epstein, 217–36, West Lafayette: Purdue.

Erdrich, Louise (1988), *Tracks*, New York: Henry Holt & Company.

Erikson, Erik (1954), "The Dream Specimen of Psychoanalysis," in *Psychoanalytic Psychiatry and Psychology: Clinical and Theoretical Papers*, eds. Robert P. Knight and Cyrus R. Friedman, 131–70, New York: Hallmark-Hubner.

Fairbairn, W.R.D. (1952), *An Object Relations Theory of the Personality*, New York: Basic Books.

Falzeder, Ernst, ed. (2002), *The Complete Correspondence of Sigmund Freud and Karl Abraham 1907–1925*, trans. Caroline Schwaracher, London: Karnac Books.

Felman, Shoshana (1987), *Jacques Lacan and the Adventure of Insight: Psychoanalysis in Contemporary Culture*, Cambridge: Harvard University Press.

Fichtner, Gerhard, Ilse Grubrich-Simitis, and Albrecht Hirschmüller, eds. (2011; 2013), *Die Brautbriefe, Band I Sei Mein, Wie Ich Mir's Denke*, and *Band II, Unser Roman in Fortsetzungen*, Frankfurt am Main: S. Fischer Verlag.

Fiorini, Leticia, Thierry Bokanowski, and Sergio Lewkowicz, eds. (2009), *On Freud's "Mourning and Melancholia,"* London: Karnac Books.

Fish, Stanley (1967), *Surprised by Sin: The Reader in Paradise Lost*, Cambridge: Harvard University Press.

Fish, Stanley (1991), "Biography and Intention," in *Contesting the Subject*, ed. William H. Epstein, 9–16, West Lafayette: Purdue University Press.

Fonagy, Peter (2001), *Attachment Theory and Psychoanalysis*, New York: Other Press.

Foucault, Michel (1977), "What Is an Author?" in *Language, Counter-Memory, Practice: Selected Essays and Interviews by Michel Foucault*, ed. Donald Bouchard, 113–38, Ithaca: Cornell University Press.

Foucault, Michel (1978), *The History of Sexuality, Vol. 1*, trans. R. Hurley, New York: Pantheon.

Frank, Lawrence (1989), "Freud and Dora: Blindness and Insight," in *Seduction and Theory: Readings of Gender, Representation and Rhetoric*, ed. Dianne Hunter, 110–32, Urbana: University of Illinois Press.

Freud, Anna (1974), *Introduction to Psychoanalysis: Lectures for Child Analysts and Teachers, The Writings of Anna Freud, Vol. 1*, Madison, CT: International Universities Press.

Freud, Ernst L., ed. (1970), *The Letters of Sigmund Freud and Arnold Zweig*, trans. Elaine and William Robson-Scott, New York: Harvest/Harcourt Brace Jovanovich.

Freud, Ernst L., ed. (1975), *The Letters of Sigmund Freud*, trans. Tania and James Stern, New York: Basic Books.

Freud, Martin (1957), *Glory Reflected: Sigmund Freud—Man and Father*, London: Angus and Robertson.

Freud, Sigmund (1986), *The Standard Edition of the Complete Psychological Works of Sigmund Freud*, ed. and trans. James Strachey et al., 24 Vols., London: Hogarth.

Freud, Sigmund (1893–95), *Studies on Hysteria*, S.E. 2: 1–305.

Freud, Sigmund (1899), "Screen Memories," S.E. 3: 301–22.

Freud, Sigmund (1900), *The Interpretation of Dreams*, S.E. 4: 1–338.

Freud, Sigmund (1901), *The Psychopathology of Everyday Life*, S.E. 6: 1–279.

Freud, Sigmund (1905), "Fragment of an Analysis of a Case of Hysteria," S.E. 7: 1–122.

Freud, Sigmund (1908), "Creative Writers and Daydreaming," S.E. 9: 141–54.

Freud, Sigmund (1909), "Analysis of a Phobia in a Five-Year-Old Boy," S.E. 10: 1–149.

Freud, Sigmund (1910a), "A Special Type of Choice of Object Made by Men," S.E. 11: 163–75.

Freud, Sigmund (1910b), *Leonardo da Vinci and a Memory of His Childhood*, S.E. 11: 59–137.

Freud, Sigmund (1912a), "Recommendations to Physicians Practising Psycho-Analysis," S.E. 12: 111–20.

Freud, Sigmund (1912b), "The Dynamics of Transference," S.E. 12: 97–108.

Freud, Sigmund (1913a), "The Theme of the Three Caskets," S.E. 12: 289–301.

Freud, Sigmund (1913b), *Totem and Taboo*, S.E. 13: 1–16.

Freud, Sigmund (1914), "On the History of the Psycho-Analytic Movement," S.E. 14: 7–66.

Freud, Sigmund (1915), "Observations on Transference Love," S.E. 12: 157–71.

Freud, Sigmund (1917a), "Mourning and Melancholia," S.E. 14: 237–58.

Freud, Sigmund (1917b), "A Metapsychological Supplement to the Theory of Dreams," S.E. 4: 219–35.

Freud, Sigmund (1920), *Beyond the Pleasure Principle*, S.E. 18: 1–64.

Freud, Sigmund (1923), *The Ego and the Id*, S.E. 19: 1–66.

Freud, Sigmund (1925a), *An Autobiographical Study*, S.E. 20: 7–74.

Freud, Sigmund (1925b), "Some Psychical Consequences of the Anatomical Distinction Between the Sexes," S.E. 19: 241–58.

Freud, Sigmund (1931), "Female Sexuality," *S.E.* 21: 221–43.
Freud, Sigmund (1933), "Femininity," *S.E.* 22: 112–35.
Freud, Sigmund (1935), "The Subtleties of a Faulty Action," *S.E.* 22: 233–35.
Freud, Sigmund (1937), "Analysis Terminable and Interminable," *S.E.* 23: 209–51.
Freud, Sigmund (1939), *Moses and Monotheism, S.E.* 23: 1–137.
Frey, James (2003), *A Million Little Pieces*, New York: Random House.
Friedan, Betty (1963), *The Feminine Mystique*, New York: Norton.
Frosh, Stephen (2013), *Hauntings: Psychoanalysis and Ghostly Transmissions*, New York: Palgrave Macmillan.
Gabbard, Glen (1995), "Countertransference: The Emerging Common Ground," *International Journal of Psychoanalysis* 76: 475–85.
Gallop, Jane (1982), *The Daughter's Seduction: Feminism and Psychoanalysis*, Ithaca: Cornell University Press.
Gardiner, Judith (1985), "Mind Mother: Psychoanalysis and Feminism," in *Making a Difference Feminist Literary Criticism*, eds. Gayle Greene and Coppélia Kahn, 113–45, London: Methuen.
Garner, Shirley Nelson (1989), "Feminism, Psychoanalysis and the Heterosexual Imperative," in *Psychoanalysis and Feminism*, eds. Richard Feldstein and Judith Roof, 164–81, Ithaca: Cornell University Press.
Gay, Peter (1988), *Freud: A Life for Our Time*, New York: Norton.
Gilbert, Sandra and Susan Gubar (1979), *The Madwoman in the Attic: The Woman Writer and The Nineteenth-Century Literary Imagination*, New Haven: Yale University Press.
Gilbert, Sandra (1989), "Life's Empty Pack: Notes Toward a Literary Daughteronomy," in *Daughters and Fathers*, eds. Lynda Boose and Betty S. Flowers, 256–77, Baltimore, MD: Johns Hopkins University Press.
Gilligan, Carol (1982), *In a Different Voice: Psychological Theory and Women's Development*, Cambridge: Harvard University Press.
Gilroy, Paul (2005), *Postcolonial Melancholia*, New York: Columbia University Press.
Gordon, Avery (1997), *Ghostly Matters: Haunting and the Sociological Imagination*, Minneapolis: University of Minnesota Press.
Griffin, Fred (2004), "One Form of Self-Analysis," *Psychoanalytic Quarterly* 73: 683–715.
Grosskurth, Phyllis (1986), *Melanie Klein: Her World and Her Work*, New York: Knopf.
Grosskurth, Phyllis (1991), *The Secret Ring: Freud's Inner Circle and the Politics of Psychoanalysis*, Reading: Addison-Wesley.
Guntrip, Harry (1968), *Schizoid Phenomena, Object Relations and the Self*, London: Hogarth Press and Institute of Psychoanalysis.
Hampl, Patricia (1999), *I Could Tell You Stories*, New York: Norton.
Hardin, Harry (1987), "On the Vicissitudes of Freud's Early Mothering: Early Environment and Loss," *Psychoanalytic Quarterly* 56: 628–44.

Hardin, Harry (1988a), "On the Vicissitudes of Freud's Early Mothering: Alienation from His Biological Mother," *Psychoanalytic Quarterly* 57: 72–86.

Hardin, Harry (1988b), "On the Vicissitudes of Freud's Early Mothering: Freiberg, Screen Memories and Loss," *Psychoanalytic Quarterly* 57: 209–23.

Harris, Adrienne (2005), *Gender as Soft Assembly*, Hillsdale, NJ: Analytic Press.

Harris, Adrienne (2011), "Transference, Countertransference, and the Real Relationship," in *Textbook of Psychoanalysis, Second Edition*, eds. Glen O Gabbard, Bonnie E. Litowitz, and Paul Williams, 255–68, Washington, DC: American Psychiatric Publishing.

Hartman, Frank (1983), "A Reappraisal of the Emma Eckstein Episode and the Specimen Dream," *Journal of the American Psychoanalytic Association* 31: 555–86.

Heilbrun, Carolyn (1989), "Afterword," in *Daughters and Fathers*, eds. Lynda Boose and Betty S. Flowers, 418–29, Baltimore, MD: Johns Hopkins University Press.

Heller, Judith Bernays (1973), "Freud's Mother and Father," in *Freud As We Knew Him*, ed. Hendrick M. Ruitenbeck, 334–40, Detroit, MI: Wayne State University Press.

Herman, Judith (1992), *Trauma and Recovery*, New York: Basic Books.

Hersh, Thomas R. (1995), "How Might We Explain the Parallels Between Freud's 1895 Irma Dream and His 1923 Cancer?" *Dreaming* 5: 267–87.

Hertz, Neil (1983), "Dora's Secrets, Freud's Techniques," *Diacritics* 13: 65–76.

Hirsch, Marianne (1989), *The Mother/Daughter Plot: Narrative, Psychoanalysis, Feminism*, Bloomington: Indiana University Press.

Holland, Norman (1968), *The Dynamics of Literary Response*, New York: Oxford University Press.

Holt, Robert R. (1992), "Freud's Paternal Identification as a Source of Some Contradictions Within Psychoanalysis," in *Freud and the History of Psychoanalysis*, eds. T. Gelfand and J. Kerr, 1–28, Hillsdale, NJ: Analytic Press.

Homans, Peter (1989), *The Ability to Mourn: Disillusionment and the Social Origin of Psychoanalysis*, Chicago: Chicago University Press.

Irigaray, Luce (1981), "And the One Doesn't Stir Without the Other," trans. Helene Vivienne Wenzel, *Signs* 7: 60–67.

Irigaray, Luce (1985), *Speculum of the Other Woman*, trans. Gillian C. Gill, Ithaca: Cornell University Press.

Iser, Wolfgang (1974), *The Implied Reader*, Baltimore, MD: Johns Hopkins University Press.

Jacobs, Theodore (1991), *The Use of the Self: Countertransference and Communication in the Analytic Situation*, Madison, CT: International Universities Press.
Jacobs, Theodore (1999), "Countertransference Past and Present," *International Journal of Psychoanalysis* 80: 575–94.
Janet, Pierre (1901), *The Mental State of Hystericals*, trans. Caroline Rollin Corsen, New York: Putnam.
Jones, Ernest (1953, 1955, 1957), *The Life and Work of Sigmund Freud*, 3 Vols, New York: Basic Books.
Jonte-Pace, Diane (2001), *Speaking the Unspeakable: Religion, Misogyny and the Uncanny Mother in Freud's Cultural Texts*, Berkeley: University of California Press.
Joyce, James (1922), *Ulysses*, Paris: Shakespeare and Company.
Jung, Carl (1916), *Psychology of the Unconscious: Transformations and Symbols of the Libido*, trans. B. Hinkle, New York: Moffat.
Kahn, Coppélia (1986), "The Absent Mother in *King Lear*," in *Rewriting the Renaissance: The Discourses of Sexual Difference in Early Modern Europe*, eds. Margaret Ferguson, Maureen Quilligan, and Nancy Vickers, 33–49, Chicago: Chicago University Press.
Kandel, Eric (2006), *In Search of Memory: The Emergence of a New Science of Mind*, New York: Norton.
Karr, Mary (1995), *The Liar's Club*, New York: Viking Penguin.
Kerr, John (1993), *A Most Dangerous Method: The Story of Jung, Freud, and Sabina Spielrein*, New York: Knopf.
Klein, Melanie (1935), "A Contribution to the Psychogenesis of Manic-Depressive States," in *Selected Melanie Klein*, ed. Juliet Mitchell (1986), 116–145, London: Hogarth Press.
Klein, Melanie (1940), "Mourning and Its Relation to Manic-Depressive States," in *Selected Melanie Klein*, ed. Juliet Mitchell (1986), 146–171, London: Hogarth Press.
Klein, Melanie (1975a), *Envy and Gratitude & Other Works 1946–1963*, New York: Delacorte.
Klein, Melanie (1975b), *Love, Guilt and Reparation & Other Works 1921–1945*, New York: Delacorte.
Koestenbaum, Wayne (1988), "Privileging the Anus: Anna O and the Collaborative Origin of Psychoanalysis," *Genders* 3: 57–80.
Krakauer, Jon (2011), *Three Cups of Deceit*, New York: Random House.
Kris, Anton (2013), "Unlearning and Learning Psychoanalysis," *American Imago* 70: 341–55.
Kristeva, Julia (1977), *About Chinese Women*, trans. Anita Barrows, New York: Urizen.
Kristeva, Julia (1986), "Stabat Mater," in *The Kristeva Reader*, ed. Toril Moi, trans. Leon S. Roudiez, 160–86, New York: Columbia University Press.

Kristeva, Julia (1989), *Black Sun: Depression and Melancholia*, trans. Leon Roudiez, New York: Columbia University Press.
Krüll, Marianne (1986), *Freud and His Father*, trans. Arnold J. Pomerans, New York: Norton.
Kulish, Nancy and Deanna Holtzman (2008), *A Story of Her Own: The Female Oedipus Complex Reexamined and Renamed*, Lanham, MD: Rowman and Littlefield.
Lacan, Jacques (1977a), *Écrits: A Selection*, trans. Alan Sheridan, London: Tavistock.
Lacan, Jacques (1977b), "The Mirror Stage as Formation of the Function of the I as Revealed in Psychoanalytic Experience," in *Écrits: A Selection*, ed. Alan Sheridan, 1–7, London: Tavistock.
Lanzmann, Claude (1991), "The Obscenity of Understanding: An Evening with Claude Lanzmann," *American Imago* 48: 473–95.
Launer, John (2015), *Sex Vs. Survival: The Life and Ideas of Sabina Spielrein*, London: Peter Meyer Publishers, Inc.
Lear, Jonathan (2005), *Freud*, New York: Routledge.
Lehman, David (1983), *Signs of the Times: Deconstruction and the Fall of Paul de Man*, New York: Poseidon Press.
Lehmann, Herbert (1991), "Reflections on Freud's Reaction to the Death of His Mother," *Psychoanalytic Quarterly* 52: 237–49.
Lehrer, Jonah (2007), *Proust Was a Neuroscientist*, New York: Houghton Mifflin.
Lepenies, Wolf (1992), *Melancholy and Society*, trans. Jeremy Gaines and Doris Jones, Cambridge: Harvard University Press.
Levine, Howard B., Gail S. Reed and Dominique Scarfone, eds. (2013), *Unpresented States and the Construction of Meaning: Clinical and Theoretical Contributions*, London: Karnac Books.
Lévi-Strauss, Claude (1989), *The Elementary Structures of Kinship*, ed. Rodney Needham, trans. James Harle Bell, John Richard von Sturmer, Boston, MA: Beacon Press.
Lilienfeld, Jane (1980), "Reentering Paradise: Cather, Colette, Woolf, and Their Mothers," in *The Lost Tradition: Mothers and Daughters in Literature*, eds. E.M. Broner and Cathy Davidson, 160–75, New York: Frederick Ungar.
Loewald, Hans (1960), "On the Therapeutic Action of Psychoanalysis," *International Journal of Psychoanalysis* 4: 16–33.
Loewald, Hans (1989), "Perspectives on Memory," in *Papers on Psychoanalysis*, 148–73, New Haven: Yale University Press.
Macey, David (1988), *Lacan in Contexts*, London: Verso.
Mahler, Margaret (1968), *On Human Symbiosis and the Vicissitudes of Individuation*, New York: International Universities Press.

Mahony, Patrick (1992), "Freud as Family Therapist," in *Freud and the History of Psychoanalysis*, eds. Toby Gelfand and John Kerr, 307–17, Hillsdale, NJ: The Analytic Press.

Malcolm, Janet (1993), "Annals of Biography: The Silent Woman," *New Yorker* August 23 & 30: 84–159.

Marcus, Steven (1985), "Freud and Dora: Story, History, Case History," in *In Dora's Case: Freud-Hysteria-Feminism*, eds. Charles Bernheimer and Claire Kahane, 56–71, New York: Columbia University Press.

Marks, Elaine and Isabelle de Courtivron, eds. (1981), *New French Feminisms*, New York: Schocken Books.

Masson, Jeffrey Moussaieff (1984), *The Assault on Truth: Freud's Suppression of the Seduction Theory*, New York: Farrar, Straus and Giroux.

Masson, Jeffrey Moussaieff, ed. and trans. (1985), *The Complete Letters of Sigmund Freud to Wilhelm Fliess 1887–1904*, Cambridge: Harvard University Press.

McCann, Colum (2009), *Let the Great World Spin*, New York: Random House.

McGrath, William (1987), *Freud's Discovery of Psychoanalysis: The Politics of Hysteria*, Ithaca: Cornell University Press.

McGuire, William, ed. (1974), *The Freud/Jung Letters: The Correspondence of Sigmund Freud and C.G. Jung*, trans. Ralph Manheim and R.F.C. Hull, Princeton, NJ: Princeton University Press.

Miller, Nancy (1991), *Getting Personal*, New York: Routledge.

Mitchell, Juliet (1974), *Psychoanalysis and Feminism*, New York: Pantheon.

Mitchell, Stephen (1993), *Hope and Dread in Psychoanalysis*, New York: Basic Books.

Mitscherlich, Alexander and Margarete (1975), *The Inability to Mourn*, trans. Beverly R. Placzek, New York: Grove Press.

Moi, Toril (1981), "Representation of Patriarchy: Sexuality and Epistemology in Freud's Dora," *Feminist Review*, October: 60–73.

Moi, Toril (1986), *Sexual/Textual Politics: Feminist Literary Theory*, London: Methuen.

Morrison, Toni (1972), *The Bluest Eye*, New York: Knopf.

Morrison, Toni (1987), *Beloved*, New York: Knopf.

Mortenson, Greg (2006), *Three Cups of Tea*, New York: Viking Penguin.

Nabokov, Vladimir (1955), *Lolita*, New York: Putnam Publishing Group Inc.

Novy, Marianne (1980), "Shakespeare's Female Characters as Actors and Audience," in *The Woman's Part: Feminist Criticism of Shakespeare*, eds. Carolyn Ruth Swift Lenz, Gayle Greene, and Carol Thomas Neely, 256–70, Urbana: University of Illinois Press.

O'Brien, Sharon (1991), "Feminist Theory and Literary Biography," in *Contesting the Subject*, ed. William P. Epstein, 123–33, West Lafayette: Purdue University Press.

Ogden, Thomas (1994a), "The Analytic Third: Working with Intersubjective Analytic Facts," *International Journal of Psychoanalysis* 75: 3–19.

Ogden, Thomas (1994b), *Subjects of Analysis*, London: Karnac Books.

Ogden, Thomas (1997), *Reverie and Interpretation*, Northvale, NJ: Jason Aronson.

Ogden, Thomas (2001), *Conversations on the Frontier of Dreaming*, Northvale, NJ: Jason Aronson.

Phillips, Arthur (2007), *Angelica*, New York: Random House Inc.

Prager, Jeffrey (2014), "Mourning Becomes Eclectic: Racial Melancholia in an Age of Reconciliation" now titled "Melancholia and the Racial Order: A Psychosocial Analysis of America's Enduring Racism," in *The Unhappy Divorce of Sociology and Psychoanalysis*, eds. Lynn Chancer and John Andrews, 284–316, New York: Palgrave McMillan.

Proust, Marcel (1934), *Remembrance of Things Past, 2 Vols*, trans. C. K. Scott-Moncrieff, Paris: Grasset and Gallimard.

Radden, Jennifer, ed. (2000), *The Nature of Melancholy: From Aristotle to Kristeva*, Oxford: Oxford University Press.

Rank, Otto (1924; 1952), *The Trauma of Birth* [no trans listed], New York: Robert Brunner.

Rice, Emanuel (1990), *Freud and Moses: The Long Journey Home*, Albany: State University of New York Press.

Roazen, Paul (1971), *Freud and His Followers*, New York: Meridian/NAL.

Roazen, Paul (1976), *Brother Animal: The Story of Freud and Tausk*, New York: New York University Press.

Robert, Marthe (1976), *From Oedipus to Moses: Freud's Jewish Identity*, trans. Ralph Manheim, New York: Anchor/Doubleday.

Roith, Estelle (1987), *The Riddle of Freud: Jewish Influences on His Theory of Female Sexuality*, London: Tavistock.

Roth, Philip (1969), *Portnoy's Complaint*, New York: Random House.

Rubin, Gayle (1975), "The Traffic in Women: Notes on the Political Economy of Sex," in *Toward an Anthropology of Women*, ed. Rayna Reiter, 157–210, New York: Monthly Review Press.

Ruddick, Sara (1989), *Maternal Thinking*, Boston, MA: Beacon Press.

Rudnytsky, Peter (1987), *Freud and Oedipus*, New York: Columbia University Press.

Rudnytsky, Peter (2002), *Reading Psychoanalysis: Freud, Rank, Ferenczi, Groddeck*, Ithaca: Cornell University Press.

Saussure, Ferdinand (1977), *Course in General Linguistics*, eds. C. Bally and A. Sechehaye, trans. W. Baskin, Glasgow: Fontana/Collins.

Schacter, Daniel (1996), *Searching for Memory*, New York: Basic Books.

Schafer, Roy (1992), *Reading a Life: Narrative and Dialogue in Psychoanalysis*, New York: Basic Books.
Schiesari, Juliana (1992), *The Gendering of Melancholia: Feminism, Psychoanalysis, and The Symbolics of Loss in Renaissance Literature*, Ithaca: Cornell University Press.
Schore, Allan (1994), *Affect Regulation and the Origin of the Self*, Hillsdale, NJ: Erlbaum.
Schorske, Carl (1981), *Fin-de-Siecle Vienna: Politics and Culture*, New York: Vintage/Random House.
Schur, Max (1966), "Some Additional 'Day Residues' of the Specimen Dream of Psychoanalysis," in *Psychoanalysis—A General Psychology: Essays in Honor of Heinz Hartman*, eds. Rudolph M. Loewenstein, Lottie M. Newman, Max Schur, and Albert J. Solnit, 45–85, New York: International Universities Press.
Schur, Max (1972), *Freud: Living and Dying*, New York: International Universities Press.
Seligman, Steven (2000), "Clinical Implications of Attachment Theory," *Journal of the American Psychoanalytic Association* 48: 1189–96.
Shakespeare, William (1992), *Hamlet*, ed. C. Hoy, New York: Norton.
Showalter, Elaine (1977), *A Literature of Their Own: British Women Novelists from Brontë to Lessing*, Princeton, NJ: Princeton University Press.
Silverman, Kaja (1988), *The Acoustic Mirror: The Female Voice in Psychoanalysis and Cinema*, Bloomington: Indiana University Press.
Slater, Lauren (2000), *Lying*, New York: Random House.
Slipp, Samuel (1988), "Freud's Mother, Ferenczi and the Seduction Theory," *Journal of the American Psychoanalytic Association* 16: 155–65.
Smith, Sedonie and Julia Watson (2010), *Reading Autobiography*, Minneapolis: University of Minnesota Press.
Smith, Zadie (2012), *NW*, London: Hamish Hamilton.
Spence, Donald (1982), *Narrative Truth and Historical Truth: Meaning and Interpretation in Psychoanalysis*, New York: Norton.
Sprengnether, Madelon (1985), "Enforcing Oedipus: Freud and Dora," in *The (M)other Tongue: Essays in Feminist Literary Interpretation*, eds. Shirley Nelson Garner, Claire Kahane, and Madelon Sprengnether, 51–71, Ithaca: Cornell University Press.
Sprengnether, Madelon (1990), *The Spectral Mother: Freud, Feminism and Psychoanalysis*, Ithaca: Cornell University Press.
Sprengnether, Madelon (1995a), "Reading Freud's Life," *American Imago* 52: 9–54.
Sprengnether, Madelon (1995b), "Mourning Freud," in *Psychoanalysis in Contexts*, eds. Anthony Elliott and Stephen Frosh, 142–65, London: Routledge.

Sprengnether, Madelon (2003), "Mouth to Mouth: Freud, Irma, and the Dream of Psychoanalysis," *American Imago* 60, 259–84.

Sprengnether, Madelon (2016), "Literature and Psychoanalysis," in *The Routledge Handbook of Psychoanalysis in the Social Sciences and Humanities*, eds. Anthony Elliott and Jeffrey Prager, 300–13, London and New York: Routledge.

Stanley, Liz (1992), *The Auto/biographical I: The Theory and Practice of Feminist Auto/Biography*, Manchester: Manchester University Press.

Stepansky, Paul E. (1999), *Freud, Surgery, and the Surgeons*, Hillsdale, NJ: The Analytic Press.

Stern, Daniel N. (1985), *The Interpersonal World of the Infant*, New York: Basic Books.

Stoppard, Tom (2003), *The Coast of Utopia*, New York: Grove/Atlantic Press.

Suleiman, Susan (1985), "Writing and Motherhood," in *The (M)other Tongue: Essays in Feminist Psychoanalytic Interpretation*, eds. Shirley Nelson Garner, Claire Kahane, and Madelon Sprengnether, 352–77, Ithaca: Cornell University Press.

Suleiman, Susan (1990), *Subversive Intent: Gender, Politics and the Avant-Garde*, Cambridge: Harvard University Press.

Sulloway, Frank J. (1979), *Freud, Biologist of the Mind*, New York: Basic Books.

Sulloway, Frank J. (1992), "Reassessing Freud's Case Histories: The Social Construction of Psychoanalysis," in *Freud and the History of Psychoanalysis*, eds. Toby Gelfand and John Kerr, 153–92, Hillsdale, NJ: The Analytic Press.

Swales, Peter (1982), "Freud, Minna Bernays, and the Conquest of Rome: New Light on the Origins of Psychoanalysis," *New American Review* 1: 1–23.

Swales, Peter (1983 copyright), "Freud, Martha Bernays & the Language of Flowers," Privately published paper.

Swan, Jim (1974), "Mater and Nannie: Freud's Two Mothers and the Discovery of the Oedipus Complex," *American Imago* 31: 1–64.

Thornton, E.M. (1986), *The Freudian Fallacy: Freud and Cocaine*, London: Paladin/Collins.

Torok, Maria (1995), "The Illness of Mourning and the Fantasy of the Exquisite Corpse," in *The Shell and the Kernel, Vol 1*, Nicolas Abraham and Maria Torok, ed. and trans. Nicholas T. Rand, 107–24, Chicago: University of Chicago Press.

Van Herik, Judith (1982), *Freud on Femininity and Faith*, Berkeley: University of California Press.

van der Kolk, Bessel, Lars Weisaeth, and Onno van der Hart, eds. (1996), "History of Trauma in Psychiatry," in *Traumatic Stress: The Effects of*

Overwhelming Experience on Mind, Body and Society, eds. Bessel van der Kolk, Alexander McFarlane, and Lars Weisaeth, 47–74, New York: Guilford Press.

van der Kolk, Bessel and Onno van der Hart (1991), "The Intrusive Past: The Flexibility of Memory and the Engraving of Trauma," *American Imago* 48: 425–53.

Walker, Cheryl (1991), "Persona Criticism and the Death of the Author," in *Contesting the Subject*, ed. William H. Epstein, 109–21, West Lafayette: Purdue University Press.

Wallace, David (1996), *Infinite Jest*, New York: Little, Brown and Company.

Whitebook, Joel. (1917), *Freud: An Intellectual Biography*, New York: Cambridge University Press.

Willis, Sharon (1983), "A Symptomatic Narrative," *Diacritics* 13: 46–66.

Winnicott, D.W. (1971), "Mirror Role of Mother and Family in Child Development," in *Playing and Reality*, 148–59, London: Tavistock.

Wolff, Larry (1988), *Postcards from the End of the World: Child Abuse in Freud's Vienna*, New York: Atheneum.

Woodward, Kathleen (1991), "Between Mourning and Melancholia: Roland Barthes' *Camera Lucida*," in *Aging and Its Discontents: Freud and Other Fictions*, ed. Kathleen Woodward, 110–29, Bloomington: Indiana University Press.

Yerushalmi, Yosef Hayim (1991), *Freud's Moses: Judaism Terminable and Interminable*, New Haven: Yale University Press.

Young-Bruehl, Elisabeth (1988), *Anna Freud: A Biography*, New York: Summit/Simon and Schuster.

Zaretsky, Eli (2004), *Secrets of the Soul: A Social and Cultural History of Psychoanalysis*, New York: Random House.

INDEX

Note: Locators with letter "n" refer to notes.

Abraham, Karl 15, 115 n.3, 198–201, 204, 208–14, 217, 221, 227–8, 231, 238 n.5, 238 n.8, 243
Abraham, Nicolas 15, 209
addiction 8, 97, 104, 109, 111–13, 131, 153
Adler, Alfred 29, 103–4, 182 n.3
adolescence 6, 30, 40, 44, 51, 123, 132, 145
adult mourner 203–4
ambivalence 2, 42, 48, 55, 82–3, 110, 194–6, 198, 201, 203, 215, 218, 227, 244
Andreas-Salomé, Lou 127
anger 4, 6, 47, 51–2, 54–5, 79, 83, 195
anthropology 3, 66, 120
anti-Vietnam war movement 167
anxiety 8, 14, 26, 28, 42–3, 51, 73, 80–1, 97, 100, 102, 112–13, 124, 129, 165, 173, 178
attachment 5, 11, 30, 40, 69, 100, 107, 111–13, 131, 169, 193, 195–7, 209, 211, 218, 227, 236–7, 241
autonomy 125, 133, 135, 226, 228–9

Barthes, Roland 163, 178, 212–13, 231
  "Death of the Author, The" (1989) 163

betrayal 25, 28, 43, 76–7, 79, 90 n.12, 125, 128, 208
biographers 22–4, 37, 39, 56, 57 n.2, 59 n.10, 61 n.19, 68, 126, 184 n.12
Bion, Wilfred 161 n.16, 175
Blum, Harold P. 93
Boose, Lynda 10, 119–22, 125, 130–2, 136
  Daughters and Fathers (1989) 10, 119–21, 128, 132, 134, 136
Breuer, Josef 25, 28–9, 47–8, 58 n.7, 97, 184 n.12
Brome, Vincent 128
Burlingham, Dorothy 11, 33–4, 59 n.13, 60 n.16, 138 n.13
Butler, Judith 172, 214–16, 227–31, 236
  Gender Trouble (1990) 172
  "Melancholy Gender: Refused Identification" (1997) 214

Carotenuto, Aldo 126
Carton, Evan 121
Caruth, Cathy 223
castration 5, 10, 66, 85, 103, 108, 110, 121, 123, 132, 158 n.2, 165–6, 170, 174, 183 n.5, 197, 204–5, 232, 242
childhood
  anxieties 82
  development 5, 195

loss 81, 243
memory 107, 142–50, 152, 157
sexual abuse 6, 141
children
  neuroses 75
  perversions against 73
  preschool-age 173
  reality of loss 219
  sexual desire in 3, 6–7, 103
Civil Rights movement 167
Cixous, Hélène 170
Clément, Catherine 170
cocaine 26–8, 97, 111
countertransference theory 155, 161 n.15, 174–5, 184 n.11
Cullingford, Elizabeth 121–2
cultural achievement 51–2, 125
cure, effected by love 234–7

Dadaism 169
death instinct 15, 176, 243–4
death-in-life 211, 214
deconstructive theory 13–14, 153
DeLillo, Don 179
denial 52, 104, 207–8, 216, 241
depressive position 91 n.21, 201–3, 201–5, 205
Derrida, Jacques 2, 185 n.13
detachment 25, 198, 212, 218
Deutsch, Felix 104–5, 116 n.16
Deutsch, Helene 11, 127
Diehl, Joanne 121
displacement 3, 38, 52, 122, 140, 165, 195
Dora case history 3–4, 11, 106, 126–8, 131, 157 n.1, 159 n.6, 185 n.3
dream 7–8, 31, 52, 57 n.4, 70–2, 75, 77–8, 86
dream of Irma's injection 70, 93, 99, 112–13. *See also Interpretation of Dreams, The* (1900)

dreamer 31, 200
drive theory 5, 87 n.3, 243

Eagleton, Terry 1–2
early loss 6, 215
Eckstein, Emma 8, 11, 70, 89 n.10, 96, 100–2, 104, 106, 110, 113, 114 n.1, 126, 137 n.7
ego
  Butler's concept 227–8
  elegiac construction 92 n.24, 230
  gendered character 214–15
  introjections and 210
  Klein's account 201, 203, 214
  Lacan's account 34–5, 169–70
  melancholia and 84, 195–8, 216
  normal mourning 82–3
  pathological mourning 111, 193
  structural model of mind 164
ego development 1–2, 34–5, 82–4, 111–12, 146, 164, 169–71, 193, 195–9, 201, 203–4, 210, 214–17, 227–8, 230–2, 235, 243
Erdrich, Louise 179
Erikson, Erik 94, 114 n.1
erotic wishes 7, 82, 102, 106, 109, 113, 122, 125, 127
exchange of women 10–11, 120–2, 124–5, 130, 132, 135

Fairbairn, W.R.D. 167
family structure 119–20, 125, 131–2, 242
fantasy 7–8, 30, 43, 48–51, 68–9, 76, 90 n.12, 101, 107–9, 124, 132, 135, 140, 147, 200, 210
  sexual fantasies 101, 109

father–daughter relationship 10, 120–2, 124–5, 128, 130–3, 135–6, 138 n.14
fellatio 4, 106–8, 131
Felman, Shoshana 65, 234
female sexuality 4, 167
feminism. *See also Spectral Mother, The :Freud, Feminism, and Psychoanalysis* (1990)
daughter–father relationship 123
French 171, 173
psychoanalysis and 65, 68, 86, 243
second-wave 10, 167
Ferenczi, Sándor 60 nn.14–15, 129–30, 182 n.13, 210, 238 n.5, 238 n.8
Fliess, Wilhelm 7–8, 11, 23, 31, 54, 70, 89 n.10, 98, 114 n.1, 126, 141, 182 n.3, 184 n.12
Flowers, Betty S. 119
Daughters and Fathers (1989) 10, 119–21, 128, 132, 134, 136
Fluss, Frau 41–2, 44, 53, 62 n.21
Fluss, Gisela 41–2, 44, 51, 159 n.8
Foucault, Michel 56 n.2, 88 n.6, 171–3, 175
fraternal clan 66
Freud, Amalia 9, 53–4, 62 n.25, 77, 79, 88 n.9, 90 n.14–15, 124
Freud, Anna 11, 23, 33–4, 48, 59 n.13, 60 nn.13–15, 62 n.23, 70, 80, 89 n.9, 99–100, 104–5, 114 n.1, 115 n.3, 124, 128–32, 138 n.13, 141, 167–8, 179, 183 n.3
Freud, Ernst 6, 51–5, 62 n.22, 159 n.7, 219

Freud, Jacob 6, 36, 70, 72, 79–81, 85–6, 89 nn.10–11, 90 n.15
Freud, Martha Bernays 6, 8, 22–3, 26–7, 40, 44–51, 53, 55, 62 n.23, 70, 96, 97, 99–100, 104–5, 116 n.5
Freud, Martin 62 n.25
Freud, Mathilde 8, 96, 115 n.3
Freud, Sigmund
letters
to Anna 129
to Ferenczi 130
to Fliess 38, 54, 72–4, 79, 100–1, 103, 109, 142
to Jones 129
to Jung 239 n.11
to Martha 6, 40, 44–6, 49–51
to Silberstein 40–1, 53
life of
addiction to cigars 8, 113
autobiographical effort 68
biographical portrait 35–9 (*see also* Gay, Peter; Jones, Ernest)
brother's (Julius) death 9, 79–80
coping with loss 52–4
death instinct 15
early childhood, 75, 81, 85, 195, 243
encounters with Fluss women (*see* Fluss, Frau; Fluss, Gisela)
failure to mourn 54, 62 n.26
father's death 6–7, 38–9, 55, 65, 70–7, 79, 81–6, 89 n.11, 142
"fort-da" game 6, 51–3
friend's (Weiss) death 50
friend's (von Marxow) death 97
homoerotic aspect of friendship 102, 113

Jewishness 25, 59 n.10
  as literary writer 140–1
  Martha, relationship with
    40, 44–51, 53, 55, 62
    n.22–3
  melancholia, description
    83–5, 193–7
  memories of his early years
    80–1
  mother's death 53–4, 88 n.9
  nickname for Martha 47–8
  personal crisis 73, 81
  personal destiny 25, 30
  quarreling and
    reconciliation 45, 49, 53
  relationship with Silberstein
    40–4, 53, 55
  resistance to repetition 33,
    45, 52–3, 60 n.16
  screen memories 11,
    142–52, 155, 157
  self-analysis 31–8, 56,
    141–2
  self-characterizations 29, 33
  self-construction 26, 55, 68,
    155, 157
  self-fashioning 22–31
  self-image 5, 9, 22, 56, 70,
    103
  theorization of femininity
    112–13
  traffic in women 123–31
  trip to U.S. (1909) 26
  unauthorization 39–56
  understanding of memory
    12–13
  undoing oedipus 131–6
  writings
    "Analysis Terminable and
      Interminable" (1937)
      31–2, 59 n.12
    An Autobiographical Study
      (1925) 24–5, 28–9
    *A Metapsychological
      Supplement to the
      Theory of Dreams*"
      (1917) 112, 114
    *Beyond the Pleasure
      Principle* (1920) 6, 16,
      51, 210–20
    "A Special Type of Choice
      of Object Made by Men"
      (1910) 66
    Ego and the Id, The (1923)
      214, 216, 230–1
    "Femininity" (1933) 55
    *Fragment of an Analysis of a
      Case of Hysteria* (1905)
      3–4
    "On the History of
      the Psycho-Analytic
      Movement" (1914) 29,
      31
    *Interpretation of Dreams,
      The* (1900) 3, 7, 12, 31,
      38–9, 58 n.9
    *Leonardo da Vinci and
      a Memory of His
      Childhood* (1910b) 3
    Moses and Monotheism
      (1939) 3, 30, 86 n.1
    "Mourning and
      Melancholia" (1917)
      7, 15, 82, 84, 91 n.22,
      111–12, 193–4, 212,
      216, 218, 230, 243
    Preliminary Communication
      (1893, Freud and Breuer)
      29, 58 n.7
    *Psychopathology of
      Everyday Life, The*
      (1901) 124, 159 n.7
    "Recommendations to
      Physicians Practicing
      Psycho-Analysis" (1912)
      31

"Screen Memories" (1899) 12, 126, 139, 142–3, 150–1, 155, 157
"Some Psychical Consequences of the Anatomical Distinction between the Sexes" (1925) 85
Studies on Hysteria (1895, Breuer and Freud) 25, 29, 58 n.7
"Subtleties of a Faulty Action, The" (1935) 32
"Theme of the Three Caskets, The" (1913) 34
Totem and Taboo (1913b) 3, 30, 66, 86 n.1
Frey, James 153
A Million Little Pieces (2003) 153
Friedan, Betty
Feminine Mystique (1963) 167
Froula, Christine 121
frustrations 1, 4, 37, 44, 55, 111–13, 132, 202, 228

Gardiner, Judith 121
Gay, Peter 5, 9, 22, 36, 56 n.2, 58 n.8, 68, 88 n.5, 116 n.5, 129, 131, 159 n.6, 182 n.2, 183 n.4
Genet, Jean 171
gestation 220
ghosts
  ancestors and 16, 194, 210, 213, 226
  in Homer's *Odyssey* 189–92
Gilbert, Sandra 121–2
GLBT (gay/lesbian/bisexual/transgender) 172
Gordon, Avery 225–6
Ghostly Matters (1997) 214, 224
Great War, 176, 193

grief 7, 49, 52–5, 61 n.18, 72, 75, 79, 81, 86, 88 n.9, 200, 202, 204–5, 212–13, 215, 228–9

Haney-Peritz, Janice 121
hatred 83, 133–4, 195–6, 198, 202
haunting 4, 16, 191, 211–15, 217–18, 220, 223–7, 239 n.10
Heilbrun, Carolyn 134–5
helplessness 3, 7, 39, 51, 94, 109, 123, 125, 228–9, 232
Hill-Miller, Katherine 121–2
Holocaust 14, 177, 219, 222–3, 227, 233, 239 n.10
Homer (Book XI) 189, 192
homophobia 102, 215–16, 227
hostility 7, 23, 38, 53–5, 75, 242
human development 2, 184 n.8, 202, 205–6

id 164–5, 174, 230
illness 31, 74, 83–4, 97, 105, 128, 197, 202
incest 4, 10–11, 55, 76, 104
  Freud's taboo 123–5, 131
  Lévi-Strauss's depiction 121
incorporation, reality of loss 15, 84, 198–9, 210, 212–13
infant development 167, 169, 204–5
  unverbalized life 201
infantile dependency 125, 132
internalized object 198, 200
intersubjective theory 13, 88 n.4, 155–6, 161 n.15, 173, 175 n.17
introjection 15–16, 185 n.14, 198, 200–1, 208, 210–11, 222, 238 n.8
Irigaray, Luce 170
isolation 25–6, 71, 230, 233

INDEX

Janet, Pierre 26, 28–9, 220–2
Jones, Ernest 5, 9, 11, 22–3, 35, 37, 56 n.2, 68–9, 88 n.4, 105, 128, 183 n.3
Joyce, James 171
Jung, Carl 11, 29, 65–6, 86 n.1, 104, 114 n.1, 126–7, 182 n.3, 185 n.12, 224, 234, 239 n.11
Transformations and Symbols of the Libido (1911–12) 66

Kann, Loe 11, 128–30
Karr, Mary 154
Liar's Club, The (1995) 154
Klein, Melanie 5, 15, 91 n.21, 116 n.9, 167–8, 175, 201–5, 208–9, 212, 214, 227–8, 231, 238 nn.5–6, 243–4
"Mourning and its Relation to Manic-Depressive States" (1940) 202
Koestenbaum, Wayne 102
Koller, Carl 26–7
Kristeva, Julia 15, 91 n.21, 170, 184 n.29, 205–9, 211–12, 214–15, 221, 227–8, 231–3, 243
Black Sun (1989) 91 n.21, 205, 209

Lacan, Jacques 5, 13, 15, 65, 91 n.21, 161 n.16, 169–71, 173–5, 204–6, 208–9, 220, 227, 232, 243
mirror stage concept 34–5, 183 n.8, 204
languageless condition 15, 204–5, 211, 227
Lanzmann, Claude 177, 223, 234
Law of the Father 66, 204–9
Lehman, David 21

l'écriture féminine. 13, 171, 184 n.9
Lévi-Strauss 10–11, 121–2, 125, 128, 169. *See also* exchange of women
libido theory 65–6, 185 n.12, 193, 195–6, 198–9
literature
 avant-garde forms 171, 181
 modernism 178
 post-war American culture 166–7
 psychoanalysis and 163–5, 172, 175, 177–8, 197
lived experience 68, 154
living with the dead 192–3, 213
Loewald, Hans 16, 185 n.14, 191–2, 210, 213–14, 226, 235–6, 237 n.1, 241–2
loss
 absence and 55
 of mother 15, 51, 54, 63 n.26
 separation and 16, 49, 52
 traumatic 5
lost object 82, 111, 193–5, 197–200, 207, 209–10, 212
love and loss 83, 214, 232, 235, 237
love-object 83, 122, 198

Malcolm, Janet 21
male bonds 11, 127, 130
male sexual development 10, 67
masculinity 5, 87 n.2, 101, 108, 110, 112, 166, 172, 242
Masson, Jeffrey Moussaieff 100–1, 111
masturbation 4, 89 n.10, 100, 109, 131
maternal desire 77, 123, 125
maternal subjectivity 4, 87 n.4
matriarchy 66, 86 n.1
McCann, Colum 179
McFarlane, Alexander 176

melancholia
  as bleeding wound 111, 242
  contemporary theories 194, 209
  death-in-life 211
  dynamics of 7, 9, 83–4
  ego development and 196, 198–9
  forms of 15–16, 112
  Kristeva's discussion 205, 208, 221–2, 227
  psychoanalytic theories 213, 234–5
  trauma theory and 220
memoir genre 152–5
memory
  contemporary neuroscience on 151–2
  distortion of memory 77
  functions and dysfunctions 176
  in psychoanalysis 155–7
  traumatic 221, 223, 238 n.9
Mitscherlich, Alexander and Margarete 216–18
  The Inability to Mourn (1967/1975) 216–17
morality 30, 164, 168
Morrison, Toni 133, 179, 224, 226–7, 234
  Bluest Eye, The (1972) 132
mother-right 66
mother–infant relations 1, 67, 85, 167, 169–70, 242
mother–son relationship 10, 55, 63 n.26, 76, 110, 112
mourning
  concept 2, 7, 15–16
  failures 241–4
  normal 82, 84, 91 n.22, 200, 202, 227
  process 37–9, 74, 81–2, 85–6, 193, 197, 199–204, 206, 209–14, 216–18, 228, 232–3

Nabokov, Vladimir 14
  Lolita (1955) 166
narcissism 85, 113, 196, 198
narrative memory 14, 220–2
negation 15, 207
neuroscience 11–13, 16, 151–2, 176–7, 221
  cognitive neuroscience 221
neuroscientists 155, 176–7, 220
neuroses 25, 29, 31, 52, 58 n.7, 65, 70, 74–5, 100–1, 141
  sexual origins 25, 29
New Criticism 166, 184 n.11
Night of the Living Dead (1968, movie) 190
nonfiction writing 11–12, 21, 143–4, 153–4, 160 nn.11–12, 161 n.13, 164
nonverbal interaction 175–7, 181, 205, 208

object relations theory 5, 13, 62 n.21, 67, 87 n.2, 167–9, 173, 191, 194, 228
obstacles 23, 32, 45, 196, 215, 220, 223
Odyssey (Homer) 189–92
oedipal theory 1, 3–6, 8–9, 13, 15, 38–9, 55–6, 61, 65, 67, 70, 73, 75–82, 85, 87, 103, 106, 122, 124, 134–5, 167, 169–70, 205, 242–3
Oedipus complex 2, 5–7, 9–11, 36–9, 55, 60–1 n.8, 65–9, 73, 81–2, 87 n.4, 88 n.7, 91 nn.19–21, 94, 101, 113, 114 n.1, 120–5, 128, 135, 137 n.4, 140–2, 158 n.2, 163–5, 167–8, 172–3, 231, 242
  as autobiography 68–9
  formulation 73, 78, 81, 124, 135, 142, 166, 169–72, 174–6, 181, 200

libido theory 65–6
shadow background 81–6
Oedipus Rex (Sophocles) 65, 69, 75–6, 80–1, 85, 140, 158 n.2
Ogden, Thomas 161 n.18, 175
oral phase 83, 201
oral violation 8, 94, 103, 112–13

paranoid-schizoid position 205, 214
patriarchal family 10–11, 86 n.11, 120, 131–2
personal narratives 3, 14
phallic concerns 5, 7, 85–6, 94, 103–4, 107, 109–10, 113, 166, 232
Phillips, Arthur
  Angelica (2007) 189
Plath, Sylvia 21
posterity 9, 23–5, 59 n.11
postmodernism 10, 15, 152, 165, 172–4, 178–9, 182, 233
preoedipal period 1–2, 5–6, 8–9, 15–16, 82, 109, 112, 167–72, 174–7, 180–1, 191, 204, 241–3
Proust, Marcel 171
psychoanalytic theory
  analyst's role 174
  childhood development 5
  contemporary theories 181, 243
  disciplinary developments 172
  evidence for 156
  feminist perspectives 65, 68, 86, 167
  Lacan's reformulation 170
  literary investigation 13, 163
  melancholia 197, 213, 222
  mourning and ego in 234–5
  neuroscientific research 176, 220
  Oedipus complex 67, 81–2, 121

  philosophic discourse 165
  post-Freudian developments 2, 13, 15, 241
  postmodernism 178–80
  social developments 9–10
  sociology and 224
  trauma theory 14, 173, 177, 208

Rank, Otto 168
reenactment 51, 134, 191, 205, 220–1, 235
religion 30, 66, 180
repetition compulsion 4, 6, 45, 181, 210, 221
representation
  language and 204–5, 208
  modes of discourse 164
  narrative organization and 14
  selfhood and 191
retrieval cue 151–2
Roth, Philip 14
  Portnoy's Complaint (1969) 167
Rubin, Gayle 126, 128
Rudnytsky, Peter 126

sadism 197, 201
Sadoff, Dianne 121
same sex love/desire 215
Schacter, Daniel 151–2, 154–5, 159 n.9, 177
Schur, Max 94, 104–6, 114 n.1, 116 n.6
seduction theory 6–7, 10, 36–7, 73–5, 89 n.10, 101, 103, 122–3
self-analysis 5, 8, 11–12, 22, 24, 30–9, 55–6, 65, 68–9, 74, 80, 82, 86, 88 n.5, 91 n.19, 96, 115 n.2, 123, 125, 141–2, 144, 150, 158 n.5, 161 n.17, 174, 183 n.5

self-psychology 5
selfhood 16, 150, 153, 155, 184
    n.8, 191, 204, 214, 227,
    232, 241
separation 1, 16, 25, 40–1,
    46, 49, 51–2, 85, 105,
    128, 146, 202, 206, 209,
    227, 231
sexual abuse 6–7, 101, 141, 176
sexual object 10, 106, 130, 230
sexuality 4, 77, 79–80, 98, 141,
    165–7, 171–3
Shakespeare, William 135
    Hamlet 7, 23, 74–80, 82, 158
    n.2, 194
    King Lear 48, 130
Shoah (documentary film) 223
Silberstein, Eduard 6, 40–4, 53,
    55, 159 n.8
Slater, Lauren 154
    Lying (2000) 154
Smith, Sedonie
    *Reading Autobiography: A
    Guide for Interpreting
    Life Narratives* (2010) 152,
    155
Smith, Zadie 179
social loss 214–15
social order 68, 121–2, 170, 172,
    183 n.18
specimen dream 7, 70, 93
Spielrein, Sabina 11, 126–7, 137
    n.8, 224
Spillers, Hortense 121
Sprengnether, Madelon 5–6, 11,
    13, 16 n.1, 63 n.26, 65, 67,
    120, 170, 241
    *Spectral Mother,
    The: Freud, Feminism, and
    Psychoanalysis* (1990) 4–5,
    9, 16–17 n.1, 26, 62 n.23,
    62–3 n.26
Stekel, Wilhelm 103–4, 182 n.3

Stoppard, Tom
    Coast of Utopia (2003) 179
super-ego 231
Surrealism 169
Swan, Jim 62 n.25, 94, 114 n.1,
    137 n.4

Tausk, Victor 11, 127
theory of hysterical longing 11
tombs 211–12
Torok, Maria 15, 209–13, 217,
    221, 238 n.8
transference 3–4, 37, 53, 174,
    191–2, 199, 211, 234–6
transitional stage 15, 66, 86 n.1,
    99–100, 199, 205, 209–10,
    243
trauma theory 14, 16, 173, 176–7,
    179, 219–20, 243
traumatic loss 2, 5, 79, 94, 185
    n.14, 209
traumatic memory 221, 223, 238
    n.9

unconditional love 49, 55, 125,
    135
unconscious
    communication 175
    conscious awareness 14,
        147–9, 214
    desires 76, 156
    effects of trauma 176–7
    ego psychology 169
    in "feminine" writing 171
    forms of discourse 165
    Freud's investigation 2–3, 13,
        68, 70, 189–91
    introjection process 200
    Jones on 35, 37
    Loewald on 192
    mind, attention and 14, 93,
        96, 140, 141, 163–4
    unverbalized elements 176

van der Hart, Onno 177, 219–22, 238 n.9
  "History of Trauma in Psychiatry" (1996) 219
van der Kolk, Bessel 176–7, 219–22, 238
  "History of Trauma in Psychiatry" (1996) 219
Verneinumg 209
vulnerability 3, 7, 94, 102, 134, 155, 228–9, 232

Wallace, David Foster 179
war
  First World War 104, 219
  Second World War 166, 218
  Vietnam war 176
Watson, Julia
  Reading Autobiography: A Guide for Interpreting Life Narratives (2010) 152, 155
Weisaeth, Lars 176, 219
  "History of Trauma in Psychiatry" (1996) 219
Weiss, Nathan 49–51
women
  castration complex 85
  gender roles 13, 110
  paternal control 10–11
  writers 13
women writers 13, 167–8, 173
Woodward, Kathleen 61 n.18, 91 n.18, 193, 212–14, 228 n.22. *See also* living with the dead
  "Between Mourning and Melancholia: Roland Barthes's *Camera Lucida*" (1991) 212

Zweig, Arnold 23, 60 n.14

www.ingramcontent.com/pod-product-compliance
Lightning Source LLC
Chambersburg PA
CBHW052217300426
44115CB00011B/1724